2002

Video Relay Service (VRS) is introduced as a great technological opportunity to deaf, hard of hearing, and hearing people. VRS can be used for conversation or during the provision of interpreting services. (Image source: i-2-eye.)

MID TO LATE 1880S

Gallaudet College is established in Washington, DC, as the only liberal arts college for the deaf in the United States. It is first named the "National College for the Deaf and Dumb". (Image source: National Association of the Deaf [NAD].)

1880

At the first meeting of NAD in Milan, Italy, the congress supports oral education for the deaf; in the US, NAD maintains sign language as an instructional option. (Image source: NAD.)

LATE 1800S

Helen Keller and Anne Sullivan (pictured) along with Alexander Graham Bell, whose mother had a hearing loss, pioneered early oral communication methods used with the deaf. (Image source: NAD.)

1980s–Forward

Throughout the 1980s to the present, American Sign Language becomes more prominent in our society, demonstrating its presence as the fourth most common language in the United States. "Cover", from *American Sign Language Dictionary* by Elaine Costello, copyright © 1994 by Elaine Costello. Used by permission of Random House Reference and Information Publishing, a division of Random House, Inc.

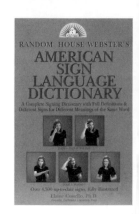

Eighteenth Century

Abbe Charles Michel De L'Eppe established the first public school for the deaf in France. (Image source: NAD.)

Early 1970s

Captioning is first seen in television broadcasting. (Image source: Photo by Lee Dray.)

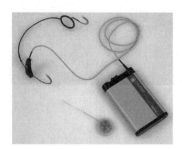

1980s

During the 1980s, the first cochlear implants are introduced. (Image source: Cochlear Implant, Nucleus 22, Cochlear Corporation.)

Mid-Twentieth Century

Members of Deaf communities across America begin to enter the mainstream job market in higher numbers. Deaf and hard of hearing subgroups settle and become more established in industrial neighborhoods. (Image source: Labor and War Effort, Gerrit A. Beneker, National Archives.)

HANDBOOK TO SERVICE THE DEAF AND HARD OF HEARING

A BRIDGE TO ACCESSIBILITY

JOHN W. ADAMS, PH.D.

AND

PAMELA S. ROHRING, M.S.

ELSEVIER
ACADEMIC
PRESS

Amsterdam • Boston • Heidelberg • London
New York • Oxford • Paris • San Diego
San Francisco • Singapore • Sydney • Tokyo

Elsevier Academic Press
525 B Street, Suite 1900, San Diego, California 92101-4495, USA
84 Theobald's Road, London WC1X 8RR, UK

Library of Congress Cataloging-in-Publication Data
Adams, John W., 1956–
    Handbook to service the deaf and hard of hearing : a bridge to accessibility / John W.
Adams and Pamela S. Rohring.
        p. cm.
Includes bibliographical references and index.
    ISBN 0-12-044141-1 (hardcover : alk. paper)
    1. Deaf—United States.   2. Deaf—Means of communication—United States.
3. Social work with the deaf—United States.   4. Deafness—Social aspects.
I. Rohring, Pamela S.   II. Title.
    HV2545.A33 2004
    362.4'28—dc22

                                                                2003023768

British Library Cataloguing in Publication Data
A catalogue record for this book is available from the British Library

ISBN: 0-12-044141-1

For all information on all Academic Press publications
visit our Web site at www.academicpress.com

Printed in the United States of America
04 05 06 07 08 09   9 8 7 6 5 4 3 2 1

DEDICATION

"Rose" by Chuck Baird

To those souls who have gone before us. We have been blessed with their love and strength. They inspire our ideas and the courage to work for others without a voice.

To my family, my mom and dad, Bill and Mary, and my siblings, Mary Ann, Bill, and Mark. Your faith, fun ways, and love of life are a part of me forever.

John

To my mother, Helen, who has a special way of caring and showing her appreciation; To my late father, Ronald, who had that way of making me feel loved, And to my wonderful sister, Judy, who continues to give me tremendous support and whose faith in me is a constant encouragement.

Pamela

ACKNOWLEDGMENTS

We want to express our deep appreciation to several individuals who have come along with us on this journey in writing *Handbook to Service the Deaf and Hard of Hearing: A Bridge to Accessibility.*

It was a pleasure and an honor to be associated with pioneers in the field of serving the Deaf and Hard of Hearing: Bernard Bragg, Karen Christie, Patricia Chute, Mary Ellen Nevins, Bernard Hurwitz, Harlan Lane, Win McChord, Catherine Morton, and Robert Pollard. Their ideas, experiences, and information will enable Deaf and Hard of Hearing people to have more of an impact on society. A special heartfelt thank you is sent to Dr. Romeria Tidwell for her friendship and mentorship over the years. Her contribution to this work provided the unique perspective from a successful, late-deafened adult professional.

We thank the artists who have contributed their work to the book that bring their culture and their experiences to life: Chuck Baird, Morris Broderson, Susan Dupor, Dana Janik, Mary Thornley, and Charles Wild-bank—your art inspires us.

In appreciation to Lee Dray for creating the concept of our cover illustration, you captured our vision. Also, Lee's illustrations concerning environmental accommodations for Deaf and hard of hearing individuals found in Chapter 6 will advance the knowledge of accessibility in the community.

Our best regards are sent to the publishing team at Academic Press, Elsevier, including Mark Zadrozny, Mara Conner, Troy Lilly, and Cate Barr. Your support, patience, and kind use of feedback helped us to develop our initial concept into this book. Your professionalism and support will have a lasting impact in the Deaf community.

And finally, a warm acknowledgement to the many Deaf and hard of hearing people in our nation. May they continue to strive to access services that would better their lives. May they be persistent in their struggle and fight!

CONTENTS

1

INTRODUCTION TO BEING DEAF OR HARD OF HEARING

2

WORLDS COLLIDE: GROWING UP WITH A HEARING LOSS

3

LANGUAGE DIFFERENCES AND COMMUNICATION ISSUES

4

DEAF CULTURE OR CONDITION?

5

ISSUES FROM THE PAST . . . ISSUES FOR THE MILLENNIUM: THE PROFESSIONALS' PERSPECTIVES

6

BEST PRACTICES WHEN COMMUNICATING WITH DEAF AND HARD OF HEARING PEOPLE

7

RESOURCES

BIOGRAPHY

John William Adams is a licensed psychologist, a certified school psychologist, and the director of the Family Center of Western New York, a mental health clinic that serves deaf, hard of hearing, and hearing individuals and their families. He attended Pennsylvania State University as an undergraduate and majored in elementary and special education. He obtained his Master of Arts degree and his Ph.D. in counseling psychology at the University of California, Los Angeles (UCLA).

Dr. Adams worked as a full-time assistant and associate professor at California State University, San Bernardino, and Rochester Institute of Technology (RIT), respectively, and as an adjunct professor at Canisius College. Specifically, he helped develop and then direct the School of Psychology and Deafness graduate program, a collaborative effort between the colleges of Liberal Arts and the National Technical Institute for the Deaf (NTID) at RIT. He also practiced as a school psychologist and as a consulting licensed psychologist at St. Mary's School for the Deaf in Buffalo, New York.

Dr. Adams has several article and book publications to his credit, specifically *You and Your Hearing Impaired Child* and the second edition of this work, *You and Your Deaf Child*, both published by Gallaudet University Press. He has lectured at numerous local, regional, national, and international conferences on such topics as mental health and Deaf and hard of hearing consumers, behavior issues and Deaf and hard of hearing children, and parent education and family issues within the Deaf and hard of hearing population.

Deaf since the age of 2 $\frac{1}{2}$ years old, **Pamela Sue Rohring** is the Deaf Studies/ASL Specialist at St. Mary's School for the Deaf in Buffalo, New York. She attended Gallaudet University as an undergraduate and majored in Biology. She obtained her Masters of Science degree at Canisius College, specializing in Deaf Education. She has a New York state Certification as a teacher of the Deaf.

Pamela has conducted many workshops and program presentations at the local, regional, and state levels on Deaf Culture, ASL, and family and child development issues. Her primary goal is to help bridge the communication and cultural gaps between hearing and Deaf people.

INTRODUCTION

This book is intended for hearing professionals in the community who provide or who may provide services to individuals with hearing loss. This book also can be used as a comprehensive resource for any person who lives or works with deaf and hard of hearing people. Up-to-date research and practical information about this diverse population as well as a guide to help improve communications and ultimately interactions between hearing people and deaf and hard of hearing individuals are at the core of its purpose.

Chapter 1 introduces the reader to basic information about hearing loss and the deaf and hard of hearing population. Medical and audiological issues are addressed, and the many primary factors that influence the development of deaf and hard of hearing individuals are presented.

Chapter 2 offers personal views of having a hearing loss from three unique perspectives: a deaf woman who is a communication and deaf studies specialist, a hard of hearing man who is a lawyer, and a late-deafened adult who is an accomplished university professor.

Chapter 3 addresses the importance of language development and how both communications and interactions are affected when the worlds of hearing and hearing loss combine and intertwine.

Chapter 4 is a comprehensive presentation of the unique culture that has arisen from a strong, steadfast community who have survived much, the least of which is a medical condition. This chapter approaches Deaf Culture in all of its beauty and opportunity.

Chapter 5 is an exciting chapter that provides the perspectives of members of the Deaf community who focus on past and current issues relevant to working and interacting with deaf and hard of hearing people. The advancements of medical technology, drama, and theatre in the deaf and hard of hearing population and their impact on society; language and communication topics; mental health issues; the cochlear implant controversy; and an inside look at the diversity within the deaf and hard of hearing population highlight this important and intriguing chapter.

Chapter 6 guides the reader on how to provide communication access within a variety of community service situations as well as during individual interactions.

The book concludes with a comprehensive list of articles, books, media, and website resources related to topic areas relevant to deaf and hard of hearing people. These resources will help those interested in being more involved in the lives of Deaf people who make up a portion of this incredible population with its own unique language, culture, and influence on current society.

Mr. Winfield McChord, Jr. is a son of Deaf parents who has been a driving force within the field of deaf education for the past 40 years. For example, for 20 years he was the chief administrative officer at the American School for the Deaf (the oldest permanent school for the deaf in the New World). His reaction to this book helps culminate a description of the book's purpose and significance:

> "Handbook to Service the Deaf and Hard of Hearing: A Bridge to Accessibility" by John W. Adams, Ph.D. and Pamela S. Rohring, M.S. is a comprehensive resource on deafness addressing medical issues, language development, communication access, and psychology and sociology topics. Whether regarded as a minority group or members of a linguistic minority, there are 28 million deaf and hard of hearing Americans.

> The majority of Americans, their hearing counterparts, have little or no knowledge about our fellow deaf and hard of hearing Americans due to communication differences. These differences often affect a level of comfort during current or potential interactions and the quality of interactions between hearing and deaf and hard of hearing individuals. These interactions will affect future comfort levels and ultimately the familiarity with this segment of our American society.

> No reader will close this book without learning something new about the world of the deaf, appreciating the ramifications of hearing loss more deeply, or confronting their views and opinions of longstanding challenges faced by deaf and hard of hearing Americans. It is the ultimate hope of the authors that you will open up your hearts, minds, and your places of service to provide more access to this diversified population in our society and more importantly, that you will enjoy access to a beautiful people whose culture, language, and experiences can affect us all."

1

INTRODUCTION TO
BEING DEAF OR
HARD OF HEARING

*No otherwise qualified handicapped individual in the
United States—shall, solely by reason of his handicap,
be excluded from the participation in, be denied the
benefits of, or be subjected to discrimination under
any program of activity receiving federal financial
assistance.*

United States Congress
Section 504, The Rehabilitation Act of 1973 (PL
93–11)

*The Americans with Disabilities Act (ADA) is a
new civil rights law that gives individuals on the basis
of race, gender, national origin, or religion, equal
protection. It guarantees equal opportunity for individuals with disabilities in employment, public accommodations, transportation, state, and local government
services and telecommunications.*

Americans with Disabilities Act, July 26, 1990

*In March 1998, President Clinton signed an executive
order 13078 establishing the Presidential Task Force
on Employment of Adults with Disabilities. Its charge:
To create a co-ordinated and active national agenda
to bring adults with disabilities into the workplace at
a rate similar to that in the general population.*

SBA Information Notice, 1999 (Control No.:
3000–1856)

These acts and executive order provide for equal protection under the
law so that individuals with disabilities receive fair and equitable treatment
in relation to employment opportunities and access to community services.

Deaf individuals and hard of hearing people are identified by law as members of disability groups (see Appendix A for state definitions). Deaf and hard of hearing people are a diverse group who are often denied access to job opportunities or community services because of their unique and varied characteristics.

INDIVIDUALS WHO ARE DEAF
AND HARD OF HEARING

A 7-year-old boy has a moderately severe hearing loss in his right ear and a moderate loss in his left ear. He was born with a mild hearing loss due to unknown causes. When he was 3, he fell in a playground and hit his head. His hearing loss became progressively worse. He attends a regular classroom in a rural school district with some hearing and speech–related services.

A 12-year-old girl with a severe hearing loss attends a school for the deaf. She is enrolled in a sixth-grade classroom with children who have good oral skills. She communicates with both spoken English and sign language. Both of her parents are Deaf.

A 40-year-old woman who is a college professor was diagnosed with a progressive hearing loss in her early 20s. She had functioned with behind-the-ear hearing aids most of her adult life. She communicates with spoken English and has adapted devices to amplify sound on her telephones. At the age of 35, she decided to undergo a cochlear implant operation and her functioning level seemed to have increased dramatically. At the age of 38, she no longer used her cochlear implant as she reported that she no longer received the benefits.

A 15-year-old young man had struggled with academics throughout his school experience. At the beginning of one academic year, he was diagnosed with central auditory processing (CAP) disorder. He has good hearing acuity but his brain does not process the sounds in a meaningful way or processes them in a slower than usual manner. He attended a mainstream program with visual communication support and then transferred to a school for the deaf after 1 year. He has progressed in learning sign language so that he can process the meaning of language more readily.

An 18-year-old young man is about to graduate from a school for the deaf. He communicates using American Sign Language with his friends and other Deaf adults but uses Contact Language (Pidgin Sign English) and writing when communicating in the community and when conversing with hearing people. He has no intelligible speech. He has worked as a waiter at a local restaurant for the past 2 years.

A 10-year-old young girl with hearing parents has a severe to profound hearing loss. She responded well to hearing aids and has good speech production. She received a cochlear implant, which helped her continue to improve her oral skills as her primary mode of communication, and she has sign language support. Her parents are very active in her cochlear implant programming and auditory training experiences.

A 6-month-old baby girl is the fourth child born to a suburban couple. The entire family is hearing. This child's hearing loss, a profound loss in both ears, will not be diagnosed until she is $1\frac{1}{2}$ years old. The parents had noticed that their baby babbled at a young age but then did not respond to her name consistently. The parents will experience a year of anxiety, frustration, and concern until the diagnosis is finally made by staff at a local speech and hearing center.

The individuals just described offer a kaleidoscope picture of a specific population in America in terms of age and life circumstances. However, they are set apart by a unique characteristic that affects a very small portion of the population—hearing loss. The diversity of the deaf and hard of hearing (D/HOH) population is reflected in their life scenarios, including diversity in age, socioeconomic status, communication abilities, onset of and degree of hearing loss, cause of the condition, and family circumstances.

A person who is deaf or hard of hearing may be the only individual with a hearing loss in that person's area. For example, in some rural areas, no other person with the condition exists for hundreds of miles. Or, he or she may live in a larger city such as Rochester, New York, where about 10,000 people are Deaf and another 60,000 are hard of hearing (Marschark, 1997).

PREVALENCE

Estimates of the number of individuals with hearing loss vary. Factors such as differences in definition, populations researched, and accuracy of reporting contribute to differences.

Approximately 1 in every 1000 babies is born deaf, and half of these young children are not identified with a hearing loss until the age of 3 (Goldberg cited in Hallahan & Kauffman, 1997, p. 396). Estimates of hearing loss in the entire population reach as high as 25 to 28 million people, or 10 to 11% of the total population including elderly persons to infants (Marschark, 1997; Wheeler, 1999). Others have estimated the prevalence of hearing loss slightly lower at 21 million persons in the United States, or about 8% of the population (Paul & Quigley, 1990). According to the 1990 and 1991 Health Interview Surveys, approximately 20 million persons, or 8.6% of the total U.S. population 3 years and older, were reported to have a hearing loss (see Table 1.1). Recent statistics have estimated that approximately 10% of the population has some degree of hearing loss and that about one third of elderly persons in the United States are hard of hearing (Hard of Hearing Advocates, n.d.). In its 1998 summary of health statistics for U.S. adults, over 17% of the responding population 18 years and older

TABLE 1.1 Estimates of the Prevalence of Hearing Loss by Age Group in the United States, 1990–1991

Age group	Population	Number of hearing impaired	Percent of population
Total	235,688,000	20,295,000	8.6
3–17 years	53,327,000	968,000	1.8
18–34 years	67,414,000	2,309,000	3.4
35–44 years	38,019,000	2,380,000	6.3
45–54 years	25,668,000	2,634,000	10.3
55–64 years	21,217,000	3,275,000	15.4
65 years and older	30,043,000	8,729,000	29.1

Source: National Center for Health Statistics. Data from the National Health Interview Survey, Series 10, Number 188, Table 1, 1994.

reported trouble hearing. (Vital and Health Statistics, 2002.) Of the large number of individuals with hearing loss, a majority, three fourths, are late-deafened adults who are different from deaf and hard of hearing people because a significant part of their experience entails the transition to deafness (Woodcock, 1996).

There are approximately 200,000 people who are born deaf or lost their hearing before they acquired spoken language and use sign language as a primary means of communication. Another 200,000 or so have a congenital or early-onset loss but use spoken language as a primary means of communication, most often because their hearing loss is less severe (Marschark, 1997).

Even though the population of deaf and hard of hearing persons is a small one, it is a population with a strong presence in our society. Also, there exists more acceptance of D/HOH people in the schools, agencies, and communities across our country. Some people with hearing loss have gained recognition in the national media and have brought attention to this low-incidence condition. The movie *Sound and Fury*, which was nominated for an Academy Award in 2001, is a documentary about a family's struggle over controversial medical technology (cochlear implants) for the deaf and hard of hearing. It premiered on the Public Broadcasting Service (PBS) for national broadcasting in 2002. Phyllis Friedman, a Deaf woman, won a Tony Award for her performance in a Broadway play. Marlee Matlin won an Oscar for her performance in a motion picture and an Emmy for a leading role in a television series. Miss America, 1995, Ms. Heather Whitestone, is a woman with a hearing loss (Kirk, Gallagher, & Anastasiow, 1997). Jeffrey T. Perri, a Deaf man, is a reputable chef in Arizona (*www.tomatochef.com*). Laurie Spagnola, a woman with a severe hearing loss, is the village trustee in Camillus, New York. Dr. Christopher Lehfeldt is one of 25 deaf dentists throughout the country, and Dr. Carolyn Stern is a deaf family physician who uses an amplified stethoscope to check the heart rate of her patients (Low, 1999). Vinton Cerf, a hard of hearing man, is credited as the founder of the Internet. More recently, conservative talk show pioneer Rush Limbaugh announced on the air that he had become deaf (Deafness Research Foundation, 2001; Drudge Report, 2001).

Several prominent Deaf people have made an impact on the international and national scene. For example, Billy Hughes, who served as Prime Minister of Australia (1915–1923), had a severe hearing loss. He had a 58-year career in politics (*DeafDigest*, 2001). More recently, a prominent professional made headlines in national newspapers in March 1988. I. King Jordan, a Deaf man, became the first Deaf president at Gallaudet University, a liberal arts university for individuals who are Deaf. Other notable D/HOH professionals may not be the subject of the national media, but they function effectively as sports figures, doctors, lawyers, coaches, directors of businesses, teaching staff, florists, printers, stockbrokers, and, yes, even writers (Ogden, 1996). There are several well-known artists who are deaf.

Mary Thornley is one such artist, whose work you will become acquainted with because her work and that of other artists who are deaf are portrayed throughout this book.

In terms of the future, the U.S. Department of Education's statistics and a Gallaudet University study indicate that about 0.14 and 2%, respectively, of the children in the school-age population from 6 to 17, are educationally identified as deaf or hard of hearing by the public school system (Hallahan & Kauffman, 1997; Marschark, 1997).

"Self-Portrait-The Blue Nose"
Created by: Mary Thornley

As an illustration of the estimate of students receiving services, the U.S. Department of Education's annual report indicated that 60,896 students between the ages of 6 and 21 received some type of specialized services in the schools during the 1992–1993 academic year. A majority of this group, 80 to 90%, is categorized as deaf, whereas only 10 to 20% are identified as hard of hearing. The total group who have some hearing loss was estimated to be 360,000 of the school-age population; therefore, a large proportion of the schoolchildren who have a hearing loss of one kind or another who could benefit are not receiving services (Hardman, Drew, & Wiston-Egan, 1996).

More recent data concerning the 1999–2000 academic year indicated that 43,861 students were seen to have some type of hearing loss, with the majority receiving a type of support service (interpreter, speech training, note taker, etc.). Of this number, approximately 50% had severe to profound hearing loss (Gallandet Research Institute, 2001). Figure 1.1 displays an image of the approximate number of children with hearing loss who are served within special education in recent years.

DEFINITION

Hearing loss, or the words deaf and hard of hearing, cannot be described by a single phrase or neatly portrayed in an audiogram picture; it is a range, a spectrum of conditions or characteristics. The D/HOH population does not constitute a homogeneous group; rather, the individuals with hearing loss form a diverse group composed of smaller subgroups (Ogden, 1996).

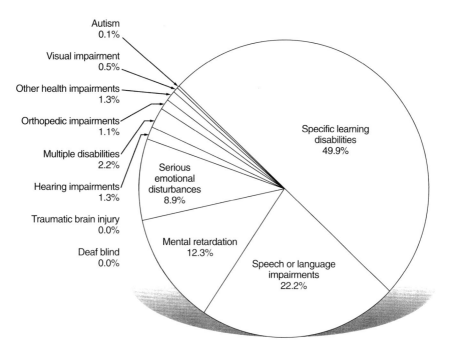

FIGURE 1.1 Percentage of special education by disability. (From *Allyn & Bacon transparencies for special education*. Boston, MA: Allyn & Bacon. Copyright 1996 by Pearson Education. Reprinted by permission of the publisher.)

Even with this in mind, there exist many definitions of and classification systems for hearing loss. By far the most common division is between deaf and hard of hearing (Hallahan & Kauffman, 1997). However, many professionals cannot agree with the exact way to separate the two groups. Two ways to view these divisions are through an audiological definition and a cultural definition. The audiological definition uses at its base the medical perspective of audition (the act or sense of hearing) and hearing loss. This definition is the one most often used in the hearing community.

However, leaders in the Deaf community view this definition as a pathological view of hearing loss because it aligns itself with the medical model of disability (Brueggemann, 1999). To the contrary, the cultural definition is examined through the cultural model as first presented by Baker and Cokely (1980). According to this definition, hearing loss is not so important as a medical condition but rather as helping to define a sociolinguistic group of people sharing a trait who also share a common language and a common culture. Individuals supporting this perspective believe strongly that the physical issue of a loss of hearing does little to define a deaf person's educational, social, intellectual status, or any significant portion of his or her overall identity.

In fact, supporters of this view believe that all Deaf and hard of hearing children who are faced with the effects of hearing loss succeed in life just as hearing children do when they are understood and fully integrated into the life of their own family (Quinn, 1996) and understood and accepted as a linguistic minority within society. Deaf people discussing their "deafness" tend not to focus on pathology or their amount of hearing loss because they believe the greatest deviation from them is "hearing" (Padden & Humphries, 1988; Wohar Torres, 1995). Those espousing the cultural perspective believe that for too long, deafness has been the subject of and subjected to rehabilitation (Brueggemann, 1999).

The audiological definition and its impact are examined in this chapter. The cultural definition will be presented and thoroughly reviewed in Chapter 4. To begin to understand the audiological definition of hearing loss, it is important to understand how the ear works in the process of audition.

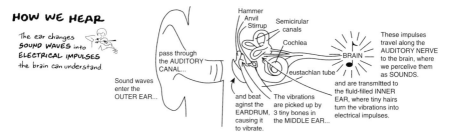

FIGURE 1.2   How we hear.

THE HEARING PROCESS

The hearing process involves the transmission of sound through the vibration of an object to a receiver (Hardman, Drew, & Winston-Egan, 1996). The displacement of air particles by the vibrator produces a pattern of circular waves that move away from the source; this movement is referred to as sound waves (see Figure 1.2). Sound waves are carried through three different parts of the ear (external, middle, and inner) (see Figure 1.3).

The external part of the ear consists of the auricle and the outer auditory canal. The auricle is the part of the ear that is visible. This external portion of the ear is the least complex and the least important for hearing, in comparison with the middle and inner ear (Hallahan & Kauffman, 1997). However, the outer ear channels air vibrations to the eardrum. Its function is one of protection and localization (Moore, 1997). Sound waves are collected by the auricle and are funneled through the outer canal to the middle portion of the ear, which includes the eardrum and the bones of the middle ear. The middle ear comprises the eardrum and three tiny bones, ossicles called the malleus (hammer), incus (anvil), and stapes (stirrup). These bones conduct vibrations to send the sound waves to its next destination, the oval window. The oval window is the link between the middle ear and the inner ear. The major function of the middle ear is to ensure the efficient transfer of sounds from the air to the fluids of the cochlea in the inner ear (Moore, 1997).

The inner ear, the most complex portion of the ear and the most important for hearing, contains two sections, the vestibular mechanism, which is responsible for the sense of balance, and the cochlea. The cochlea is the most important part of the ear, and understanding what happens in the cochlea can provide a key to many aspects of auditory perception (Moore, 1997). The cochlea contains fluid and hair cells, which enable the stimulation of the cochlear nerve, which sends electrical impulses to the brain so that sound can be heard.

In each part of the ear-the outer, middle, and inner-something can occur that causes a hearing loss.

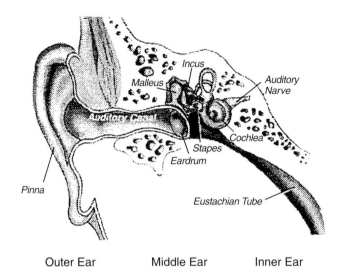

Outer Ear   Middle Ear   Inner Ear

FIGURE 1.3   The parts of the ear. (From National Association of the Deaf. *The Red Notebook*, 2001; Silver Springs MD: National Association of the Deaf.)

TYPES OF HEARING LOSS

A hearing loss can occur in the outer ear if it is obstructed, causing sound waves not to reach the middle or inner ear areas. A conductive hearing loss can occur in the outer or middle ear area that involves poor conduction of sound along the passages leading to the inner ear. Sound is not conducted efficiently and is transmitted in a weaker and muffled manner. These types of losses are typically not as severe as the sensorineural kind and can often be helped by hearing aids and/or surgery.

A sensorineural hearing loss occurs in the inner ear, which involves damage to the hair cells in the cochlea or nerve endings. Sounds are not heard, heard with distortion, or heard incorrectly. Within the past several years, audiologists have been able, in many cases, to diagnose auditory dyssynchronization, a condition in which the sound waves enter the cochlea and functioning hair cells send the neural information to the brain, but the neural component receives the data in an unsynchronized fashion and therefore the message is garbled. Otoacoustic Emissions Testing is a procedure that can be used to help determine this condition, pinpointing the breakdown of the hearing process by separating the neural and sensory components (Starr, Pictin, Sininger, Hood, & Berlin, 1996; K. Wilson-Ward, personal communications, January 5, 2002).

Although more rare than the other two kinds of hearing loss, a mixed hearing loss involves a combination of conductive and sensorineural problems.

MEASURING HEARING LOSS

Behavioral audiometry, often referred to as pure tone audiometry, is the most common way to measure hearing loss and is used effectively at any age. Behavioral audiometry is designed to measure an individual's threshold for hearing a variety of different frequencies. Technically, a threshold is the level at which a stimulus or change in stimulus is just sufficient to produce a sensation or an effect (Stach, 1997). More simply, a person's threshold is simply the level at which he or she can first detect a sound and how intense that sound must be for it to be heard (Hallahan & Kauffman, 1997). A speech audiometer is used to measure hearing acuity by presenting tones as well as speech stimuli to an individual through the use of a headset or insertion of ear phones. Speech audiometry is used to establish levels of detection, reception, and perception of speech.

Sound is a physical event consisting of frequency, intensity, and duration (Candlish, 1996). An audiologist presents a range of sounds through the audiometer and measures the person's reactions to the frequency perceived as pitch in cycles per second, called hertz (Hz). One hertz equals one cycle per second. The hertz measurement is the number of times a sound wave vibrates in 1 second. Intensity involves the loudness of the sound, which is described in a common unit of measurement, the decibel (dB) (Marsharck, 1997). The higher the number of decibels, the louder the sound.

A response from a person, either a raising of the hand or speaking into a microphone or other agreed upon behavior, lets the examiner know whether the person hears the particular sound. The responses are then recorded on a graph called an audiogram. An audiogram is a graphic representation of pure frequency high or low, loud or soft sounds (Candlish, 1996) (see Figure 1.4).

Behavioral observation and play audiometry are often used with individuals who are difficult to test. For example, in certain settings, an individual is placed in a room with a range of items (such as attractive toys or objects) and the audiologist notes the reactions of the individual (head turns, eye blinks, smiles, movements, and lack of responses). These reactions are recorded as sounds are introduced into the room. In play audiometry, the audiologist may set up the testing room as a game. Using pure tones or speech, the examiner may teach the child to do various activities when he or she hears a signal, for example, pick up a book, squeeze a toy, or get a block (Hallahan & Kauffman, 1997).

Electrophysiological tests are administered to the difficult-to-assess individuals or to the side of a lesion if known or suspected. These tests are especially useful for infants, children, or individuals with severe multiple needs because they do not require the client to raise a hand or respond to words (Schwartz, 1996). The reception of sound is recorded on a graph that indicates the brain's responses to the vibrations (Johnson, Benson, & Seaton,

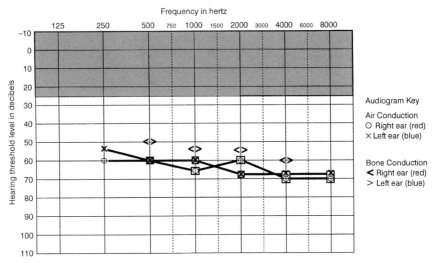

FIGURE 1.4   An audiogram depicting a bilateral sensorineural hearing loss. (From Transparencies to Accompany Exceptional Children and Youth, 6th ed. Copyright 1994 by Macmillan College Publishing Company.)

1997). This technique involves measuring the brain wave activity through the use of an electroencephalograph (EEG) (Hallahan & Kauffman, 1997).

Auditory Brainstem Response (ABR) testing is used to measure the hearing of infants and young children. It is sometimes referred to as Brainstem Auditory Evoked Response (BAER) or Brainstem Evoked Response (BSER). A relaxed state is required to obtain accurate results. In some cases, sedation may be needed. With earphones on the individual's head, clicking noises are presented. A computer monitors the response to the clicking noises and hearing status can then be determined (Schwartz, 1996).

Evoked Otoacoustic Emissions Screening (EOAES) are sounds that are generated in the cochlea in response to stimuli presented in the ear. They travel through the middle ear and into the ear canal, where they can be measured with a miniature microphone. These emissions are thought to be generated by hair cells. Because most hearing loss involves loss of outer hair cells, the lack of an emission is a good predictor of hearing loss (Spivak, 1998). The clinical application of otoacoustic emissions with children and adults has profoundly altered audiology, and given the numerous advantages of this technique, more useful roles of the method should be discovered (Hall, 2000).

Currently, a crusade is on for universal hearing screening of newborns. For example, in New York, following birth, it is required that all infants be screened for a hearing loss before they go home from the hospital, with 6-month follow-up visits (Kwiatkowski, 2000). The National Institutes of Health (NIH) convened a consensus panel that recommended universal newborn screening of infants within the first few months of life. The panel further recommended that screening of infants ideally could occur before the infants leave the hospital through a two-stage process—EOAE screening testing followed by ABR testing if the EOAE screen is failed (Spivak, 1998).

Once a hearing loss is discovered, it is important to examine several variables that have an impact on the development of the individual who is deaf or hard of hearing. The factors that have appeared in the literature as the most important ones affecting development are addressed in the following pages.

FACTORS OF HEARING LOSS AFFECTING DEVELOPMENT

DEGREES OF HEARING LOSS

Hearing loss can be described in terms of decibel loss from mild to profound (Paul & Quigley, 1990). The severity of hearing loss is determined by the individual's reception of sound as measured in decibels. In the 1950s, a diagnosis of a significant hearing loss involved a description of the percentage of hearing lost or available (Candlish, 1996). The use of percentages oversimplified the complexity of a hearing loss, and they are not useful or used in most professional settings.

A person classified as deaf is a person who has a profound loss with a complete inability to hear the spoken language, and a person classified as hard of hearing is one in any of the other categories (mild, moderate, moderately severe, severe) with the capability of hearing speech or of doing so when assisted with hearing aids (Kirk et al., 1997). In order to understand some of what the degrees of loss may limit in terms of hearing environmental sounds, we show Figure 1.5. This figure illustrates what individuals may hear with certain degrees of loss in particular environments such as at school, home, or work. As Figure 1.5 indicates, a person who has a moderate degree of hearing loss may hear speech at a distance of 3 to 5 feet (face to face) and only if the vocabulary is controlled, whereas a person with a profound hearing loss is aware of vibrations but not speech patterns. Most people with a profound loss rely primarily on receiving and sending cues through visual communication. Individuals with borderline to mild losses have a degree of difficulty in hearing related to the noise level and distance from the speaker.

For most individuals with hearing loss in the range of moderate to profound, speaking across a room is a waste of energy. Your face must be clearly visible so that the person may elicit some information from reading your lips and facial expressions (parts of visual communication).

In order to convey a more personal understanding of the impact of hearing loss on understanding speech, Kinsella-Meier (1994) presented an example of what a child with a hearing loss may hear from a formal presentation at school:

Degree of Hearing Loss Based on modified pure tone average (500-4000 Hz)	Possible Effect of Hearing Loss on the Understanding of Language & Speech	Possible Psychosocial Impact of Hearing Loss	Potential Educational Needs and Programs
NORMAL HEARING -10- +15 dB HL	Children have better hearing sensitivity than the accepted normal range for adults. A child with hearing sensitivity in the -10 to +15 dB range will detect the complete speech signal even at soft conversation levels. However, good hearing does not guarantee good ability to discriminate speech in the presence of background noise.		
MINIMAL (BORDERLINE) 16-25 dB HL	May have difficulty hearing faint or distant speech. At 15 dB student can miss up to 10% of speech signal when teacher is at a distance greater than 3 feet or when the classroom is noisy, especially in the elementary grades when verbal instruction predominates.	May be unaware of subtle conversational cues which could cause child to be viewed as inappropriate or awkward. May miss portions of fast-paced peer interactions which could begin to have an impact on socialization and self concept. May have immature behavior. Child may be more fatigued than classmates due to listening effort needed.	May benefit from mild gain/low MPO hearing aid or personal FM system dependent on loss configuration. Would benefit from soundfield amplification if classroom is noisy and/or reverberant. Favorable seating. May need attention to vocabulary or speech, especially with recurrent otitis media history. Appropriate medical management necessary for conductive losses. Teacher requires inservice on impact of hearing loss on language development and learning.
MILD 26-40 dB HL	At 30 dB can miss 25-40% of speech signal. The degree of difficulty experienced in school will depend upon the noise level in classroom, distance from teacher and the configuration of the hearing loss. Without amplification the child with 35-40 dB loss may miss at least 50% of class discussions, especially when voices are faint or speaker is not in line of vision. Will miss consonants, especially when a high frequency hearing loss is present.	Barriers beginning to build with negative impact on self esteem as child is accused of "hearing when he or she wants to," "daydreaming," or "not paying attention." Child begins to lose ability for selective hearing, and has increasing difficulty suppressing background noise which makes the learning environment stressful. Child is more fatigued than classmates due to listening effort needed.	Will benefit from a hearing aid and use of a personal FM system in the classroom. Needs favorable seating and lighting. Refer to special education for language evaluation and educational follow-up. Needs auditory skill building. May need attention to vocabulary and language development, articulation or speechreading and/or special support in reading. May need help with self esteem. Teacher inservice required.
MODERATE 41-55 dB HL	Understands conversational speech at a distance of 3-5 feet (face-to-face) only if structure and vocabulary controlled. Without amplification the amount of speech signal missed can be 50% to 75% with 40 dB loss and 80% to 100% with 50 dB loss. Is likely to have delayed or defective syntax, limited vocabulary, imperfect speech production and an atonal voice quality.	Often with this degree of hearing loss, communication is significantly affected, and socialization with peers with normal hearing becomes increasingly difficult. With full time use of hearing aids/FM systems child may be judged as a less competent learner. There is an increasing impact in self-esteem.	Refer to special education for language evaluation and for educational follow-up. Amplification is essential (hearing aids and FM system). Special education support may be needed, especially for primary children. Attention to oral language development, reading and written language. Auditory skill development and speech therapy usually needed. Teacher inservice required.
MODERATE TO SEVERE 56-70 dB HL	Without amplification, conversation must be very loud to be understood. A 55 dB loss can cause child to miss up to 100% of speech information. Will have marked difficulty in school situations requiring verbal communication in both one-to-one and group situations. Delayed language, syntax, reduced speech intelligibility and atonal voice quality likely.	Full time use of hearing aids/FM systems may result in child being judged by both peers and adults as a less competent learner, resulting in poorer self concept, social maturity and contributing to a sense of rejection. Inservice to address these attitudes may be helpful.	Full time use of amplification is essential. Will need resource teacher or special class depending on magnitude of language delay. May require special help in all language skills, language based academic subjects vocabulary, grammar,pragmatics as well as reading and writing. Probably needs assistance to expand experiential language base. Inservice of mainstream teachers required.
SEVERE 71-90 dB HL	Without amplification may hear loud voices about one foot from ear. When amplified optimally, children with hearing ability of 90 dB or better should be able to identify environmental sounds and detect all the sounds of speech. If loss is of prelingual onset, oral language and speech may not develop spontaneously or will be severely delayed. If hearing loss is of recent onset speech is likely to deteriorate with quality becoming atonal.	Child may prefer other children with hearing impairments as friends and playmates. This may further isolate the child from the mainstream, however, these peer relationships may foster improved self concept and a sense of cultural identity.	May need full-time special aural/oral program for with emphasis on all auditory language skills, speechreading concept development and speech. As loss approaches 80-90 dB, may benefit from a Total Communication approach especially in the early language learning years. Individual hearing aid/personal FM system essential. Need to monitor effectiveness of communication modality. Participation in regular classes as much as beneficial to student. Inservice of mainstream teachers essential.
PROFOUND 91 dB HL or more	Aware of vibrations more than tonal pattern. Many rely on vision rather than hearing as primary avenue for communication and learning. Detection of speech sounds dependent upon loss configuration and use of amplification. Speech and language will not develop spontaneously and is likely to deteriorate rapidly if hearing loss is of recent onset.	Depending on auditory/oral competence, peer use of sign language, parental attitude, ect., child may or may not increasingly prefer association with the deaf culture.	May need special program for deaf children with emphasis on all language skills and academic areas. Program needs specialized supervision and comprehensive support services. Early use of amplification likely to help if part of an intensive training program. May be cochlear implant or vibrotactile aid candidate. Requires continual appraisal of needs in regard to communication and learning mode. Part-time in regular classes as much as beneficial to student.
UNILATERAL One normal hearing ear and one ear with at least a permanent mild hearing loss	May have difficulty hearing faint or distant speech. Usually has difficulty localizing sounds and voices. Unilateral listener will have greater difficulty understanding speech when environment is noisy and/or reverberant. Difficulty detecting or understanding soft speech from side of bad ear, especially in a group discussion.	Child may be accused of selective hearing due to discrepancies in speech understanding in quiet versus noise. Child will be more fatigued in classroom setting due to greater effort needed to listen. May appear inattentive or frustrated. Behavior problems sometimes evident.	May benefit from personal FM or soundfield FM system in classroom. CROS hearing aid may be of benefit in quiet settings. Needs favorable seating and lighting. Student is at risk for educational difficulties. Educational monitoring warranted with support services provided as soon as difficulties appear. Teacher inservice is beneficial.

NOTE: All children with hearing loss require periodic audiologic evaluation, rigorous monitoring of amplification and regular monitoring of communication skills. All children with hearing loss (especially conductive) need appropriate medical attention in conjuction with educational programming.

FIGURE 1.5 Relationship of degree of long-term hearing loss to psychosocial impact and educational needs.(From Anderson, K. L., & Matkin, N. D. [1991]. Relationship of degree of long-term hearing loss to psychosocial impact and educational needs. *Educational Audiology Association Newsletter, 8*, 17–18.)

The setting: An elementary school assembly with a famous person speaking to the children about his career in space.

Question to the guest speaker as stated:
"What would you tell kids who want to be an astronaut?"

Question to the guest speaker possibly heard by child:
_a_ _ou _ you _e_ _i_ _ _o _an_ _o be a_ a__onau_?

Speaker's response as stated:
"Remember that there are lots of opportunities in the future for more astronauts to visit Mars and the moon. NASA needs people who are not discouraged if they suffer a loss or don't achieve every goal they've set. If you miss the goal, try again. And remember to reach for the stars". (Risell cited in Kinsella-Meier, 1994).

Speaker's response possibly heard by child:
" _emembe_ __a_ __e_e a_e _o__ o_ oppo__uni_ie_ in __e
_u_u_e _o_ mo_e a__onau__ _o _i_i_ Ma__ an__ __ e
moon. NA_A nee__ peop__ __o a_e no_ _i___ou_a_e_ i_
__ey _u__e_ a _o__ o_ _on'_ a__ie_e e_e_y _oa_ __ey'_e
_e_. I_ you mi__ __e _oa_, __y a_ain. An_ _ememb__ _o
_ea__ _o_ __e __a__."

If this case scenario represents a possible result for a child with a specific type of loss without hearing aids during a presentation at school, it shows great frustration and suffering for the child but little understanding or gained knowledge. What the child specifically would receive with a hearing aid is not known. However, most children, adolescents, and adults can benefit from hearing aids to amplify the sounds they hear. However, they will still experience gaps in what spoken language or sounds are heard or can be ascertained from their environments. Trying to amplify your own voice to help a person understand what you are saying is often not helpful; raising your voice to a person with a hearing loss can distort your words because shouting changes the form of the consonants and your message will be garbled (Candlish, 1996).

The degree of hearing loss is seen as an important influence on a deaf or hard of hearing person's development. For example, the degree of hearing loss helps classify children for receiving special education services and helps to ascertain whether an individual can receive Supplemental Security Income (SSI) or Social Security Disability (SSD) benefits. Appendix A shows the definitions described in the state education laws from California and New York. These state education regulations are in compliance with federal law 94–142 currently reauthorized in the Individuals with Disabilities Education Act (IDEA), 1990.

Besides affecting educational placement and performance, degrees of hearing loss have been found to affect social and emotional development. People in the general population may think that the more serious the hearing loss, the more problems encountered by hearing family members. However, some researchers have found that children with lesser degrees of loss (mild to moderately severe) were rated by parents as having more behavior problems than deaf or hard of hearing children with greater degrees of loss (severe to profound) (Adams & Tidwell, 1989). Hearing individuals interacting with individuals with lesser degrees of loss may believe that the hard of hearing person can understand more of what is happening in his or her environment because of use of a hearing aid. However, these persons may receive distorted information or may misinterpret information. This situation may get worse over time due to additional frustration, and more adjustment problems may be seen. Parents, teachers, or employers who interact with individuals with greater degrees of loss may understand that the hearing loss will not change. These persons may communicate with the individual using a variety of means (including visual means) to be sure about understanding (Adams, 1997). It should be noted that even in the classroom, a child with a mild to moderate hearing loss may appear to be fine. However, in reality, the child may hear the teacher's voice and some of the intonation patterns but may not hear individual speech sounds clearly enough to differentiate one word from the other (Bless cited in Candlish, 1996). Now place the deaf or hard of hearing person in an employment setting that includes competing noise within the work environment, and the individual with a hearing loss is up against impossible odds if only spoken language is used.

As described before, an audiologist completes an evaluation with a report that can be used to determine whether a loss exists and whether the person has a mild, moderate, moderately severe, severe, or profound loss across specific frequencies. Unfortunately, some have used these descriptions as "labels" to pigeonhole individuals and paint profiles of their cognitive, language, social, employment, relationship, and adjustment capabilities (Tucker, 1998). These misguided people can destroy the importance of the use of this piece of information by the tendency to make invalid assumptions. One must be careful how one estimates a person's overall functioning from an audiogram.

When interacting with D/HOH people, one will discover amusing anecdotes describing their attempts to try to fool the audiologist when taking their hearing test.

For example:

A Deaf adult explained how she cheated on audiological examinations in the past. When she went into the testing room, she was given a headset to put on. When she was asked if she felt comfortable, she adjusted the headset so that it pushed the backs of her earlobes forward. This enabled her to feel the vibrations of the high-pitched sounds, which she was able to detect readily. She was able to indicate which ear the tone was going to because she felt the vibrations.

Another example:

A 10-year-old deaf young boy talked about his experiences since the age of 7 when he used the reflections from a glass-framed picture or the audiologist's glasses to see the lights indicating when a sound was transmitted. He hoped that the angle was good so that he could get a good read on when the tones were appearing and "beat the test."

Even though these stories are often shared in humor, they highlight the care one must take in labeling any persons with specific skills or personality characteristics on the basis of one piece of data received. All assessment procedures administered are subject to error no matter what the area of functioning.

Whatever degree of hearing loss is discovered, individuals who are either deaf or hard of hearing do not or receive minimal linguistic information from their hearing; therefore, they *require a visual base to the communication* used with them, whether this means using sign language, providing consistent eye contact, lip-reading, using pictures to enhance the spoken words, writing, or a combination of these.

AGE OF ONSET OF HEARING LOSS

The age of onset of hearing loss is important as a base for acquiring and using spoken language. Individuals who experience a hearing loss before they acquire speech and spoken language, typically before the age of 3, are considered to have prelingual hearing loss. For example, Pamela Rohring, who cowrote this book, was diagnosed with her hearing loss before language development, at the age of 2. She has a prelingual hearing loss. On the other hand, Rush Limbaugh, who was recently diagnosed, has a postlingual hearing loss. Persons who acquire hearing loss after acquiring spoken language, typically after the age of 3, are considered to have a hearing loss that is postlingual. This is important in our society because spoken and written English is the foundation of our culture and educational system.

Individuals with prelingual hearing loss as it relates to being exposed to spoken English are often delayed in English language achievement because they primarily use visual means to communicate rather than oral or aural means.

FAMILY STRUCTURE

Most parents of deaf and hard of hearing children (90–95%) are hearing themselves (Marschark, 1997). The largest problem facing these parents is communication in the family (Adams, 1997). Problems in deaf and hard of hearing children and the social and emotional difficulties appearing in some D/HOH youth and adults are seen as resulting from breakdowns in family communication. The social-emotional problems in these individuals often relate to attempts to communicate thoughts, feelings, and desires to family members that have been thwarted. Family communication is frequently strained. The development of an optimal communication system between parents and children is critical in the emotional development of deaf and hard of hearing children (Luterman, 1996; Stinson, 1991).

Families with deaf or hard of hearing members encounter a unique challenge to the family. Because most parents of deaf and hard of hearing children are themselves hearing, they experience the feeling of being "different" from their offspring. After the diagnosis of hearing loss, some parents feel that the deaf child became a stranger with whom they had little in common. The hearing loss in their child was a real difference that seemed to set them apart.

For example:

> One Deaf adult stated that the communication between her and her parents was almost non-existent based solely on rudimentary gestures indicating sleep, eat, yes, no (Sevigny-Skyer, 1990).

The fact that hearing parents and deaf children do not experience the world in the same way demands adjustment in the family system (Henderson & Hendershott, 1992). Hearing parents need to make adjustments in their family unit or in their expectations for their family to include an individual who has a hearing loss and experiences the world differently from them. Creating an early family communication system that is inclusive of the deaf or hard of hearing member is a difficult challenge and becomes a hurdle not often overcome in many families. In fact, only 10 to 15% of all hearing parents use primarily visual communication such as sign language effectively with their children.

Once a child is diagnosed as deaf, the family unit is no longer considered "hearing"; the parents may be hearing, the other children may be hearing, but the family unit becomes "hearing and deaf" (Henderson & Hendershott, 1992). Within this new family unit, the problem is not that deaf and hard of hearing children are being deprived of sounds as much as they are being deprived of language and communication (Meadow, 1980). Being deaf per se does not lead to problems in communication as Deaf parents communicate quite well with their Deaf children (Sloman, Perry, & Frankenburg, 1987). Good communication patterns established early in the home have been related consistently with positive child development (Garbarino, 1992; Marschark, 1997; Nowell & Marschark, 1994).

Communication affects every aspect of our human development from dealing with feelings to managing behaviors and disseminating information about our culture. Communication is critical in our lives and the lives of all people. A deaf or hard of hearing individual will have difficulty communicating wants, needs, thoughts, and feelings if a strong early communication base is not established in the home. When communication is inadequate, the outlets for venting frustration and working through difficult situations as well as celebrating happy moments or subtle enjoyments are often limited. The single largest issue facing parents in maintaining a family unit is that of involving all family members in communication in the home. Research has shown that Deaf children with Deaf parents, who share a common language and communication system, have an advantage when attempting a variety of life's tasks. Deaf parents and Deaf adults are resources to all parents of deaf and hard of hearing children and to all members of the community who provide services to the D/HOH population.

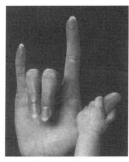

"Parent-Child"
Created by: Dana Janik

The lack of a strong communication base within the family affects how deaf and hard of hearing youth and adults seek out interactions with hearing individuals and ultimately how they feel about those interactions in school, the workplace, and the community. In the absence of a shared communication system, a general sense of isolation can exist (Kluwin & Gaustad, 1992).

ETIOLOGY OF DEAFNESS

The etiology (causes) of deafness has an important influence on development. In the majority of cases, the cause of hearing loss is unknown (Gallandet Research Institute, 2001). There exist many causes of hearing loss that originate outside the body (a disease such as meningitis, an injury, or drugs) or inside the body (genetics) (Paul & Jackson, 1993). Causes of hearing loss include heredity, blood incompatibility, accidents, medications, drug and alcohol addiction syndromes, poisons, allergies, bacterial infections (meningitis), viral infections (cytomeglavirus [CMV], mumps, rubella, measles), otitis media (ear infections), and birth accidents (prematurity, birth injury) (Adams, 2001; Quigley & Kretschmer, 1982; Vernon & Andrews, 1990) (see Figure 1.6 for a comprehensive list of etiologies of deafness).

Heredity	Both parents deaf	Unknown	No known cause of hearing loss
	One or more deaf siblings		
	Deaf relatives		
	History of family hearing loss and prematurity	Other	Acquired Immune Deficiency Syndrome (AIDS)
	History of family hearing loss and rubella		Adenoids or tonsil problem
	History of family deafness and childhood illness		Anoxia
			Birth complications
			Bone cancer
Meningitis	Hearing loss formed by meningitis		Chicken Pox
	Hearing loss formed by tuberculous meningitis		Complications during pregnancy
	Possible meningitis		Complications of several illnesses
	History of family hearing loss and meningitis		Cyclomegavirus (CMV)
	Prematurity and meningitis		Ear infections
	Prematurity and tuberculous meningitis		Encephalitis
			Fetal Alcohol Syndrome
			Functional hearing loss
Prematurity	Birthweight 5 lbs, 1/2 oz, or less		Head injury
	Maternal rubella and prematurity		High fever
	Rh and prematurity		Mastoid problems
	Possible prematurity		Maternal Flu or virus
	History of family hearing loss and prematurity		Maternal scarlet fever during pregnancy
	Meningitis and prematurity		Maternal use of drugs during pregnancy
	Tuberculous meningitis and prematurity		Mumps
			Pneumonia
Rh Factor	Rh factor and full-term pregnancy		Polio
	Rh factor and prematurity		Scarlet fever
	Possible Rh		Virus
			Whooping cough
Rubella	Maternal rubella and full-term pregnancy		Whooping cough and measles
	Prematurity and maternal rubella		
	Possible rubella		
	History of family hearing loss and rubella		
	Other measles and rubella		

FIGURE 1.6 Causes of hearing loss. (Adapted, from Adams, J.W. [2001, July]. *Mental health issues and the deaf consumer.* Paper presented at the biannual meeting of the Empire State Association for the Deaf, and Vemon, M., & Andrews, J.F. (1990). *The psychology of deafness.* New York: Longman.

The causes of the hearing loss are important because some of the conditions that cause deafness may cause problems in health, learning, and social and emotional functioning. Some of the leading causes of deafness can also cause behavior or learning problems. For example, Attention Deficit Hyperactivity Disorder (ADHD) is found to a higher degree in the D/HOH population. Vision problems are found in 30% of those diagnosed with hearing loss. Caution must be used, however, in diagnosing physical and neurological disorders in deaf and hard of hearing individuals. Some studies have shown that ADHD is no more prevalent in the deaf and hard of hearing population than in the hearing population and that differences found may be due to the consequences of language differences and communication needs mistakenly perceived as symptoms of a biological disorder by hearing parents (Hindley & Kroll, 1998).

Also, it is estimated that Pervasive Developmental Disorder, Not Otherwise Specified (PDD NOS) will probably be found to be higher in the D/HOH population because of the suggested etiology of neurological involvement (C. M. Oliver, M.D., personal communication, December 10, 2001).

DEAF AND HARD OF HEARING
PEOPLE AND THE LAW

Given the many factors affecting the development and experiences of individuals who are deaf or hard of hearing, they have specific needs. By audiological and medical definitions, deaf and hard of hearing people belong to a minority group, those with disabilities. Persons with disabilities have won several victories for their advancement and equal protection under the law in education (PL 94–147) and in the private sector (The Rehabilitation Act of 1973, PL 93–11, Section 504; Americans with Disabilities Act [ADA], 1990).

In 1973, the Vocational Rehabilitation Act, Section 504 (the precursor to PL 94–147 and ADA) provided for a number of advances in access to businesses, employment opportunities, and college placements. For example, the act provided for interpreters for the national mainstreaming of deaf students in post-secondary institutions (Sanderson, Siple, & Lyons, 2000).

In 1990, ADA provided legislative protection against discrimination in employment of all those with disabilities. Without such legislation, individuals such as Chuck Lamoreaux, now an equal employment specialist, could not have obtained the quality of training necessary to help underrepresented groups. He attended Edinborough University in Pennsylvania because it was the only wheelchair-accessible campus at the time that accommodated his physical disabilities. Now, with ADA, more universities and colleges are accessible (Schneider, 1999/2000) and post-secondary education is a reality to thousands of deaf and hard of hearing students. In the 1990s each year, approximately 20,000 students attended 2- to 4-year universities and colleges where about 10,000 received interpreting services (Stuckless, Ashmore, Schroedel, & Simon, 1997). Without the availability of well-qualified interpreters, the dramatic increase in the numbers of deaf and hard of hearing students in regular colleges would not have occurred.

Specifically, Title III of the Americans with Disabilities Act gives rights of equal access to places of public accommodation. For deaf and hard of hearing people, Title III requires businesses and agencies to remove many frustrating barriers to communication (National Association of the Deaf, 1997–1998). Title III addresses accommodations in a wide range of places such as retail stores; hotels; theaters; doctors', lawyers', dentists', and psychologists' offices; museums; and social service agencies, covering both profit and nonprofit organizations. Places of public accommodation must give persons with a hearing loss equal opportunity to participate in and to benefit from their services regardless of the size of their business or service.

For example:

> A place of business shall furnish appropriate auxiliary aids and services where necessary to ensure effective communication with individuals with disabilities (28 C.F.R. 36.303 (c), 1990).

A list of auxiliary aids and services required by ADA for deaf and hard of hearing people includes qualified interpreters, notetakers, computer-aided transcription services, written materials, telephone handset amplifiers, assistive listening devices, telephones compatible with hearing aids, closed caption decoders, open and closed captioning, telecommunication devices for the deaf (e.g., teletypewriters, TTYs), videotext displays, or other effective methods of making aurally delivered materials available to individuals with hearing loss (National Association of the Deaf Law Center, n.d.).

A national class action lawsuit was initiated against the United Parcel Service (UPS) by the Disability Rights Advocates in Oakland, California. The claimants reported UPS' failure to allow deaf and hard of hearing workers to drive delivery vehicles; its failure to provide accommodations such as interpreters or captioning at interviews, trainings, and other meetings; its failure to promote deaf and hard of hearing workers beyond entry-level positions (Dralegal, n.d.). The alleged failures are common complaints heard from many deaf and hard of hearing employees from small businesses to government organizations around our country.

Our laws protect individuals who are deaf and hard of hearing in gaining employment and in obtaining services. However, Schneider (1999/2000) points out that individuals with disabilities should not need to prove themselves as competent workers or individuals who have a right to receive services as do all others in our society, despite their limitations. *However, in the year 2004 equal protection is still needed.*

THE LAW AND ACCESSIBILITY

THEIR STORIES . . .

Several years ago, a man was arrested in Washington, DC. The police pushed the man to the floor as he was struggling to communicate; the man was Deaf. The man had difficulty breathing but was unable to tell the police that he could not breathe because his arms were constrained. The man suffocated and died.

A young deaf man was leaving a college party and clearly had too many drinks. He got into his car and was driving on campus. The police stopped him and told him to take the series of field tests for sobriety. The man told the officers that he needed an interpreter before he could answer any questions. They told him to sign a waiver that he refused the field tests. He did not understand the legal words on paper, and again he requested an interpreter. The young man was arrested.

THE LAW . . .

State and local law enforcement agencies have a federal mandate to ensure adequate and appropriate communication with D/HOH persons. For example, qualified sign language interpreters for communication with persons who rely on sign language are required. If a deaf or hard of hearing individual is arrested, a Miranda warning should be given in printed form and the arrestee must be advised that the law enforcement agency has an obligation to offer an interpreter when available without cost and will defer interrogation until a qualified interpreter is available. If this is not done, serious violations of constitutional and civil rights can occur (National Association of the Deaf, 1997–1998).

THEIR STORIES . . .

A young Deaf man was admitted to the psychiatric unit of the main hospital in a large city. He requested an interpreter to discuss his problems and why he needed to be admitted (severe depression). The staff reported that they would look for one. The man called Deaf Adult Services in the city and asked for someone to advocate for him. They were understaffed. The doctors were ready to discharge him the next day even though he had signed to his Deaf girlfriend that he was thinking of killing himself and sometimes he had homicidal feelings. The psychiatrist on duty reported that the Deaf person was reserved and was not a threat to self or others. The staff asked the girlfriend to tell all she knew from their conversations, and they would follow up.

A 55-year-old Deaf woman cut herself on her arm with a wire. On the assumption that it was a suicide attempt, she was admitted to the psychiatric ward. At no time was an interpreter available for the woman during her admission, treatment, or discharge meetings. The nurses and doctors wrote notes to her. They never became suspicious concerning her understanding of the written word even when she refused a tetanus shot. Later, when questioned by a friend who knew sign language, she reported that she did not know what the injection involved and had never seen the word "tetanus" before.

A young teenage girl who had a severe hearing loss was at the hospital and needed to be admitted for possible seizure activity. She requested a television with captioning and, most important, a TTY so she could call her mother directly. The staff could not find a television with captioning during her week and a half stay, and a TTY was delivered 2 days later to the nurses' station because they needed to obtain it from another section of the hospital.

THE LAW ...

The Department of Health and Human Services' Office of Civil Rights (OCR) has determined that effective communication must be provided at "critical points" during hospitalization. Critical points are considered to be as follows: when critical medical information is communicated, such as at admission; when explaining medical procedures; when an informed consent is required for treatment; and at discharge. Deaf or hard of hearing persons must also relate their communication needs. It is important to determine the extent to which communication is needed in a sign language base or another visual means.

In 1980, Stewart (Director of OCR) reported that physicians wonder why the exchange of written notes will not suffice with a deaf patient. There is a distinction between English and ASL. ASL is a visual means of communication separate and distinct from English regardless of whether it is in spoken or written form.

No distinction is made between inpatient and outpatient treatment. All of the services provided in health care facilities *must be* accessible. Inpatient facilities also have the responsibilities under ADA to ensure that their telephone, television, and other services are accessible and usable by D/HOH individuals (National Association of the Deaf Law Center, n.d.). Services must be equivalent for both hearing and deaf and hard of hearing patients. Deaf patients should have TTYs and televisions equipped for captioning (National Association of the Deaf, 2000).

THEIR STORIES ...

Two Deaf women attended a conference in a large northeastern city. They obtained accommodations at a well-known hotel and made reservations well in advance. They requested accommodations for people who are deaf and hard of hearing—a TTY and a television with captioning. When they arrived to check in, the registration clerk reported that they had a "handicapped-accessible room," which meant that they had a large door for a wheelchair to get through, located on the first floor, and had rails in the bathtub. No TTY or television with captioning was found. Finally, when a maintenance person brought the decoder in several hours later, it was dusty and he had no idea how to connect it.

THE LAW ...

Title III also requires public accommodations to provide TTYs upon request when such facilities offer a customer, client, patient, or participant the opportunity to make outgoing telephone calls on more than an incidental convenience basis. Hotels should also provide a TTY at the front desk in order to take calls from guests who use TTYs in their rooms (National Association for the Deaf, 2000).

THEIR STORIES . . .

"A professor objects to providing real-time captioning transcripts to deaf and hard of hearing students in class because the regular (hearing) students do not receive the same benefits. The professor forbids tape-recording of the lecture" (Rawlinson, 1998, pp. 339–340).

THE LAW . . .

The professor does not have the right to refuse the student real-time captions during class. The issue of supplying a transcript of the class lecture from a tape recording is separate from providing captions during class. A notetaker could be provided to this student in addition to the real-time captions (Rawlinson, 1998).

CONCLUSION

ADA is the law that formally protects the rights of individuals with disabilities. However, when interacting with deaf and hard of hearing people, some common sense would further the cause in providing access to communication and interactions. This was not the case on October 3, 2000, when hundreds of people gathered together in Washington, DC for a rally demanding the protection of ADA, the very law that proclaims their rights. Upon arrival at the Supreme Court, interpreters tried to stand on the steps so that they could be visible to deaf and hard of hearing participants. The court security banned the interpreters from the steps. They could not accept the logic that the interpreters needed to be only a few steps higher than the crowd to provide accessible communication to all (Brick, 2000).

2

WORLDS COLLIDE: GROWING UP WITH A HEARING LOSS

The following personal accounts represent three people who have grown up with a hearing loss and are successful in their lives. Their life stories illustrate the experiences of having a hearing loss, dealing with the ups and downs that contributed to their growth, and how they have become positive role models for the deaf and hard of hearing population and for society as a whole.

"Sarah and Garrett"
Created by: Mary Thornley

PAMELA S. ROHRING, M.S.

ASL/Deaf Studies Specialist
St. Mary's School for the Deaf,
Buffalo, New York
Hearing Status: Bilateral Profound
Sensorineural Hearing Loss

I was 2 years old and experienced a high fever. In March 1967, I was playing in the backyard of my parent's house. My mother, Helen, was trying to call my name and I did not hear her. My sister, Judy, approached me and tapped on my right shoulder. I was surprised and puzzled by my sister's actions. I was not aware that I couldn't hear. My mother and father began to realize that I did not hear at all. My parents discussed seeing a doctor; however, my father was in denial that his daughter Pamela was deaf. My father's reactions are fairly typical of many hearing parents who do not want their child to be different from themselves (Adams, 1997).

"Tapestry"
Created by: Morris Broderson

A few weeks later, or perhaps more like over the next 2 years, they took me to see a variety of doctors searching for help. I remember going with my parents, sister, and Aunt Alice to Buffalo, where I took many hearing tests and evaluations. I remember the events that took place in a small room extremely well. After the evaluation, the audiologist showed my family and me a body hearing aid. I was puzzled. The specialist explained to me how to use it. I looked at my sister and wondered why she did not have a hearing aid. I knew, then, that something was wrong with me. I gestured to the audiologist and pointed (at my sister), indicating that she should have one too. "No, it is for you," his gestures and facial expressions told me. He put the hearing aid in both of my ears. I started to recognize environmental sounds including the "sound of voices" (which did not make sense). At that moment, at the age of 4, I learned that I was deaf.

My parents enrolled me in speech therapy at Mt. View Hospital in my hometown of Lockport, New York. My father drove me to this hospital three times a week for speech therapy classes. While sitting with my mother in the waiting room, I looked around and noticed something odd. I learned that most people were elderly and had a difficult time using their speech. I was only 4 or 5 years old at that time. I became aware that I was the only child there with a speech teacher, whose name was John. I practiced how to use my speech again. I hated it because there was so much repetition. I could never get it right. This, I will never forget! Every time I came home from speech therapy, my mother would pull out a long rectangular mirror and we continued practicing how to enunciate each word. After I mouthed the word approximately right, we would place a picture illustrating it in a scrapbook. For example, my mom showed me how to say "ball" and I had to watch her mouth to see how she formed her lips into the specific morphemes. I then would try to say "ball" in front of the mirror.

The process was tedious, with constant drills and repetitions. These experiences were exhausting. I used to become angry and frustrated about these "speech" exercises. I missed the real time alone with my mother because she spent a great deal of time on "teaching" words. As I look back on these experiences, my mother was stuck in the role of teacher and educator and not always in the role of my mother.

In 1970, when I was 5 years old, I was enrolled St. Mary's School for the Deaf in Buffalo, New York. My mother, sister, and Aunt Alice visited St. Mary's School for the Deaf with me. The philosophy at the school was to use an oral/aural approach, which was compatible with the speech therapy I received before school age. When I was 6, the school changed to a total communication philosophy, which included the use of all visual and aural means to make communication more effective. Sign language was a part of this philosophy. Although we had no knowledge of sign language at the time, my mother and my sister were enrolled in sign language classes. My father was not interested in learning sign language. He communicated with me by gestures or body language. He always communicated with me with a few signs such as EAT, SLEEP, WORK, and GO OUT EAT. I always wanted to communicate with my dad in sign language, but communication remained in gesture or body language. My home life centered around what little communication was provided by my mother and sister.

Most educators of deaf students who favor Total Communication stress the use of auditory and oral skills, including speech reading and manual skills such as some signing English system. Signing English systems follow the same word order as spoken English and are therefore not a separate, distinct language. Signing English systems are more comfortable for hearing people to use at home and in teaching because they have English at their base. This is not true for Deaf people. American Sign Language (ASL) is rarely used in the schools, and I was not exposed to it in formal situations. ASL is a grammatically sophisticated, highly evolved language of its own (Hallahan & Kauffman, 1997).

Even with the use of the total communication philosophy, academic achievement of deaf students with severe to profound hearing losses is lower than that of their hearing counterparts. Studies have shown that when the language is the same in the home between parents and children (spoken English for hearing, sign language for deaf), children's reading achievement is higher than when children who are deaf grow up in English-speaking families. This is because both sets of families are able to communicate more easily with their children through their native home language (Marschark, 1997).

I did my best in an educational program that used a sign system that related to English and a home environment where I was able to sign only with my sister. For most deaf children, only about 10% of hearing parents can communicate effectively with their children (Lane, Hoffmeister, & Bahan, 1996). At least my sister was my communication outlet.

By the time I graduated from high school, I quit using my hearing aid. I knew that hearing aids never helped me to hear or recognize words. They helped me only to be aware of environmental sounds (a car honk, a siren, people's talking [no recognizable words], and other, very loud sounds) when these sounds were amplified greatly. This amplification of noise caused me a great deal of headaches. The sounds were very annoying. I have a very low tolerance for such noises and sensations.

As I looked back on my youth, I recalled that most educators were concerned primarily with the extent to which the hearing loss affects the ability to speak and understand spoken language. Educators often refer to people with hearing impairment who cannot process spoken linguistic information as deaf and those who can as hard of hearing. Persons who are deaf at birth or before language develops are referred to as having prelingual deafness (Hallahan & Kauffman, 1997). Those who acquire their deafness after spoken language starts to develop are referred to as having postlingual deafness. I am considered to be prelingually deaf because my hearing loss occurred before the foundation of a spoken language started. The approach that addresses speech and emphasizes use of lipreading and residual hearing and a signed English system would be of more benefit to those who are postlingually deaf. It is not surprising to me now that even though I was successful in school and as an adult professional, it was a tremendous struggle year after year in my educational years.

Some people who are deaf resent being defined as "disabled" at all and prefer to be considered as part of a cultural or language minority. I prefer to be considered as part of a cultural minority because my whole existence relates to my identity as a Deaf woman who identifies with other deaf people and who uses a common visual language, ASL.

When I was 9 or 10 years old, I communicated with my mom and dad in sign language. Often, they misunderstood what I said with my "deaf" voice. I had temper tantrums and struggled to tell them what I wanted. Home signs (homemade signs unique to each family) were developed. This form of communication limits and restricts interaction between hearing parents and their Deaf child. The results of this communication system were reflected in my temper tantrums, which were often the product of frustrated attempts to communicate even simple ideas. I frequently displayed long moments of staring during communicative interactions out of feelings of confusion or a sense of futility. These staring episodes may have exacerbated my parents' fear and self-doubt. Communications with my parents and extended family members were events of constant frustration.

I always depended on my sister in most communication situations because she knew how to interact with me more readily in sign language. For example, when my parents were trying to tell me something and I didn't understand what was said, I often asked my sister to fill in the blanks. She was my "interpreter." I knew that it was not fair for her to be an interpreter because she was not allowed to have a typical sister relationship with me, and this also placed her in a working relationship (a communication interpreter) during family functions instead of having fun.

At other times, I forced myself to focus on my parents' speech when they were talking by using my best asset, my eyes. I learned by necessity to read my parents' lips well. I was lucky, however, because lip-reading is an inefficient means of gathering meaning from spoken language. Only 25% of what is said can be seen formed on the lips. Most of the phonemes are formed inside the mouth, making them invisible to the lipreader. Therefore, the best lip-reader receives only a small portion of the message by using this method (Hallahan & Kaufman, 1997).

When we had our Thanksgiving, Christmas, birthdays, and wedding parties and other celebrations, my parents always encouraged me to go to my extended family's house. I didn't like to attend these gatherings because no one in our family was willing to communicate with me in sign language. They treated me differently, as a disabled person, when in truth their behavior was "disabling" me. I remembered that to keep busy, I always brought a book or something to read. I watched with envy as my sister talked with our cousins, grandparents, uncles, or aunts. I always sat by myself or next to my sister. These visits exhausted me. My extended family members would always ask me, "HOW ARE YOU?" "HOW WAS YOUR SCHOOL?" "DO YOU HAVE ANY BOYFRIENDS?" and "WOULD YOU LIKE SOMETHING TO EAT?" My family members did not communicate with me in in-depth conversation. The same questions came up every time through my sister's sign language interpreting. When non-signers wanted more of a conversation, they called my sister's name or grabbed my sister to interpret. It was not a perfect solution because it was not fair for my sister to be an interpreter everywhere I went; however, it seemed the only choice, or so I thought. To be honest, I often felt deep inside that my sister was my "mother" because she was always there for me. She was my voice and my ears, and I depended on her. Our family had a different family structure. We had different relationships and roles within my family compared with those developed by other families.

When we were sitting at the table and passing the bowls of food, everyone was talking to each other. I was not able to understand everyone by lipreading at the same time. I always finished eating and then left the table to watch television or read a book. I felt too bored or left out with no one trying to communicate with me. Table conversation is a well-known factor in positive language development (Bodner-Johnson, 1988). I missed out on these experiences and in part missed out greatly in language enrichment that would have enhanced my language development.

When growing up, I always complained when we were to go to visit my extended family because they did not make the effort to communicate with me. The situation was unfair. I felt that I was a different person, an outcast in my own family. I often thought that other people saw me as a limited, handicapped child.

Because of the problems finding people with whom to communicate, individuals who are deaf and hard of hearing are at risk for loneliness (Pollard, 1998). Some, or people who have hearing parents, may experience more unhappiness because of the difficulty they have in communicating with their parents (Adams, 1997).

My self-esteem was very low. At every stage of my growth, I was never challenged to solve problems and my family always tried to protect me out of concern for my welfare. They really did not understand that what I really needed was a family within which to interact and involve myself in communication. When I was in my teens, my parents gave up and let me do what I wanted. I did not need this freedom; I needed the freedom and the independence that a good family communication system would have provided. I rebelled. For example, when it was my grandfather's or grandmother's birthday, I would visit them, and before the rest of the family arrived, I often walked home myself. I had no foundation for a relationship with any of my extended family members. I looked back at my youth and often wish my family had had exposure to the Deaf community. The Deaf community and its culture met my needs. I wish my family could have been exposed to Deaf people in the community because then they would have been exposed to at least a part of me.

My hearing parents may have resorted unwittingly to practices that actually inhibited my growth because of their lack of knowledge about hearing loss and their lack of communication with me. A survey at one school for the Deaf found that only 1 parent in 10 could communicate well with his or her deaf child (Lane et al., 1996). Because of this limited ability to communicate, hearing parents tend to control their interactions and dictate the topics of the interactions. For example, they may set very strict rules to prevent their child from exploring the physical and social environment out of a misplaced concern for the child's welfare. For me, it was difficult to manage my own turn-taking in play when I was young or in a discussion when older, a basic social skill, because my parents often responded to their own questions that they would introduce. Most hearing parents talk *to* their deaf children, not *with* them (Lane *et al.*, 1996).

Reliance on spoken English as the sole means of communication with a deaf child restricts parent–child interaction severely and interferes with the natural bonding process. When communication breaks down, the child's cognitive, linguistic, emotional, and educational progress suffers. My parents were unable to communicate information, rules of behavior, and values to me, a Deaf person, their daughter. This lack of communication therefore inhibited me from obtaining the bases for independent decision making.

It is very important for parents to begin early communication efforts so that the deaf and hard of hearing child will reap the benefits of these early efforts by strengthening their cognitive ability, helping them acquire knowledge of the world, and enabling them to communicate fully with the surrounding world, living fully in the worlds of the hearing and of the Deaf.

As I grew older, I recognized myself as culturally Deaf. This process slowly began in high school. When in secondary school I was involved with sports. As I think back, I often chose events such as going to basketball games or track and field tournaments rather than to family gatherings. I chose the sport tournament because I was starved for social interaction and ease of communication that met my personal needs. It was very important for my growth as a Deaf person to attend these events. Often, Deaf young adults talk about school as their primary family environment compared with their own actual family unit (Padden & Humphries, 1988).

After I graduated from St. Mary's School for the Deaf in 1985 I attended Gallaudet University in Washington, DC, the only liberal arts university established for the deaf. When I arrived at Gallaudet University, I experienced true culture shock and my cultural ties with the Deaf community continued to grow.

The impact of this experience changed my life because my experiences with my family and school did not prepare me for this exposure to Deaf Culture.

I began to evaluate my life and understand my parents more fully. I looked back at every experience and tried to gain new insight into behaviors and actions. I had always struggled with the hearing culture. Hearing parents are so vulnerable, perhaps to the shock of discovering that their child, whom they had considered normal in every way, is in fact unable to hear. Identity is a major issue for deaf people. I was very angry with the people who were not preparing my parents about my future life as a Deaf young adult or who were not preparing me concerning my goals after graduation. I realized that my hearing parents and some hearing professionals were clueless about the needs of young deaf adults. I had to rediscover myself again and again.

Isolation from the hearing community on the part of many people who are deaf is seen as sign of social pathology. Often, however, Deaf people who believe in the value of having their Deaf Culture are seeking the enjoyment of finally belonging and finding a place in their culture, a true identity. What appears to be isolation is really the natural response of a person who discovers the common bond of sign language and sense of community.

With the experiences at Gallaudet University as a young adult, I finally recognized myself with a Deaf attitude and identity—I am a DEAF person. Slowly, I acquired a positive attitude as a culturally deaf person. I am proud of my Deaf culture and heritage. Being deaf has little to do with a person's hearing acuity, which is a major focus in the hearing community. The Deaf community has its own set of norms with regard to such behaviors as eye contact, physical touching, and communication techniques.

I will never forget that one time during my freshman year (1986) at Gallaudet University, I invited home two friends who were from Texas and California. They were coming to my house for Thanksgiving. It was a good experience for my family. We were so involved with our Deaf Culture that my family experienced this immersion first hand. We communicated in ASL and used cultural ways to get each other's attention during our Thanksgiving dinner. My family were now the "outsiders." I remembered that I tried to communicate with my sister and she had a hard time following our conversation because her use of signing English was so different from the language of ASL.

It seems that my family's knowledge was very limited about Deaf issues throughout my life. My parents learned from hearing professionals, whose knowledge about Deaf people and their needs is almost always limited. My parents readily took the advice of these professionals. This advice was often outdated and old fashioned. Even schools for the deaf have very few Deaf people in the positions of teachers and administrators.

In 1988, the Deaf President Now (DPN) protest occurred in Washington, DC. Gallaudet University never had a Deaf president in modern times. The board of trustees hired a hearing person for the position. The protest that followed was "heard" around the world and culminated the selection of a Deaf president. This event was an important cultural milestone and inspired recognition of the Deaf as having a separate culture with its own language. This protest raised awareness of many hearing and deaf individuals around the world. During my sophomore year at Gallaudet University, the DPN protest was a life-changing experience for me. Deaf people had solidarity and a cultural "voice."

In April 1991, I was hired as a teaching assistant at St. Mary's School for the Deaf. While working with the children, I noticed that some deaf children had low self-esteem similar to what I experienced in my youth. I started to flash back to my younger years.

For many years, Deaf people struggled with oppression, and were being treated as second-class citizens. I wanted to become a role model for deaf and hard of hearing children so that they could be proud of themselves and their Deaf heritage. This goal remains a challenge as we struggle with cultural differences, true learning deficits related to second language acquisition, and hearing and deaf people working as a team to provide effective educational programming.

As I examined what could be my future contributions to the growth of all deaf and hard of hearing children, I realized that no Deaf Culture or American Sign Language classes were being offered at our school. I spoke with the president at St. Mary's School for the Deaf. From this conversation, a position of ASL/Deaf Studies Specialist was born. I never imagined that I would be the person to guide educators, students, and parents concerning effective communication and bring issues related to Deaf Culture to a school for the deaf, much less to my alma mater.

I dedicated myself to a career as a Deaf Studies and ASL teacher. I would like to see our deaf children learn how to interact with other deaf and hard of hearing children. I care about our children becoming role models for future generations of Deaf and hard of hearing youth.

I want others to share in my appreciation of Deaf Culture and educate them about the beauty of our language. I want to demonstrate to others how to communicate with our children in a way that creates accessibility when meeting our specialized needs. I want our future generations of deaf and hard of hearing children to understand and know each other personally within both the hearing and the Deaf communities.

I continue to educate and be educated by people in the workplace environment. Even though we work at a school for the deaf, we still struggle with culture and language issues within our walls. Barriers to effective communication exist in our school such as interpreting services, deaf hiring practices, and staff sign communication competence in a variety of modes. These barriers will inhibit the provision of full access to services in a Deaf-friendly environment. I want the children of our cultural future to experience their education and their community with models from both the Deaf community and the hearing world that have a positive impact on their growth. When I was a child, very few Deaf role models were available and I always felt different and out of place. It is my hope that this publication will help us work together to make each and every child have a future in which they have a strong sense of self in a community that experiences awareness of their needs.

My major goal, in which I solicit your help, is to teach our deaf and hard of hearing children to advocate for themselves and to be respectable citizens in our society without limitation.

BERNARD R. HURWITZ, ESQ.

Attorney
Rochester, New York
Hearing Status: Hard of Hearing

Often when I was growing up and my parents introduced me to a deaf friend of theirs, that person would shake my hand and ask if I was hearing or deaf. Sometimes, the person would just point at me as if I were a lamppost and ask my parents "Hearing?" as if it were a foregone conclusion.

I may never understand why many deaf people think it is necessary to label a person "hearing" or "deaf" immediately upon meeting that person. It seems to be one of those things that people like to defend by saying, "that's just the Deaf way" or "that's just Deaf culture." Whatever the reason, the problem is that some people are square pegs that do not quite fit into those neat, round hearing and deaf holes. I am one of those people.

According to my audiogram, I have a moderate hearing loss of between 50 and 65 dB. A dispassionate observer might review the audiogram and decide that I am "hard of hearing" or "hearing impaired." I am, of course, just that. But that doesn't always accurately describe who I am.

For example, I have gone long stretches of time without wearing hearing aids. I rarely wore them in college, for example, except in class. I do not wear them at work unless I am attending a meeting. When I go to the store, I don't wear my aids. Most of my childhood friends are hearing, as are most of my professional colleagues. Someone who meets and converses with me when I am "aidless" might conclude that I am hearing. But I'm not.

And yet, I was raised by profoundly deaf parents, have a profoundly deaf sister, and married a profoundly deaf woman. Most of the people in my social circle these days are deaf. My hearing loss is equal to or greater than that of plenty of people who call themselves deaf, to unquestioning acceptance. Someone who sees me with my family or friends in public, conversing almost entirely in sign language, might conclude that I too am deaf. But I'm not.

So what am I?

At various times throughout my life, I have given different answers to that question. I've never said I was hearing, although I once liked to say that in certain situations I "function as a hearing person." Often, particularly when I was younger, I have identified myself as hard of hearing. Sometimes, recognizing that the word deaf encompasses not only those with profound hearing losses but also those with significant residual hearing who are steeped in deaf culture or are considered to be members of the deaf community, I just say that I am deaf. My favorite answer, however, is, "It depends on who I'm with."

I have found, as have most other deaf or hard of hearing individuals, that hearing people often judge us on how well or poorly we speak. My own speech has occasioned a variety of reactions from others.

On more than one occasion—usually when I was in college—I have been introduced to someone who after a few minutes would ask, "Where were you born?" I knew what that meant. Usually I would just answer "St. Louis" and leave the inquirer to fumble visibly for a response. I never said, "I'm hard of hearing; that's why I sound like this," not because I was embarrassed by my hearing loss but because I considered the question to be insensitive and rude.

Other times, someone who knew of my hearing loss would comment, "But you speak so *well*." Some people have assumed that I had extensive speech therapy when I was younger and are shocked to learn that this wasn't the case. I'm never sure how to respond to that, either. I know their intentions are perfectly good. Still, like many deaf people, I consider it to be one of the most backhanded of compliments.

As an aside, most of the speech-related comments I have heard of late have been directed toward our daughter, Susan Juliette, who is hearing and who has talked (and signed) a blue streak since before the beginning of her second year. "She speaks so *well*!" some people exclaim. Of course she does, we reply; why wouldn't she? "But how can she speak so well when her parents are deaf?" they ask.

On the surface, I suppose that's a compliment. But the underlying message, I think, remains not so complimentary. My wife, who is profoundly deaf, received extensive speech training as a child but still speaks with an unmistakably "deaf" voice. Others, as deaf as my wife or more so, speak with only a slight deaf accent. And yet, she is one of the brightest people I know. By the same token, there are hearing people who have unbelievably mellifluous voices and absolutely nothing to say. (Certain politicians and attorneys come to mind.)

My point is that speech and intelligence are, I think, wholly unrelated. And yet, in this overwhelmingly oral society of ours, people equate good speech with intelligence. Those of us who do not speak well are at a certain disadvantage, but there is no reason why this should be the case.

When I was an infant and toddler, chattering away and reasonably responsive to hearing relatives, my parents (as well as my hearing relatives) assumed that I was hearing. My mother is, to her knowledge, the only deaf person in her family, and although my father's parents were deaf, his mother had no deafness in her family, so on the whole there was little reason to suspect that hearing loss had been passed on to me. My parents also came from an environment where one was either hearing or deaf; the concept of being hard of hearing was relatively foreign to them. So it wasn't until I was a relatively advanced 3 years old that an audiologist finally determined that I was hard of hearing.

I had masked my hearing loss through adeptly using my residual hearing as well as by becoming an accomplished lip-reader, a skill that has served me quite well throughout my life. For example, when Roger Clemens, the outstanding but volatile major league pitcher, once profanely criticized an umpire, he was thrown out of the game and suspended for several more. Clemens appealed his suspension and baseball officials employed a deaf consultant from the New York League for the Deaf and Hard of Hearing to examine the videotape of Clemens' supposed transgression. The consultant concluded that it was impossible to tell whether Clemens had used the language of which he was accused, and his suspension was reduced. They should have asked me. I watched the tape, and I can say without reservation that Clemens used quite a bit of language unsuitable for printing in this and most other reputable publications.

But I digress. The point is that throughout my life I have employed the compensating strategies that allowed me to "hide" my hearing loss for my first 3 years, and this has not always worked to my advantage. Teachers, coaches, and scout leaders, to name just a few, often doubted the severity of my hearing loss and were quick to blame my academic and social failings on other factors.

"You hear what you want to hear," my fifth-grade teacher once declared in front of the entire class when I claimed that I had not heard the previous day's homework assignment. (That's my story, Mr. Ludwig, and I'm still sticking to it.) He then told the class a story about his grandfather, who claimed to be as deaf as a post but who, when a flock of geese flew far overhead, would say, "Listen to those birds." The class got a good laugh out of it. I did not.

Although I began my education after the passage of Public Law 94-142 (now known as the Individuals with Disabilities Education Act), I was never classified as having a disability and so never had an individualized education plan (IEP), an interpreter, or a notetaker. I say I was "mainstreamed," but in truth I was not, not in the legal sense of the word. Absent any disability classification, I was treated just like any other student, although my elementary school principal usually made sure to assign me to a male classroom teacher on the theory that I would be able to hear and understand a male's deeper voice than a female's high-pitched one. I thought little of not having support services because I knew that my profoundly deaf father had likewise been mainstreamed throughout high school and college without services.

I probably would not have benefited much from an interpreter, in any case, because my sign language skills were nothing to write home about. That, because I come from a deaf family, comes as a surprise to many deaf people. But my parents, although fluent in ASL, were raised oral—both attended the Central Institute for the Deaf in St. Louis—and we conversed for the most part without sign language for my first 25 or so years. (Today, however, now that my signing skills have improved by leaps and bounds thanks to my wife and an increased involvement in the deaf community, we converse in simultaneous speech and sign.) In any case, my residual hearing has often made it difficult for me to focus on an interpreter while also being able to hear the teacher. Even today, I often find myself evaluating the interpreter's proficiency instead of watching for content. I probably could have benefited more from computer-assisted real-time captioning (CART), but such technology was not widely available, if at all, when I was younger.

At various times as a child, I was asked if I thought I needed a notetaker. I declined; my notetaking skills were actually superior to those of most of my classmates, who often asked to borrow *my* notes. I sat in the front row and concentrated—or didn't concentrate, depending on how interested I was in the class. I usually had little trouble understanding teachers and professors, but upon reflection I know I missed a great deal in the way of my classmates' contributions, particularly if they sat near the back of the room. (Those who have attended law school will probably consider this to be a blessing in most respects.)

The period between sixth and ninth grades was the most difficult time for me, as it is for most children. That is the age of puberty, and I was significantly behind most of my classmates in that respect. When I entered high school, I was all of 5 feet 3 inches and 98 pounds, and athletically I was at least 2 years behind my peers, which was doubly disappointing to me because I loved sports. Today, 8 inches taller and 80 pounds heavier, I can hold my own in a number of sports, but in middle school I was always the last one picked in gym class. In addition, I was in advanced classes, I wore thick glasses, and I was hardly a stylish dresser. I was, I am sorry to say, the prototypical nerd.

That alone would have made middle school a thoroughly unpleasant experience. My hearing loss made it worse. I wore two conspicuous behind-the-ear aids that never seemed to stay behind my earlobes and always seemed to whistle at the quietest possible moment. My speech was hardly perfect; I paid less attention to proper enunciation than I do now, and growing up in a deaf household, there were some words I simply did not know how to pronounce correctly.

My social difficulties in middle school translated, as one might expect, into academic difficulties. "Potential" was the word that appeared most often on my report cards, as in "he has potential if he would just apply himself." That led to a visit to the school psychologist, who was no help at all. Most of the details of our conversation have faded into the hazy recesses of my memory, but I recall that once he found out I was hard of hearing, he decided that that was the root of all my problems. Not surprisingly, I disagreed. I had grown up in a household in which there was no shame in being deaf or hard of hearing and had been raised by parents who taught me that hearing loss was no impediment to success.

The psychologist also decided, to my surprise, that a good dose of speech therapy would solve everything. I asked him specifically to describe what was wrong with my speech; he could not, saying only that "I notice you have trouble with certain words." Which words? I asked, but he couldn't, or wouldn't, say. He asked me to meet with a speech therapist, and, in the interest of getting out of his office more quickly, I agreed.

A few days later, I was sitting in my seventh-grade homeroom when someone appeared at the door and loudly asked for me by name. I didn't hear her, and amid some tittering one of my classmates got my attention. I looked up to see a portly, middle-aged woman waddling toward me with an armful of children's games and books. Loud enough for everyone to hear, she told me that the school psychologist had arranged for her to give me speech therapy, and would I mind coming with her? My cheeks reddening, I looked at her as if she was from Mars. Part of me wanted to say, "Do you know what the word 'discreet' means?" Instead, I said, "I don't know what you're talking about. You must have the wrong person." She insisted that I come with her anyway; I, just as resolutely, refused. As the class exploded in laughter, the woman left, never to return. I never saw her—or the psychologist—again.

The school psychologist wasn't the first, or the last, professional to decide that all of my troubles stemmed from my hearing loss. At around the same time, another psychologist decided that I would be much happier if I would just admit that I was ashamed and embarrassed that (a) I was hard of hearing and (b) my parents and sister were deaf. I suppose I could have played along the way I initially did with the school psychologist, but admitting I needed speech therapy was admitting some measure of truth, whereas admitting that I was ashamed of my condition would have been a flat-out lie. So I refused, and the psychologist threw up her hands, left the room, and told my mother that I was "not ready to be helped."

Time passed. I finally hit my growth spurt at around the age of 15, and although it came too late for me to crack the high school varsity lineups, my confidence surged and my academic performance improved. I got mostly A's from tenth grade on, wrote a series of well-received pieces for the school newspaper, and even earned a few awards for my performance in Model United Nations, which was largely based on my vastly improved public speaking skills. And yet, my hearing had not improved. So the problem was not, after all, that I was hard of hearing. The problem was that

I was shorter, smaller, and in many ways just plain different from my peers. As those differences eroded, my difficulties abated.

I suppose what I have learned from this is that people who work with deaf and hard of hearing individuals—whether they be teachers, counselors, psychologists, coaches, or other professionals—must remember that hearing loss does not always define the individual, nor is it always the crucial factor that, when addressed, solves all other problems. Sometimes it is, of course, particularly in cases where the hearing loss is most profound or when the deaf or hard of hearing child has not been well prepared by parents and family to overcome obstacles.

In my case, self-confidence and self-esteem were crucial to my success. Even during the darkest days of middle school, while being teased mercilessly by my peers, I never doubted my intelligence or the promise of my eventual success. I even assured myself, in a fit of youthful cruelty, that someday my worst tormentors in middle school would be those who would deliver my mail and pump my gas. Several years later, in fact, both of those promises came to pass: my office was on one of my chief harassers' Federal Express route, and another tormentor filled my gas tank on more than one occasion!

I did not lack self-confidence in large measure because of my parents. Deaf themselves, they repeatedly told me that hearing loss was no impediment to my success. Long before Gallaudet's first deaf president, Dr. I. King Jordan, told the world that "Deaf people can do anything but hear," I knew it to be the truth because of my own parents' assurances and accomplishments. That was a legacy handed down from my father's mother, also deaf, who often shared with him articles about successful deaf professionals and said, "See, they did it! You can do it, too." He did, and so have I.

I graduated from high school ranked 27th in a class of 365, although my standing would have been higher if not for my academic problems in ninth grade, and was accepted to every college to which I applied. I chose to attend Princeton University, where I majored in politics and also earned a social studies teaching certificate, doing my student teaching at mainstream public and private high schools.

After college, I worked for $2\frac{1}{2}$ years as a legislative assistant to a local state senator and then headed off to law school. I spent 2 years at the State University of New York at Buffalo before spending my final year at Cornell Law School, graduating with high honors. As before, I received no support services, but upon reflection I think I would have done better, particularly in college, if I had availed myself of CART, a servic which was in its infancy in the late 1980s and early 1990s while I was at Princeton.

Upon graduation from law school, I joined a 100-attorney firm in Rochester, where I practiced management-side labor, employment, and education law for 2 years before moving to an even larger firm, where I represented colleges, universities, and various other kinds of nonprofit organizations. Although I serve on the board of directors of the Rochester School for the Deaf, my client base has been almost exclusively hearing, not necessarily by choice but because the legal fields and the environment in which I have chosen to practice do not often lend themselves to representing deaf individuals.

This has occasioned some criticism, some of it direct and much of it indirect, from deaf people who want me to represent them in their own personal legal dealings and also from other deaf and hard-of-hearing attorneys who have chosen to focus on improving deaf people's access to legal services. I do not fault them for their career choices; in fact, I admire them. They obviously enjoy their work, and they are very good at what they do. By the same token, I do what I do because I enjoy it, and I like to think I am good at it. (There's that self-confidence again!)

In our own way, I and the handful of deaf and hard of hearing attorneys who practice in the mainstream, representing hearing clients and working with almost exclusively hearing colleagues, are striking our own blow for the cause. After all, if deaf people can do anything except hear, why should our career options be limited to serving and working with other deaf people?

Over the last 2 or 3 years, I and several others have worked to build an e-mail listserv, called "Surduslaw," that is limited exclusively to deaf and hard of hearing attorneys and law students. Found at *http://groups.yahoo.com/group/surduslaw*, the listserv provides "a comfortable place for deaf and hard of hearing lawyers and law students to gather and swap notes." Currently, there are 73 members, from across North America (including Alaska and the far northern reaches of British Columbia) and in several foreign countries, including Australia.

We also established a public website, at *http://www.deaflawyers.org*, and are currently in the process of establishing a nonprofit, tax-exempt Deaf and Hard of Hearing Bar Association. Our mission, broadly defined, will be "to promote the professional advancement of deaf and hard of hearing attorneys, and to advance the causes of the general deaf and hard of hearing population."

Several of these deaf and hard of hearing attorneys have become some of my best friends, and as I am the only deaf/hard of hearing attorney in Rochester, this electronic community—with over 21,000 messages since its inception in August 1999—has been a godsend to me as well as to many other relatively isolated deaf and hard of hearing attorneys and law students.

When I was in high school and college, my social circle was almost exclusively hearing. That continued into my first job, as a legislative assistant for a local state senator, where my friends and professional colleagues continued to be almost all hearing.

That changed when I met my wife, Stacy, in a chance encounter in Rochester in 1994. Stacy is, as previously mentioned, profoundly deaf and as a graduate of Rochester Institute of Technology, moved and still moves in a social circle composed almost entirely of deaf people and hearing signers. Her friends quickly became my friends, and my signing—rusty as it was from years of nonuse—gradually improved. Now my social circle encompasses many deaf and hard of hearing friends in addition to the hearing friends I still have from my childhood and college days, and although my work environment remains exclusively a hearing one, Surduslaw has provided me with a number of deaf and hard of hearing professional colleagues.

So the question of what I am—hard of hearing, deaf, or hearing—is no easier to answer today than it was when I was a child. My audiogram still says I am hard of hearing, and my hearing aids amplify that status, so to speak. Many of my professional clients, with whom I deal over the telephone and via e-mail, have no reason to suspect that I am not fully hearing. And my social circle and family life are little different from those of a profoundly deaf individual. So what I am often still depends on who I am with. But instead of compartmentalizing the various aspects of my identity, I am now much more comfortable with the sum of my parts.

ROMERIA TIDWELL, PH.D.

University Professor
Counseling Psychology
University of California, Los Angeles (UCLA)
Hearing Status: Severe to Profound
Progressive Hearing Loss,
Late-Deafened Adult

I am a full professor at a major university, and I have a hearing loss. My association is with 28 million others in this country who share this condition. For many, age-related hearing loss is a normal change that occurs gradually. I found it ironic that my loss progressed at an age at which, like so many others in academics, I was nearing my highest professional rank. During this time I was called upon to engage in many important tasks, such as graduate teaching, academic administration, 2nd student advisement, which all greatly depend upon the quality of listening skills.

THE PROGRESSION OF MY HEARING LOSS

As a university professor with a hearing disability, I consider myself the "invisible" faculty member. My condition is invisible to others and not readily discernible. The consequences of the hearing loss often leave me "invisible" in the interactions around me. It is hoped that my story will lead to a better understanding of hearing loss and result in the improvement—and sometimes the creation—of academic environments that allow accessibility and the facilitation of scholarly activities.

The slow development of the hearing loss left me unaware of its impact or its extent. Not knowing that I had lost much of my acuity in the upper frequency ranges, I first noticed having difficulty when trying to hear female students in my classroom. Frequently, it was necessary to request that students who spoke in softer tones repeat their dialogue. The range and severity of my loss gradually increased. In time, I not only could not understand students in the classroom but also had difficulty understanding conversations with colleagues, friends, and all others.

Every case of hearing loss is unique, so it is important to understand the dynamics of each and every individual case. My condition was diagnosed and progressed in adulthood as a severe to profound loss, significant enough to necessitate the use of hearing aids. I was totally unprepared for the consequences of the loss for my everyday communications, particularly when it came to performing my work responsibilities at the university. At the beginning stages, I was unaware that my ability to hear had diminished. However, I now remember times when I thought that I could not hear students because they mumbled, hesitated in their speech, or covered their mouths when speaking. I often put the responsibility on the student for not communicating adequately. Increasingly, I became frustrated, annoyed, impatient, and resentful in my class encounters and during office visits.

On particular days when I was mentally fatigue, overstressed, and psychologically worn down, I even had delusions that the students were intentionally making it more difficult for me to hear; they were rejecting me or not taking me seriously. In addition, I began to believe that they were not using their best efforts when communicating with me. Simmons, Rosenbaum, and Sheridan (1996) noted that when there is frequent confusion in communication, often feelings concerning intentional deception by the listener occur. Sometimes, I interpreted my students' reactions and responses during my lectures as actively commenting on what I would say or do, especially when the lecture was not as "tight" as I might have wished. It is likely that these misinterpretations or misperceptions affected the students present and led to an unhealthy learning environment.

Like most people with a hearing loss, I had begun to depend and rely strongly on visual cues when communicating with others. I became acutely aware of nonverbal behaviors of students and began to think that they were hesitant and uncomfortable speaking to me or addressing questions to me. Overall, what resulted in the classroom was an atmosphere that was tainted with suspicion, rigidity, and, at times, alienation.

ADJUSTMENT TO MY HEARING LOSS

In performing my duties as a professor, I attempted to adapt to my loss by pretending to hear. Sometimes, I adapted to missing details by filling in information. Both of my personal coping strategies were quite easy to implement because, as a professor, I structured and established the context and boundaries in the classroom and during student advisory meetings. Several tactics were used to hide my condition. However, I could not always hide what I could not hear. For example, during a classroom lecture on suicide assessment, a female student with a relatively soft speaking voice inquired about the most important component of a suicide assessment. Believing I understood most of the question, I thought I could successfully fill in the pieces I had not heard. Unfortunately for me, I had not heard the student's words "most important." Hence, I continued on with my lecture, addressing all the components of a suicide assessment. It was not until I realized that the class had become silent and the students seemed to be staring at me in bewilderment that I realized something was wrong.

One student astutely informed me that I had incorrectly heard the student's question. Had I acknowledged my difficulty in hearing the student and asked her to cue me in to the parts of her question that I had missed, this embarrassing situation would not have occurred and 100% access to appropriate information would have been achieved.

Deceptive adaptations to hearing loss and the cognitive efforts required often result in mental fatigue. These techniques inevitably fail at some point, leading to additional stress, embarrassment, and anxiety. Regardless of individual circumstances, issues related to denial which include adaptive deceptive responses are a distinguishing characteristic of those dealing with any loss, such as a loss of hearing (Trychin, 1991).

Even for a licensed psychologist, an educational psychologist, and a professor whose specialty is counseling psychology, the process of acknowledging my hearing loss and moving forward constructively was a slow and somewhat painful one. It required 5 years to recognize fully that my deteriorating hearing was the cause of many of the unpleasant experiences in class, at meetings, and on campus.

Given my knowledge and practice of psychology, one would think that I might have been more aware of the denial process and how maladaptive responses could occur. However, I was involved in a lengthy process of adaptation. Others without sensitivity to issues such as dealing with loss may be caught indefinitely in the process of shame and blame that proceeds from denying the hearing loss condition. This process evokes fear and anxiety and is uniquely uncomfortable for a university professor, who may feel the hearing loss is a direct threat to his or her professional standing (Trychin, 1991). In American society there is a more general social stigma attached to deafness. Students and professorial colleagues assess one's cognitive abilities on the basis of what is verbally provided. Verbal intelligence, rightly or wrongly, is perceived as most important in academia. Because professors with hearing loss are less involved verbally, they say less, they have fewer social interactions, and their conversational style is often awkward, misperceptions about their intellectual capabilities can occur.

Individual differences exist with regard to how professors adapt to their condition, and these differences interact with differences in age, teaching style, and teaching assignments. For example, research findings suggest that older adults experience greater difficulty understanding speech than younger adults under equivalent hearing thresholds (Heifer & Wilber, 1990; Humes & Christopherson, 1991). However, older professors whose academic careers primarily involve autonomous research activities, and who have limited teaching responsibilities, may be, overall, less impacted by their hearing loss.

The invisibility of the hearing loss often depends on the parameters of their teaching assignments. The verbal demands on a professor teaching a calculus or physics class, for example, contrast sharply with the verbal demands on a professor teaching a course in counseling, where ongoing dialogue between the students and the instructor is integral to the therapeutic process and therefore to classroom instruction. Wide differences exist in how professors adapt to their loss in the classroom, and wide differences exist in the range of consequences that professors experience as a result of their principal function at the university. For instance, professors who teach multiple classes, work with many graduate students, serve on several departmental and intramural committees, or consult and interact extensively with those in the hearing world will be significantly affected on a personal and professional level because of their hearing limitations. Faculty who have less responsibilities requiring daily interaction may be not be as affected by their condition.

STRATEGIES FOR COPING
WITH A HEARING LOSS

It is not uncommon for deaf and hard of hearing individuals to be unaware of how they compensate to hear and gather meaning from interactions with others. For example, at times I would dominate conversations for the purpose of minimizing the necessity of understanding students, colleagues, and others. This type of strategy would unknowingly give me control of the verbal interactions in which I was involved. Another technique I used, as have others with hearing loss, was avoiding the stress when attempting to hear in various situations. This is a relatively easy strategy for professors to engage in because of their high degree of autonomy. However, avoiding certain activities at the university can weigh heavily on one's academic career advancement and one's overall quality of life. Too often, I sat on committees and wondered, "What did that person say?" These experiences are so aversive that there is a natural tendency to avoid them. Specifically, this included committee assignments and faculty meetings, where there is a great amount of verbal interaction.

Long-term use of denial and specific control techniques such as avoidance are, of course, detrimental. The *deliberate* use of effective coping resources is the most desired. For example, individuals with hearing loss will deliberately position themselves in the most advantageous position and proximity to understand others. For example, I informed the staff person who schedules classrooms that it is necessary for all of my classes to be scheduled in rooms that permit me the opportunity to walk so that I can stay in close proximity to my students.

When a professor must also confront classroom noise, the resulting stress is even more acute. Requesting room assignments that are less susceptible to noise helps reduce competitive sounds in the classroom environment and moves toward maximizing the acoustics. I scheduled frequent visits to my medical specialist (i.e., ear-nose-throat physician), sessions with a licensed psychologist also certified as an audiologist, and attended workshops, seminars, lip-reading classes, and other activities especially designed to address the needs of professionals with hearing problems. These resources were vital to my daily functioning inside and outside the university environment.

The longer one adapts daily to a hearing loss, the more practiced and more flexible one becomes in making the necessary adjustments to this condition.

The most important step I took within the classroom was informing my students of my hearing loss on the first day of classes. This action lessened the misunderstandings that some may have received from my nonverbal and verbal messages when teaching. For example, one student commented that when she was answering a question, I turned away before she finished talking. At that point she was not sure whether I understood her, heard all that she said, or did not like the response. Students felt comfortable to comment about the impact my hearing loss had on them in the classroom, which certainly helps in more effective, clear communication access.

Using all of my resources, I began to take constructive action. For example, I planned active strategies as simple as asking for repetition if something was not understood. Aural rehabilitation programs often teach listeners to use methods for obtaining successively more information. A vital component in taking constructive action is learning to use visual information skillfully. Visual information includes sign language (if known), visual images, the written word, gestures, body language, and facial expressions. Most individuals underestimate the amount and the quality of information relevant to communication that can be obtained by using visual, nonverbal information. In fact, research has shown that almost 80% of the meaning of a communication is gained through the nonverbal cues (Anderson, Bergan, Landish, & Lewis, 1985).

Some professors whose hearing loss is experienced over time require more support services in using visual communication. If the person is skilled in sign language, he or she can take advantage of interpreters in a variety of communication situations occurring in the classroom, at meetings, in social gatherings on the campus, or in the community. Or, if the person is primarily oral, like myself, he or she can use a variety of other methods such as visual representation of what is presented and can take advantage of an oral interpreter who uses different techniques optimizing lip-reading and understanding the meaning of oral communications. All of these strategies have in common the acknowledgment by the person with the hearing loss that the loss exists at a level necessitating the disclosure of the condition. Also, it involves taking constructive action to improve limiting circumstances.

THE ROLE OF SUPPORT SERVICES

Family and social support (an active social support system) is correlated with greater levels of independence in adaptive functioning (Kapetyn, 1977a, 1977b) as well as with successful hearing aid use (Becker, 1980;

Kapetyn, 1977a, 1977b; Nowak & Tesch-Romer, 1994; Weinberger & Radelet, 1983). Support is needed to deal with the predictable series of psychological consequences that accompany the hearing loss. One of the most common concerns and anxieties for the professor in the classroom is simply wondering whether the students' communications are heard correctly. After all, one primary goal of higher education is to encourage the higher level thinking and intellectual curiosity of students. It can be psychologically damaging to the classroom instructor having to wonder whether the comments, insights, and questions of students are truly heard and fully understood. Also, the professor may experience continuous anxiety regarding whether the student believes the deaf or hard of hearing instructor is really paying attention or instead ignoring parts of the student's communication.

Personal counseling can play an important role in assisting the professor with a hearing loss in dealing with the many issues involved in the classroom and in the general university environment, although few mental health professionals are trained to serve those with hearing loss (Pollard, 1998; Simmons, Rosenbaum, & Sheridan, 1996). A mentor could fill this void. A professional who functions with the condition can assist the professor in dealing with some coworkers whose behavior and attitudes appear intolerant of those with poor hearing (Colella, 2001).

Others' rejection, lack of conversation, impatience, and limited social interactions impact the professor's overall feeling of well-being. Common are feelings of isolation, alienation, inadequacy, and anxiety (Gersick, Bartunek, & Dutton, 2000). The professor with a hearing loss needs support services when attempting to adapt to different communication situations on the campus.

The "invisible" professor may become more visible with the use of supportive technology. Technology is at the forefront on the university campus. Campus e-mail, faxes, the Internet, distance learning options, and pagers can be used to enhance learning. I recommend daily workshops for

"Mono (woman) ET
Wanted to Call me Too"
Created by: Mary Thornley

professors and other staff members in order to stay knowledgeable concerning the advances in the cyberworld.

However, accommodations are needed in typical workshop or inservice formats because group instruction in computer use is often not feasible due to inaccessibility of the communication.

It is recommended that the "invisible" professor take a more active role in establishing access to communication and interactive situations. Shown in Figure 2.1 are steps that can support communication accessibility in one's classroom as well as during other activities on campus.

I. The professor must identify his or her unique work situation. If the problem is acoustics, then accommodation in the assignment of classrooms is necessary. Classrooms located where there is less noise and that are carpeted and have acoustic tile are ideal.

II. The work environment needs to be made "deaf friendly." Assignment of office space on low-traffic floors, where air conditioners are quiet, and where reduced noise is generated outside the office window, is necessary. Chairs in the professor's office must be placed so that visitors are seated reasonably close and directly in front of the professor for optimal lip-reading and analysis of facial expressions and body language.

III. It is critical to know the available resources on campus. Workshops on reasonable accommodations for people with hearing loss and the type of support services would be invaluable.

IV. The deaf or hard of hearing professor must incorporate into the workplace better and more adaptive communication strategies. If the professor is in a teaching situation where he or she controls most of the interactions, role playing is needed to communicate skills such as clarifying, rephrasing, repeating, or requesting written material prior to meetings (Baldridge & Viega, 2001; Sanders, 1982; Schein, 1998). Also, if the professor is using an oral or sign language interpreter, meeting with the interpreter in advance helps to establish a working relationship and set up expectations of individual styles and needs.

V. The instructor must be up front and direct with students and colleagues about his or her hearing problem. This behavior not only models appropriate disclosure about individual needs but also models for counseling students the importance of awareness and addressing their challenges in a constructive, adaptive way.

FIGURE 2.1   Establishing communication accessibility on campus.

Communication is a two-way interaction in which it is the responsibility of both parties to contribute to the discourse. As the person with the hearing loss, I cued others into the best way to respond in a particular communication situation. Other hearing persons adapt to interactions to accommodate new strategies for interaction. When a student has a pronounced foreign accent and has difficulty getting a message across, writing down one's ideas during the interaction or using a computer-based word processing method is an acceptable way for both to adapt to the communication situation.

Along my journey as a professor with a hearing disability, my "invisible" condition dissipated through the use of a variety of techniques. I learned that those in the university environment often need *education* regarding the best ways for communicating when a person's hearing is limited. Listed below are some suggestions I have often provided to others wishing to interact with a deaf or hard of hearing person who uses primarily an oral–aural mode of communication. I learned these techniques as my hearing loss became progressively worse. Chapter 6 expands on these ideas and introduces some "best practices" when interacting with individuals who are deaf or hard of hearing in differing communication situations.

Communication suggestions:

1. Before speaking, make sure you have eye contact with the deaf or hard of hearing person and get his or her full attention. Face the individual and continue eye contact. If you cannot get attention, wave in his or her direction or tap slightly on the hand or shoulder.
2. Make sure your face is not in a glare, shadow, or obscured.
3. Stay face to face while talking.
4. Speak at a pace that is natural and appropriate.
5. Speak slowly and clearly without exaggerating.
6. Keep hands away from your mouth.
7. Keep your voice at about the same volume throughout your sentence.
8. Make changes to a new subject, such as a name, number, or an unusual word, at a slower rate.
9. Pay attention to feedback about whether messages are understood. Watch the expressions of the deaf or hard of hearing person's face, and note when words may not have been received. Rephrase rather than repeat the same words.

CONCLUSION

In summary, I have shared my personal viewpoints concerning the effect my progressive hearing loss has had on my career as a professor on a university campus. It is my hope that I have shed some light on the important issues faced by those with hearing loss who hold professorships in our colleges and universities. Also, my desire is that the suggested strategies I presented in this discourse will aid others in adapting successfully to age-related hearing loss.

"College Hall"
Created by: Mary Thornley

As the number of older adults in the United States continues to grow, it is likely that there will be an increased need to help late-deafened adults maintain or improve the quality of their daily functioning. Those "invisible" professionals at our universities, colleges, and other work sites will become more visible when taking constructive action. They must use their own resources and educate those in the community concerning how to make activities and services more accessible to all.

3

LANGUAGE DIFFERENCES AND COMMUNICATION ISSUES

Dr. Paul Ogden, a profoundly deaf professional, related the following experience from his childhood. The story represents the usefulness and the complexity of visual language cues.

When he was 12 years old, his brother took him to an airport to meet his parents on an incoming flight. While waiting for the plane, his brother sat across from a row of doorless telephone booths. All, for the moment, were occupied. As Paul scanned the line of men talking on the phones, he could tell which men were enjoying their conversations and which were not, which were talking with people they liked or loved and which were talking with strangers or business associates, which were nervous about what they were saying and which were talking naturally. He could even speculate about which men were lying and which were telling the truth (Ogden & Lipsett, 1982, p. 75).

How much more could a person have learned without listening to the actual conversations of these men? As Ogden's story illustrates, nonverbal language can tell you much more than verbal language alone. In many ways, visual cues and nonverbal aspects of language add meaning and verify what you said and did. Hearing loss affects hearing and speech but not the ability to communicate. Deaf and hard of hearing individuals have their hands, arms, faces, eyes, and bodies with which to communicate (Ogden, 1996).

When interactions with a deaf or hard of hearing person involve verbal language only and nonverbal language is disregarded, the possibility of actually experiencing a meaningful interaction with a deaf person is reduced. Nonverbal language should be viewed as a deaf or hard of hearing individual's innate talent to express him or herself. This does not mean that nonverbal language should be used instead of verbal or spoken language for some deaf and hard of hearing people. Nonverbal language supplements and enhances these forms of communication. If hearing people hold back the important visual sources of information, such as nonverbal behaviors, limiting this information can only hinder their ability in accurately receiving your verbal messages. Gestures, body movements, and eye contact are all aspects of visual communication that are under your control.

A large portion of all human communication is nonverbal. Infants use extensive body language, facial expressions, and all sorts of movements to interact with those around them (Garcia, 1999). We, as adults, transmit and read body language all the time. For the most part, however, we do it unknowingly (Ogden & Lipsett, 1982; Walters, 1989). For example, let's say that a man you know is giving a speech to a large audience. Before beginning, he fidgets with materials on the table in front of him, looks through his notes, straightens his tie, and shifts his eyes back and forth. Because you know this individual is competent, you probably dismiss all of these nonverbal cues. Another person attending the same meeting does not know of the speaker's competence. That observer is probably more aware of the speaker's uncomfortable and nervous behaviors.

Nonverbal language supplements verbal language. Nonverbal language is an extremely potent part of our communication. In fact, it has been estimated that only 35% of the meaning of a social conversation is given by the words actually used (Birdwhistell, as cited in Davis, 1973). Some researchers have demonstrated that almost 80% of our daily communication is nonverbal (Anderson, Bergan, Landish, & Lewis, 1985). In addition, most people pay more attention to nonverbal language to determine the true meaning of a message (Walters, 1989). These language behaviors with no words or sounds speak volumes about our true thoughts and feelings (Body Language, 1995).

Nonverbal behaviors can be placed into three main groups: gestures, facial expressions, and body language. Other individuals may group these nonverbal behaviors differently. And some may put them all in the one category called *body language*. Gestures, facial expressions, and other forms of body language all add meaning to what we communicate. The use of nonverbal language is important in the lives of all individuals—hearing and nonhearing alike (Cavanagh, 1990). However, these behaviors are critical to the lives and the daily interactions of deaf and hard of hearing individuals.

GESTURES

Gestures involve spontaneous movements of the hands, head, or other parts of the body while speaking (McNeill cited in Marschark & Clark, 1993). Gestures help others understand what you are saying and can emphasize the spoken word. This form of nonverbal language can also be used in place of a whole sentence or a paragraph of words; for example, waving hello or holding your hand up to someone talking to let them know that you have heard enough.

FACIAL EXPRESSIONS

Your face gives important cues to your true feelings. Beyond contributing to your overall appearance, facial expressions serve as a message source to your emotional states of happiness, fear, surprise, sadness, anger, disgust, contempt, or interest. In fact, it has been estimated that our faces are capable of making 250,000 expressions (Ruben & Stewart, 1998).

Often you may be preoccupied or unaware that your facial expression does not match your words or actions. For instance, you may have made a big blunder at work and you smile nervously. Some examples of facial expressions are smiling, frowning, wrinkling the forehead (may indicate worry), pouting, and biting your lip. Facial expressions are critical to the lives and the communications of deaf and hard of hearing people. Facial expressions add meaning to their natural language, sign language. Because facial expressions help identify the intensity of the communications and add meaning to them, some hearing people may not understand the use of facial expressions by the deaf. They may think the deaf person's expressions are intense or odd. Hearing coworkers or fellow consumers may feel uncomfortable in a conversation at work or at a service agency.

Eye contact is an important skill to let people know that you are listening to them and respecting what they are saying. Eye contact for deaf and hard of hearing people is essential in every aspect of their lives. They must look intently at your facial expressions, body language, and movements, as well as visual components of the environment, in order to understand accurately all of the visual cues available to them.

BODY LANGUAGE

Body language is a set of nonverbal cues given by the body. These cues support our feelings and words. Body language is considered by many to be the most honest form of our communication (Body Language, 1995). Body language differs from culture to culture, but several types of communication have definite meanings that most people understand or pick up naturally.

Some examples of body language in American culture are making eye contact (means interest, attention), looking at another person but looking away when they return your glance (shyness, or keeping distance), blushing (embarrassment), leaning forward when someone is talking (display interest), and hanging the head or looking at the ground (sadness, guilt).

For deaf and hard of hearing people, communication is visual, different from that of their hearing friends, coworkers, and families (Greenberg, 1990). Deaf and hard of hearing individuals must receive information from their eyes. Hearing people are not accustomed to communicating within a visual framework (Trychin, 1990). Deaf and some hard of hearing individuals need to attend visually to all of the communication that happens and also to what is happening in their environment. Hearing people can visually pay attention to the environment while simultaneously hearing speech (Lederberg, 1993). Being more visually attentive to communication will help you practice your nonverbal skills and visual communication techniques with the deaf and hard of hearing people that you may come across.

Dennis Berrigan, a Deaf son of Deaf parents, is a native (signer fluent as a first language). He reported that his experiences with Deaf adults and skillful hearing signers were his saving grace in relation to his identity. He believes that the ideal situation for deaf people is "full visual access" best afforded by American Sign Language (ASL), a natural means for deaf people to acquire information (Wixtrom, 1999).

Most community service agencies or businesses are not able to provide "full visual access" to deaf consumers, but these service providers can use a variety of visual means of communication to provide as much access to their deaf and hard of hearing consumers as possible. A deaf professional also indicated that the place of business needs to be "deaf friendly." He stated it clearly when he said that at local businesses, he disliked salespeople who ignored him and talked to his wife because she was hearing. He reported that when this happens, he takes his business elsewhere where he is respected and valued as a consumer (Menchel, 2000) (please see Chapter 6 for a guide to communication access).

Many people in the hearing community believe that if one gives deaf people descriptions of their services or writes notes to them, talks to them face to face only, it will help with their basic communication. Where these techniques are forms of visual communication and are part of any person's communication strategy to interact with deaf individuals, there are limitations to these methods. These methods still involve verbal English language in written or spoken forms.

Because most deaf people are born to hearing parents, they are born into a unique linguistic environment. Their hearing loss condition inhibits them from acquiring their parents' language (spoken language) naturally in the hearing household. Because what is auditorily heard is limited, they are prevented from participating in the interactions with family members that are so crucial for language development. As a result, these individuals do not begin with a strong linguistic base with which to examine their world, make sense out of it, and express themselves fully in it (Erting & Pfau, 1997).

Research shows that to be good at reading a language, students must bring a substantial body of background knowledge to the task. A good part of this knowledge involves the rules of language in which the text is presented. Reading, however, goes beyond the most basic level of a language; it is essential to have considerable knowledge of life and the world picked up from the interactions of others. With this knowledge, people can create accurate expectations and hypotheses about the meaning of texts and develop abstract meaning from the passages, not just meanings of individual words. It involves the knowledge of English and a variety of experiences that they have acquired from shared information. Given the lack of language interaction between most deaf children and their hearing parents, the base for reading is severely limited (Lane, Hoffmeister, & Bahan, 1996).

Deaf and some hard of hearing individuals tend to experience English language delays or deficits (Schlesinger, 1985). It is important to note that English language (a second language to most deaf people) delays do not translate into intellectual or cognitive delays. Deaf and hard of hearing persons have the same range of intelligence as hearing individuals. Menchel (2000) reported that he finds it difficult to understand that although he holds a doctorate from a fine university, he is often looked on by community business people as a person without much intelligence. Many different factors affect the understanding of English, and the experiences at home and in the community can influence a deaf or hard of hearing person's English language development. Onset of hearing loss, amount of residual hearing, hearing status of parent, and so forth are but a few of these factors.

Just as in a family, the overall communication system within a classroom or within an office is affected when a deaf person is a part of the environment. When a deaf individual is part of a unit, it is no longer considered a "hearing" group; the majority in the group may be hearing, but the unit becomes "hearing and deaf" (Henderson & Hendershott, 1992).

Within an environmental unit, the problem is not that deaf and hard of hearing persons are being deprived of sounds but that they are being deprived of language. When communication is inadequate, the outlets for venting frustration and working through difficult situations as well as celebrating happy occasions are compromised. In the absence of a shared communication system or good attempts at visual communication, isolation will occur.

Deaf and hard of hearing people need to be included in conversations and dialogues as important members of the interactions (Henderson & Hendershott, 1992). Whether it is at work, when visiting an agency, or when going to the hospital, only when the deaf or hard of hearing person is accepted as an equal participant in the communication interaction will the service provider be able to provide the full range of support that the individual needs.

For example, one deaf professional told a story of how early interactions with hearing people affected his life.

> One day while having lunch with hearing friends, the deaf man ate quickly looking up only on occasion. His one friend asked if he were eating quickly, so he would have time to relax and chat after lunch. The deaf man commented that when he was growing up as a boy, dinner time was not important. He explained that his family carried on verbal conversations in which he could not participate. And, although he tried to become a part of these conversations by visually attending and speech reading, he still could not follow them. After a while, he learned to withdraw from the interactions that did not include him. Eating his meals quickly helped him to avoid frustration.

As this story indicates, the man's early interactions taught him that mealtime was not the time for dialogue, conversation, and the exchange of information, but a time of confusion and exclusion. Unfortunately, this deaf man's experience is typical of what is experienced by many deaf and hard of hearing people raised in families with hearing members and often continues within interactions in the community.

COMMUNICATION TYPES AND DEAF AND HARD OF HEARING PEOPLE

The communication issue is considered the most controversial issue related to hearing loss (Moores, 1987; Paul & Jackson, 1993; Paul & Quigley, 1990).

The best method of communication for deaf and hard of hearing children has been hotly debated for years. The conflict has focused primarily on the use of spoken language versus sign language (Meadow, 1980). Signed language and spoken English acquisition follow identical stages of development, as they are different but separate and potentially effective languages: babbling (7–10 months), first word (12–18 months), two words (18–22 months), word modification, and rules for sentences (22–36 months). Findings such as these have led scientists to conclude that the brain is programmed biologically to carry out language acquisition whatever its modality, spoken or signed (Lane *et al.*, 1996).

The choice of the method of communication used with a deaf child is that of the parents and the parents alone. The majority of parents are hearing, so therefore they rely on professional sources such as doctors, educators, audiologists, and speech pathologists to provide information to make their choices for their child. The overwhelming majority of these professionals are hearing themselves, and, unfortunately, the perspectives held by these professionals do not always have the particular deaf or hard of hearing child in mind but rather have a mission to further their philosophical cause.

For nearly a century, instruction in the classrooms where the deaf were educated concentrated on the teaching of "language," which in the United States meant the teaching of the oral production of English (Lane *et al.*, 1996).

The following paragraphs contain information about a few of the options available to parents regarding their choice for communication method today. Given that these methods have been debated for over 100 years, vast amounts of information are available discussing the merits of each method. Please look at the resources at the back of the book to find more information about each of these communication choices and other options not discussed here. The information presented in the following is for definition purposes only.

ORAL–AURAL METHOD

Individuals promoting the oral–aural communication method stress the use of speech, hearing aids, voice, and speech reading skills. People using this method are discouraged from relying on visual cues except those involved with lip movements used in speech. Proponents of this method promote the use of oral communication skills and residual hearing to facilitate spoken language and speech development (Becker, 1981; Eastabrooks, 1996). One of the primary objectives of this approach is to develop intelligible speech (Scheetz, 1993) and age-appropriate oral language (Connor, cited in Paul & Jackson, 1993). In the traditional oral approach, early amplification with hearing aids, auditory training–oral language learning activities, and speech training are critical features (Paul & Jackson, 1993). The ultimate goal of this method is to use oral skills to enable the person to function in a hearing society.

In 1995, Ms. Heather Whitestone believed that her deafness heightened public awareness of the condition and made her a symbol for many of overcoming adversity. However, some Deaf advocates condemned her preference for lip-reading and speaking rather than using sign language and interpreters (Anders, 1995). Many in the Deaf community believed she was not accountable to the majority of deaf people in our country, and these people believed she was not a good representative. The battle lines were once again drawn between those who support an oral–aural approach and those advocating a manual approach to communication and interaction.

MANUAL METHOD

Individuals promoting the manual communication method stress the use of gestures and sign language as the primary mode of communication. Individuals using this visual method use signs and finger spelling to communicate their ideas. The proponents of this method presume that the use of a manual means of communication such as signs is the most effective way to learn language. They believe that the knowledge and understanding of language are more important than the ability to speak intelligibly (Mindel & Vernon, 1987). In addition, the proponents of this method believe that because individuals who are deaf and hard of hearing use the visual mode more readily, it makes sense to communicate through this visual mode. This philosophy has been adapted to help parents communicate with their hearing infants. Because infants do not have the mechanisms developed to produce oral language immediately, sign language has been used effectively to help infants and parents to interact, to bond, and to express wants and needs (Garcia, 1999). Some researchers have also found that sign language communication has enhanced reading skills of even hearing students (Melville, 2001). Marilyn Daniels, an associate professor at the Pennsylvania State University, cited seven separate studies comparing preschoolers and kindergartners. Daniels found that students who were taught sign language (ASL) demonstrated higher reading levels than those who did not receive the sign language instruction. Specifically, vocabulary was improved 15 to 20% (Melville, 2001).

The supporters of the manual method also believe that deaf people have a better chance of developing social and language skills via sign language (Becker, 1981). Shown in Figure 3.1 is a description of the different types of visual communication (visual languages, codes, and sign systems) used with deaf people.

American Sign Language

ASL is a manual, visual language with its own syntax and vocabulary separating it from other languages (Jackendoff, 1994). Many hearing people who are unfamiliar with sign languages of people who are deaf have difficulty envisioning their use to obtain the same communicative power as the spoken word (Armstrong, 1999). It is a fact, however, that ASL is the fourth most used language in the United States (Christensen, 1990). It has been known for over 40 years that ASL is a true language as reported by Stokoe in 1960 (Drasgow, 1998). ASL's structure is different from that of English, making it a unique and independent language. In ASL, the visual capabilities of the eye and the motor capabilities of the body form the language (Paul & Jackson, 1993). Manual signs represent concepts, while nonmanual cues such as facial expressions, body movements, and use of the space in the environment are incorporated to express the meaning of the language. ASL is the preferred language for interactions among most individuals in the Deaf community.

Deaf Culture information is transmitted using ASL through conversations, storytelling, and videotapes (Padden, 1980; Padden & Humphries, 1988). Deaf adults who use ASL regard it as efficient, natural, and more

Visual Languages, Codes, and Signing Systems in Use with Deaf People

American Sign Language (ASL): The natural language of the DEAF—WORLD in the U.S. and parts of Canada and Mexico.

Contact sign: A contact language that has arisen from contact between English and ASL. Traditionally known as Pidgin Sign English (PSE). (See chapter 3)

Fingerspelling: The representation of written English words using the manual alphabet.

Simultaneous Communication (sim-com): A communication strategy in which speech and signs are produced at the same time. Also called sign-supported speech.

Total Communication (TC): Initially an educational policy that encouraged teachers to use all means of communication at their disposal, including ASL, English, pentomine, drawing, and fingerspelling. In practice, the Total Communication policy has become simply sim-com.

Manually Coded English (MCE) Systems: Any of several signing systems invented by educators to represent words in English sentences using signs borrowed from ASL combined with signs contrived to serve as translation equivalents for English function words (articles, prepositions, etc.) and prefixes and suffixes. Some functions words may be fingerspelled. The systems can be ordered approximately from fewer to more invented signs for the function words and prefixes and suffixes in English. The MCE systems are not languages. The three MCE systems most commonly used in the U.S. are:

1. Signed English: An MCE system invented by hearing Gallaudet University professor of education Harry Bornstein in 1973 that uses relatively few invented signs, mostly for articles and common inflections of English verbs.'

2. Signing Exact English (SEE 2): An intermediate form of MCE, invented by Deaf Gallaudet University professor of education Gerilee Gustason in 1969, and the most widely used MCE system in the U.S. today." The system incorporates many forms borrowed from ASL along with many invented forms, such as adding a fingerspelled – L-Y to adjectives to create adverbs. Some of the forms that were originally ASL signs have been changed extensively. SEE 2 assigns signs to English base words taking into account how those words are pronounced and spelled and what they mean. If any two of those three criteria are the same for two or more English words, then all those words are assigned the same sign. Thus, only one sign would be used for *right* (direction), *right* (correct), and *right* (privilege).

3. Seeing Essential English (SEE 1): Invented by a Deaf instructor at the Michigan School for the Deaf, David Anthony, in 1966, SEE 1 is a form of MCE that decomposes English words into their meaningful elements and uses arbitrarily created sign forms to portray them" SEE 1 signs are essentially based on the spelling of English syllables. Thus, the SEE 1 sign for *carpet* contains signs based on ASL CAR and PET (as in "to *per* a *dog*").

FIGURE 3.1   Communication systems used with deaf people. From Journey into the Deaf-World. (Reproduced with permission from DawnSign Press.) Lane, H., Hoffmeister, R., & Bahan, B. (1996) p. 270. San Diego, CA: DawnSign Press.

aesthetically pleasing than a manually encoded English signing system (Erting, 1987). Proponents of the use of ASL in the classroom believe that it affords deaf children many advantages: (1) it provides the children with a language foundation and background knowledge necessary to make the second language (English) more comprehensible, (2) it facilitates use of language to solve problems and promotes higher level thinking, and (3) it enhances the development of language literacy because the language used provides access (Erting & Pfau, 1997). See Chapter 4 for a more in-depth view of ASL and its importance to the Deaf community. ASL is also examined as a communication tool in classrooms where language barriers exist. For example, the Early Childhood Research Center (ECRC) has begun a project to explore the use of ASL as a common mode of communication among multilingual and multicultural preschool children whose English language is often impeded by barriers to communication (Donovan, 2000).

SIMULTANEOUS METHOD

Individuals promoting the Simultaneous Communication (SimCom) method stress the use of speech produced simultaneously with manual signs that represent the spoken language. Proponents of this approach assume that it is possible to represent the spoken language visually. A person can choose among a variety of manual sign systems to use simultaneously with spoken English. For example, Seeing Essential English (SEE I), Signing Exact English (SEE II), and Contact Language (Pidgin Sign English [PSE]) all can visually represent spoken English word order or portions of spoken English. Individuals supporting the use of SimCom believe that a deaf or hard of hearing person will use both spoken and visual forms of communication (Mindel & Vernon, 1987). Proponents of using this approach believe that they learn and use language in a way best suited to their needs while developing communication skills to function in the hearing world (Mindel & Vernon, 1987; Schlesinger & Meadow, 1972). The only problem is that many severely to profoundly deaf persons do not use speech well enough to use oral skills at the same time that they sign.

THE TOTAL COMMUNICATION PHILOSOPHY

Total Communication is a philosophy, a way of life (Cohen, 1990). Total Communication promotes the use of all possible methods of communication (such as listening, speech reading, signing, using visual images, and mime, . . .) to interact during a communication situation. "Total Communication is a philosophy requiring the incorporation of appropriate aural, manual, and oral modes of communication in order to ensure effective communication with and among [deaf and hard of hearing] persons" (Conference of Executives of American Schools for the Deaf, 1976, p. 358). It is a philosophy of educating deaf children by using a manual system simultaneously with residual hearing, speech reading, and spoken language. Most communication philosophies developed at schools for the deaf include the use of other means of visual communication in their definitions, including the use of ASL. The use of this philosophy has brought about many changes in the recent history of deaf education.

The history of the education of deaf children however, includes a history of barriers to language, learning, and communication because the use of an accessible language, a visual language (sign), had been viewed as detrimental to the development of English literacy. Studies have shown that first having a known language, a visual language—for example, ASL—and subsequently connecting this growing knowledge to the forms and structures and the use of a written second language (English) could result in higher English language literacy (Bailes, 2001). However, because the vast majority of young deaf children have hearing parents, less than 10 to 15% of these children could have ASL as a first language. For many who work with deaf children, it has been noted that most hearing parents cling to interventions based on speech and lip-reading and resist learning ASL (Bowe, 1998).

In the past, the consensus was made that English is the first language of children who are deaf (Schirmer, 1999). And, currently, in the school systems, English, in either spoken or signed form, is still the predominant language in educational programs for deaf and hard of hearing youth (Kannapell, 1993). According to an investigation conducted in 1992–1993 by Gallaudet's Center for Assessment and Demographic Studies, 48,300 deaf and hard of hearing children were receiving their education through speech and sign methods (SimCom) (56.1%) and through auditory–oral approaches (41.1%) (Mahshie, 1995).

"ASL (WAR), Milan, Italy, 1880"
Created by: Mary Thornley

BICULTURAL AND BILINGUAL
PHILOSOPHY

A debate has begun regarding the importance and value of bilingualism for deaf and hard of hearing children. Some educators who work with these children are supporting a bicultural and bilingual approach to educating the deaf child.

Thus, deaf students would become bilingual, knowing both English and a natural sign language (Paul & Jackson, 1993). Those who support this approach believe that deaf children should be taught in their natural, visual language and should be taught English as a second language (Schirmer, 1999). And, in a bicultural environment, deaf children would learn about famous deaf leaders, customs, values of the Deaf community, contributions made by deaf and hard of hearing people, and the historical aspects of the Deaf Culture along with information concerning the majority, hearing world. Proponents of this approach believe that sign language is a symbolic badge of the Deaf identity and that a knowledge of English is an important part of American life and culture (Higgins & Nash, 1987).

Specifically, in March 1994, the National Association of the Deaf (NAD) published a position paper supporting ASL and bilingual education. This paper proclaimed ASL to be the natural language of the American Deaf community. The authors emphasized that deaf children have the right to be educated, particularly with regard to reading and writing, in a bilingual or multicultural environment (Vernon & Daigle, 1994).

Bilingual–bicultural education is now in place in a growing number of sites across North America. Only research in such programs will determine its effectiveness with a segment of the Deaf and hard of hearing population. There is much controversy about how and when English would be taught in such programs. Some have suggested that English should be taught as a second language for reading and writing purposes. In the United States, we could learn from other countries concerning the educational programming of deaf children. For example, the educational systems in Sweden and Denmark introduce both sign language and spoken language during informal times, such as play interactions between parents and children. When the child experiences both as whole respected languages, the child then guides the parents and professionals to his or her predisposed preference in oral or more visual choices. The choice of a first language is then clearly the child's and not that of the professional or others (Mahshie, 1995).

It is believed that educating the deaf involves two languages, ASL and English, and two modes of communication, oral (speech) and manual (signs and finger spelling). Both languages and modes are combined to integrate a variety of approaches to education; for example, Total Communication, oralism, and the emerging approach—ASL-English bilingual education (Paul & Jackson, 1993).

Grossman (1999) from the University of Neuchatel, Switzerland, has discussed his thoughts about every deaf child's right to grow up bilingually by knowing and using both a sign and an oral language in its written and, when possible, in its spoken modality to attain his or her full cognitive, linguistic, and social capabilities.

Some advocates of bilingual education argue that ASL should be used as the first language in any bilingual program for several reasons: (1) ASL is a totally visual language which has been used as the language of the Deaf for hundreds of years; (2) ASL is easier to learn than manually coded signed English systems; (3) ASL gives the person entrance into the Deaf community, providing group solidarity and a sense of belonging; and (4) even though it is not the main choice in the schools or in educational programs, ASL has been the language of choice and has flourished in the Deaf community among Deaf individuals (Schirmer, 1999).

VISUAL COMMUNICATION

When hearing professionals interact with deaf and hard of hearing individuals, they need to consider all the approaches to communication. Authorities have suggested that 90% of the information we absorb is received through our vision (Garcia, 1999). Whether or not these "authorities" are correct concerning all individuals, what is clear in research and practice is that deaf and hard of hearing people process their information in the world using a visual mode of gathering information. Hence, any approach to communication chosen by those significant in the lives of deaf and hard of hearing individuals needs to include a visual means of transmitting information. Auditory information is lacking for most deaf and hard of hearing people to develop naturally an auditory–vocal (spoken English) language (Erting, 1987). Deaf and hard of hearing people process information using visual aspects of language. Visual aspects of language could include the use of space, movement, location, sign language, lipreading, visual images, eye contact, facial expressions, body language, and so forth. To illustrate this thought let us look at the idea of maintaining eye contact. Hearing people and deaf and hard of hearing people use eye contact differently relative to what is acceptable in each culture.

For example (Meador, 1994, p. 82):

> A deaf friend shared this experience at work: During a conversation with a coworker, my friend naturally maintained a steady eye gaze. The coworker told another colleague that the deaf person stares way too intently and makes her feel uncomfortable even at times when she is not talking to him. The workers had to be taught that looking at people in the environment intensely was necessary for communication and was not "staring" to be rude.

Visual aspects of language affect deaf and hard of hearing individuals in another way. Deaf and hard of hearing people need to shift their visual attention (their eyes) from the environment to the communication in order to fully receive a person's message. This shift in attention is called "divided attention" (Lederberg, 1993).

For example:

> Sam is working in a social security office. She is Deaf and she is able to handle communication with hearing people by trying to read lips and writing notes in one-on-one situations. During a workshop, no interpreter is available because the manager determines that one is not needed for a small group of six employees. Sam is having a difficult time understanding anything that is happening especially when an overhead is placed on the projector and Sam needs to look at the overhead to locate what is being discussed and then look back at the manager to try to follow the next topic. Sam's hearing colleagues can look at the overhead and still follow what is being said. Divided attention has exacerbated the strained communication situation where Sam already could not follow the manager's words.

If an interpreter was present, Sam could follow the words said by the manager at the same time as dividing her attention to the overhead if both were in her line of vision. Hearing people have this luxury afforded to them at all times because they can visually pay attention to the environment while simultaneously hearing the speech of another's communication (Lederberg, 1993).

It must be noted that when communicating with a deaf or hard of hearing person, divided attention is a natural phenomenon and has several effects:

1. It decreases the amount of interaction and communication between deaf people and their communication partners in a given time frame.
2. It causes hearing individuals to be less responsive to a deaf or hard of hearing person's attentional focus. (Items 1 and 2 have been adapted from Lederberg, 1993.)
3. It increases the amount of time it takes to communicate when competing with the environment.
4. It increases frustration levels in hearing individuals who are not used to a visual means of communicating.

Divided attention is a natural phenomenon for all deaf and hard of hearing people. This is how they visually attend to their world, learn, and interact.

Given considerations such as divided attention, the way in which communication is presented to deaf and hard of hearing people when services are provided by hearing individuals needs to be changed. Hearing people are used to an auditory–visual mode (relying on hearing and eyes) for exchanging information. Deaf and hard of hearing people tend to use a visual mode for communication. When interacting with deaf and hard of hearing persons, you must decide on which visual mode you will use to make your interactions more accessible.

Using visual communication techniques and practicing them are not natural habits for hearing people. A parent of a deaf child newly diagnosed with a hearing loss, Sid Ragona, from Rochester, New York, stated that in the past he simply avoided deaf people because he could not communicate with them (Lividas, 2000). It is understood that with efforts and breakdowns in communication, physical tension and resulting frustration naturally occur. When you are tense, tired, and/or frustrated, it is often easier to stop. However, he decided he needed to learn sign language and open himself to a whole new way of life. These are measures taken by a father to be able to provide his son with access to a fund of knowledge about the world. These measures are not necessarily taken by individuals in the community who will occasionally interact with a deaf or hard of hearing consumer. Although learning some sign language will be a step forward in providing more access to services, other visual techniques can make places of business more deaf-friendly. Waving in the direction of a deaf person to get attention and tapping the person on the shoulder to establish eye contact are not strategies that hearing people are comfortable with as they communicate; however, these are both acceptable ways to obtain the attention of deaf and hard of hearing individuals. (See Chapter 6 for more ways to make your service environment more deaf-friendly and for visual techniques that have been found to be successful and can be used with deaf and hard of hearing people.)

QUALIFIED INTERPRETER SERVICES

When the service provided is extremely important to the quality of life of the deaf or hard of hearing person, an interpreter is needed when communication access is not available. There are two common forms of interpreting: transliterating and interpreting. Transliterating involves listening to the spoken message and then signing it in the way that most approximates English. The second type, interpreting, involves listening to the spoken message and then interpreting it into ASL, which has its own grammar and syntax (Padden, 1980). An interpreter uses sign language so that the deaf person can understand what a nondeaf person is saying. If the hearing person does not know how to sign, the role of the interpreter will be expanded to include voicing what the deaf person is signing (Stewart, Schein, & Cartwright, 1998).

Interpreters play a vital role in relationships between hearing, deaf, and hard of hearing individuals. In fact, the most frequently requested support aid for members of the Deaf community is a qualified sign language interpreter (Firth, 1994). Interpreters working in educational, medical, legal, social, and rehabilitation settings generally require professional training and national certification (Scheetz, 1993). The Registry of Interpreters for the Deaf (RID) was founded in 1964. As a national association for interpreters, it has grown, adapted, and changed to meet the needs of the Deaf community. The biggest catalyst for this growth has been ADA (Hall, 2000). Within the context of ADA, it is mandated that qualified interpreter services be available. However, as seen in Chapter 1, many service providers do not know ADA law or choose to ignore it. For example, Robert Menchel, a Deaf professional, stated that he is dismayed that medical doctors are bothered when asked if an interpreter could be provided. He asked, "Don't we have the same right as hearing people to understand what the doctor is saying?" (Menchel, 2000).

Interpreters must provide "effective communication." There are many wonderful and qualified interpreters in the United States today. However, with the demand and open market, sometimes individuals who lack experience in deafness and have problems with sign language fluency are hired as freelancers or from interpreting agencies. Relying on amateurs who know some sign language is a frequent error because the ability to make or read a few signs or to fingerspell is no substitute for proficient interpreting (National Association of the Deaf, 2000). In addition, several service providers rely on family members or friends to interpret for the deaf or hard of hearing person. Although this is a quick solution to an access-to-service problem, most hearing family members or friends are not trained or proficient in interpreting. Also, the role of the family member or the friend should be one of support rather than being an interpreter. The act of using a family member as an interpreter, for example, in a hospital, legal, or social service environment, is not fair or recommended because a family member is biased and needs to be supportive of the deaf or hard of hearing person and need not be concerned about the effective communication of the words used.

Early in 1994, the National Association of the Deaf (NAD) and the RID recognized the mounting problems with the delivery of qualified interpreting services and declared a nationwide crisis (Firth, 1994). Because of the nature of their work, it is critical that interpreters are proficient in their skill area, remain impartial, and serve only as facilitators of communication (Scheetz, 1993). Most organizations, deaf and hard of hearing persons, and parents of deaf and hard of hearing children are beginning to request only nationally certified interpreters to provide this vital service.

As mentioned previously, the RID was founded in the United States in 1964. The primary mission of this organization is to provide training, to serve as a certifying body for those achieving certain skill levels, and to offer a registry for those seeking to obtain the services of a professional interpreter (Scheetz, 1993). Additional information about this organization, including the availability of interpreting services in various locations across the country, types of certification, fee schedules, and location of training programs, can be obtained by contacting:

Registry of Interpreters for the Deaf (RID)
8719 Colesville Road, Suite 310
Silver Spring, MD 20910 (301) 608-0500

4

DEAF CULTURE OR CONDITION?

As a person wanting to know more about Deaf and hard of hearing people, you may have many questions about their life experiences. What effect does a hearing loss have on day-to-day functioning? How will this condition influence overall development or, specifically, one's identity? Do most people who are Deaf or hard of hearing lead good, productive lives? Do most find happiness? This chapter will help you discover the answers to these types of questions.

In addition, you may be unaware of the current controversy concerning the Deaf community and others involving their culture versus their societal status as a group with a disability. For example, the majority of people who are Deaf view their population as a cultural linguistic minority.

However, Deaf people often see others outside their community apply a medical model to their understanding of hearing loss and perceive its effects as disabling.

> *The deaf believe that they are our equals in all respects. We should be generous and not destroy that illusion. But whatever they believe, deafness is an infirmity and we should repair it whether the person who has it is disturbed by it or not.*
> —Prosper Meniere, 1855 (Resident Physician at the Paris School for Deaf-Mutes) (cited in Brueggemann, 1999, p. 103)

Even though this quotation from a physician is almost 150 years old, many people who are deaf believe that the medical community and those who support the medical perspective still hold this view, which guides their actions.

Brown (1995) believes that the Culture versus disability question is not an easy one to answer. She reports that individuals who provide audiology and speech and language services in various settings have found themselves searching for a culturally sensitive service delivery model. However, some leaders in the Deaf community still view these professionals as controlling, self-serving, and oppressive.

Deaf people relate to the world through their eyes. Therefore, their language exists through *visual communication.* They believe it is society's task to shift from a pathological view of the hearing loss as a condition of deficit (lack of hearing; lack of the ability to use spoken language) to a view of each deaf individual as a person who is capable, if given a mode of communication (visual) without impairment, of developing a positive identity and self-concept (Finn, 1995).

Information provided in this chapter will help guide you in becoming more culturally Deaf sensitive and at the same time provide you with the information necessary to answer the question, Deaf Culture or condition?

We examine several areas deemed important to understanding Deaf people, including perspectives on their condition of hearing loss, culture, language, behaviors, traditions, art, literature, and technology. Also, having read the chapter, you will have achieved a greater understanding of the importance of the following to each Deaf and hard of hearing person's healthy identity development:

- D/HOH role models in all aspects of a deaf or hard of hearing person's life
- Sign communication as a necessary part of the deaf person's language development
- Interaction within the Deaf community
- Enrichment through the shared Deaf traditions, values, and life experiences
- Recognition of each deaf or hard of hearing individual's full potential as a vital, contributing member of the larger society (adapted from Hafer & Ditman-Richard, 1990, p. 16)

This chapter may not address all of your unanswered questions or completely satisfy your curiosity. Sources related to each area presented are provided in Chapter 7. These resources and a list of suggested reading can be beneficial in your quest for a better understanding of Deaf identity issues and the condition of hearing loss.

MEDICAL OR AUDIOLOGICAL PERSPECTIVE

In reaction to the medical model of understanding deafness, Harlan Lane (1992), a professional in the Deaf community, wrote a historic book entitled *Mask of Benevolence.* In this book he proclaimed that a positive self-concept is not based on how hearing one is, but rather on how Deaf one is. He believes that when members of the Deaf community accept a label such as hearing impaired, they surrender their own identity and accept a definition by the dominant social group. Whereas "Deaf" refers to a shared culture, language, and experience, "hearing impaired" refers to a physical defect that someone outside Deaf Culture possesses. Deaf people capitalize the word deaf to distinguish deafness as a culture from deafness as a diagnosis (Lightman, 1998). Chapter 1 outlined a detailed view of the medical and audiological perspective (see Appendix B for a comparison of two views of deafness).

CULTURAL PERSPECTIVE

One needs to distinguish between the physiological condition of hearing loss and the association of Deaf people with a language and a culture. As one might expect, individuals who are members of the Deaf community view hearing loss differently from others who see it as a handicapping condition. Deaf people regard being deaf not as a disability but as a sociocultural phenomenon. Most Deaf people are convinced that deafness is not a disability, but attitudes are the real disability (Starr quoted in Wentzel & Livadas, 1995). Deaf individuals see themselves as members of a unique group, community, and culture, whereas hearing people often understand deafness as a tragic medical condition (Glickman, 1996). For example, in contrast to hearing people, Deaf persons rarely use the term hearing impaired, which implies disability, but prefer the terms Deaf and hard of hearing (Higgins & Nash, 1987).

In the 1980s, a Deaf activist named Carol Padden defined culture as a set of learned behaviors of a group of people who have their own language, values, rules of behaviors, and traditions. A culture results from a group of people coming together to form a community around shared experiences, common interests, shared norms of behavior, and shared survival techniques.

The universal trait among all members in Deaf Culture is the inability to hear. Being Deaf binds the community together. Such groups as the Deaf seek each other out for social interaction and emotional support through a common language. Sign language and shared experiences determine this culture and its identity. It is not surprising that the cultural perspective of being Deaf was heralded concurrently with the acceptance of American Sign Language (ASL) as a bona fide language (Paul, 1998).

Specifically, Glickman (1996) identifies two conditions for having a Deaf identity: (1) viewing oneself as culturally different and (2) having fluency and respecting ASL.

Deaf Culture can be very foreign to hearing people. Cultural behaviors such as attention-getting techniques, back-channeling (providing feedback to the person speaking during a conversation), and eye contact while communicating can be observed in the Deaf community (Smith, Lentz, & Milkos, cited in Kemp, 1998). Such behaviors are not observed in the same manner when two people communicate in spoken English. The behaviors and the norms for those behaviors found in Deaf Culture are different from those found in hearing society. The cultural model of deafness highlights those differences in being Deaf and not in the condition of hearing loss itself. The conceptual framework of this model includes acknowledging that Deaf people have a unique identity with their own history. Within this framework, deafness becomes a cultural, rather than a biological, phenomenon (Drasgow, 1998). Each primary component of the cultural perspective will be examined: Deaf community; its language, art, and/or literature; and technology.

DEAF COMMUNITY

A Deaf community is a local group of Deaf and hard of hearing people who, based on shared experiences among each other and identification with one another, participate together in a wide variety of activities (Higgins & Nash, 1987). As a member of Deaf Culture, one must want to be identified with the Deaf community and desire to participate actively in it. Hearing loss is not a sufficient condition for membership (Scheetz, 1993). For example, if an individual has attended a public school, has primarily resided in an "oral" environment, and is not fluent in sign language, that person most probably views himself as a "hearing" person with a condition affecting his full participation in the hearing world rather than a Deaf person identified within the Deaf community and its culture. In contrast, a Deaf individual who has attended a residential school and is fluent in sign language most probably would be an active participant in the Deaf community. This individual would become involved in community activities on a regular basis and most probably would call him- or herself Deaf and a member of Deaf Culture.

The educational programming of the individual with a hearing loss is a critical component of the acceptance of that person as a member of Deaf Culture and of that person's identity as a culturally Deaf individual within the Deaf community. In fact, Van Cleve and Crouch (1989) attributed the very existence of the American Deaf Culture to its base in the residential schools. The educational system, therefore, in its early years, offered an opportunity and eventually the mechanism for a Deaf social movement in the Deaf community to thrive (Jankowski, 1997). Only a very small number of Deaf and hard of hearing children are born into Deaf Culture. Most children become enculturated during their teenage years or as adults as they become exposed to their language and the Deaf community mainly in residential educational settings (Paul & Jackson, 1993).

The Deaf community and its culture provide an example of how a strong system of social support can transform the lives of many people (Higgins & Nash, 1987). The peer support in this system influences the coping abilities and the self-esteem of deaf and hard of hearing children, youth, and adults throughout our country. Children need to have Deaf and hard of hearing adult and adolescent role models to help them develop a healthy self-image (Rodda & Grove, 1987). Because the majority of deaf people are born to hearing parents, they absorb their culture from their peers. Deaf children traditionally administer the rite of passage to newcomers to the Deaf community rather than adults as in hearing communities. Because, for the most part, deaf children are born into families with hearing members, this is one culture that typically is handed down, generation to generation, from child to child (Benderly, 1980). Published literature and folklore show that in Thailand, American, and other boarding schools for the Deaf, where those attending are allowed to interact in their own sign language, the children were and are reluctant to leave when their school years are over and even to leave their companions during vacation periods and visit homes where no one uses their language (Stokoe, 1995).

As with any other community, the Deaf community is a heterogeneous group. The members of the Deaf community have many different levels of hearing loss that range from slightly hard of hearing to profoundly deaf (Halpern, 1996). Therefore, the Deaf community is in itself a society. It includes a cross section of people with different hearing losses, physical builds, races, religions, intelligence, interests, and values (Rosen, 1986).

Hearing, hard of hearing, and deaf people have coexisted in the same communities for hundreds of years but live very differently. One Deaf professional, Stokoe (1995), explains the difference in living this way, "I go to work in the hearing world, but I live in the Deaf world." Communication is seen as the main reason for these two different worlds. If the communication barrier did not exist between Deaf and hearing people, a true sharing of culture and life experiences could occur; a true bicultural celebration could be achieved.

An illustration of how deaf, hard of hearing, and hearing people can exist in their cultures side by side was found in the example of the Chilmark community on the island of Martha's Vineyard. In this community, 1 in every 150 people was deaf. In one island village with about 500 residents, 1 in 25 was deaf. Hearing as well as Deaf children on the island learned the indigenous sign language naturally. The community used the language as a natural part of their lives—fisherman used sign language to communicate at a distance, and others used it in their churches. The hearing and Deaf children grew up interacting with each other in a comfortable, natural bilingual–bicultural community (Lane, 1989).

Because 90% of Deaf children are raised in hearing families, a healthy sense of biculturalism is difficult to achieve. Even though the majority of these families do not reach the level of bilingualism and biculturalism found in the Chilmark community on Martha's Vineyard, a balance of cultures must occur for a healthy Deaf identity to flourish. Thomas Holcomb, a professor of deaf education at Ohlone College in California, has identified the stages that the Deaf person from a hearing family goes through to reach what he calls a "positive bicultural identity"—comfort and competence in both Deaf and hearing situations. In his work with Deaf students at the college level, Holcomb sees the rage, depression, and confusion they experience as they struggle to develop a self-concept that includes acceptance of their own deafness. Because a crucial part of this development is dependent on social interactions, it is Holcomb's view that these deaf individuals must be exposed early and often to the Deaf community. Only a small number of students he interviewed believed their journey toward a positive, bicultural identity was not a struggle. These students had parents who learned to embrace Deaf Culture early on and who made sure their children had access to it (Lightman, 1998).

THE LANGUAGE OF DEAF PEOPLE

Following is a poem written by a Deaf girl who became deaf at the age of 9 because of mumps. She went to residential school and then to a mainstream school. She now has a bachelor of arts degree in history from Gallaudet University and a master of arts in bilingual education and Portuguese studies from Brown University. This poem expresses to all people what her cultural experiences and her language mean to her:

With My Hands I Can. . . .

With my hands I can
    Fly a plane,
    Pluck a guitar,
    Shout,
    Tell a story,
        Cry. . . .

With my hands I can
    Frown,
    Dance,
    Smile,
    Take a chance. . . .
    Tell me what you can do with
    your Voice?
        by Maria Grace Okwara (1994)*

"Divergence 6"
Created by: Susan Dupor

*Maria OKwara is a Deaf teacher of the Deaf and an amateur poet. She immigrated to the USA from Portugal and currently lives in Rhode Island with her husband and two daughters.

ASL is the preferred language for interactions among most individuals in the Deaf community (Christensen, 1990; Goodstein, 1990). This unique language is used in churches, theaters, schools, and other places where Deaf people interact. Deaf Culture and its language are unknown to many and poorly understood by most (Wentzel & Livadas, 1995). Culturally Deaf persons share the common experience of patterns of eye contact, rules governing contact and touching, and the use of facial expressions as vital parts of their language.

Deaf Culture information is transmitted using ASL through conversations, storytelling, and videotapes (Padden, 1980; Padden & Humphries, 1988). Mastery of ASL and skillful storytelling are highly valued in Deaf Culture. Deaf adults who use ASL regard it as efficient, natural, and more aesthetically pleasing than a manually encoded signing system (Erting, 1987). Many in the Deaf community believe that for Deaf children to succeed in all areas of development, they require a fully accessible and comprehensible language used within the schools. Children whose hearing loss is in the severe to profound range are not able to access spoken English naturally. Instead, these children require a language whose syntax, semantic, and pragmatic features are fully accessible by the eye. ASL is such a language (Di Perri, 1998).

ASL is the fourth most used language in the United States (Christensen, 1990). It is a manual, visual language, separating it from all other languages (Jackendoff, 1994). ASL's structure is different from that of English, making it a unique and independent language. It is not a manual representation of English, with individual signs corresponding to English words (Drasgow, 1998). For example, the phonology of spoken language involves the use of vocal organs to produce vowels and consonants to provide auditory input. ASL involves manual articulation and movement vital to the visual system with four basic articulatory parameters: hand configuration, placement, orientation, and movement (Drasgow, 1998). In ASL, the visual capabilities of the eye and the motor capabilities of the body form the language (Paul & Jackson, 1993). Manual signs represent concepts, and nonmanual cues such as facial expressions, body movements, and use of the space in the environment are incorporated to express the meaning of the language. In addition, fingerspelling, which is a manual representation of English orthography, is an integral component of ASL typically used to convey proper nouns and English words and ideas or phrases that have no sign equivalent in ASL or used simply to add emphasis to a statement (Padden & Ramsey, 1991).

ASL, as a natural language, has its own rules for generating grammatically sound phonological, morphological, and syntactical structures (Drasgow, 1998). All formal languages have the same deep grammatical structure. In other words, language is a rule-governed system. It is composed of symbols that its users manipulate to produce meaning. Sign language

teach

HANDSHAPES: Right and left open AND hands changing to closed AND hands

POSITION: 1. Near the sides of the forehead 2. At the shoulders

MOVEMENT: Hold the right and left open AND hands near the sides of the forehead with the palms facing each other. Move both hands forward while changing them to the closed AND handshape. To sign *teacher* or *professor*, add the *person* ending.

VISUALIZE: A teacher taking information from the mind and giving it to others.

teacher

HANDSHAPES: 1. Right and left open AND hands changing to closed AND hands 2. Right and left FLAT hands

POSITIONS: 1. Near the sides of the forehead 2. In front of the chest

MOVEMENT: 1. Hold the right and left open AND hands near the sides of the forehead with the palms facing each other. Point both hands forward while changing them to the closed AND handshape. 2. Sign the *person* ending. (See page 18.)

VISUALIZE: A teacher taking information from the mind and giving it to others.

art

HANDSHAPES: Left FLAT hand and right I hand

POSITION: In front of the chest

MOVEMENT: Point the left FLAT hand forward with the palm facing right; then slide the little finger of the right I hand down across the left palm with a wavy motion.

VISUALIZE: Drawing with a pencil.

artist

HANDSHAPES: 1. Left FLAT hand and right I hand 2. Right and left FLAT hands

POSITION: In front of the chest

MOVEMENT: 1. Point the left FLAT hand forward with the palm facing right. Then slide the little fingertip of the right I hand down across the left palm with a wavy motion. (This is the sign for *art*.) 2. Sign the *person* ending.

VISUALIZE: A person who draws or paints.

FIGURE 4.1   Photographs from *Talking With Your Hands, Listening With Your Eyes* by Gabriel Grayson, Square One Publishers © 2003. Used by permission.

certainly is a rule-governed communication system. For instance, in English, one can nominalize some verbs by adding a suffix -er, or -ist as in teach, teacher and art, artist. In ASL, nouns can also be derived according to the morphological rules of grammar; for example, adding the person indicator to the verb sign for teach and art to nominalize and create the concepts teacher and artist (see Figure 4.1) (Finn, 1995).

Within the Deaf community, it is believed that educating the Deaf involves two languages, ASL and English, and two modes of communication, oral (speech) and manual (signs and fingerspelling). Both languages and modes are combined to integrate a variety of approaches to education; for example, Total Communication (use of all possible communication methods—listening, speech reading, signing, using visual images, mime, etc.), oralism (use of speech, hearing aids, voice, and speech reading skills), and the new emerging approach ASL–English bilingualism (use of visual communication as a first language and English as a second language). The debate over which mode of communication (signing or oralism) should be used to teach deaf children has flourished for more than 100 years with mixed results in research as to which approach is more effective.

As a result of the findings of continued lower academic achievement of most deaf children compared with hearing children, the debate has now expanded to include the importance and value of bilingualism. Some educators who work with these children are supporting a bilingual–bicultural (Bi–Bi) approach to educating the deaf child. Thus, deaf students would become bilingual, knowing both English and a natural sign language (Paul & Jackson, 1993). In a bilingual–bicultural approach, deaf children are considered members of a linguistic cultural minority (Goldberg, 1995) who are instructed in the use of both ASL and English. The bilingual approach is based on a special curriculum that involves the dominant use of ASL and teaches English as a second language during specific school periods (Nover, Christensen, & Cheng, 1998). ASL is the language of instruction, and English is used in both written and spoken form (Goldberg, 1995).

Because the bilingual–bicultural philosophy advocates that deaf children be taught in their natural, visual language and taught English as a second language, these children would also learn about famous Deaf leaders, customs, values of the Deaf community, contributions made by Deaf and hard of hearing people, and the historical aspects of Deaf Culture along with information concerning the majority, hearing world. Proponents of this approach believe that sign language is a symbolic badge of the Deaf identity and that a knowledge of English is an important part of American life and culture (Higgins & Nash, 1987).

Although ASL is recognized as a formal language and even accepted as meeting the foreign language requirement in academic programs in the United States, there is little documented research on its use and effectiveness (McKee & McKee, 1992). Whereas many had suggested the use of ASL in classrooms, no one had directly tested the relationship between ASL and the academic performance of either deaf or hearing children (Drasgow, 1998). However, researchers have begun to examine individuals who use the language and their measured academic achievement. This research has indicated that Deaf children whose parents are fluent and acquire ASL as a first language through natural, ongoing communication at home typically achieve academic success at higher levels than their peers from homes where signed language is not a primary language (Brasel & Quigley, 1977; Ewolt & Israelite, 1992; Mahshie, 1995; Prinz, Strong, Kunze, Vincent, Friedman, Moyers, & Helman, 1996). In two studies specifically, empirical evidence was demonstrated. In 1976, Prinz and colleagues found a strong, positive relationship between ASL competence and English literacy. Strong and Prinz (1977) validated the results of the first study and also determined that the level of proficiency is related to the level of English literacy. It is believed that results such as these indicate that if a child learns one language well, it is easier to learn the second language (Goldberg, 1995).

Some have attributed the superiority of Deaf children of Deaf parents' competence in English to the visual access to language along with a corresponding exposure to and understanding of a wide range of personal and social experiences that ASL provides (Grushkin, 1998).Others have attributed the academic advantages of children of Deaf parents to the development of an internal language base stemming from exposure to a natural language (the use of ASL) that was fully accessible to them during their early childhood (Drasgow, 1998). For instance, in an examination of how Deaf mothers read to their children, it was found that these mothers naturally use strategies such as the following:

1. Sign placement—mother signs certain words or phrases on the picture or uses the book as part of the sign.
2. Text paired with signed demonstration—mother clarifies the text or picture by demonstrating the action pictured or represented in the text.
3. Real-world connection between text and child's experience—mother signs an example of an event or experience in the child's life that relates to the story text.
4. Attention maintenance—mother physically secures the child's attention to her signing or to a picture in the book.
5. Physical demonstrations of character changes—mother uses facial expressions and body posture to signal different characters in the book.

    6. Nonmanual signals as questions—mother uses facial expressions to ask questions about a picture in the book.
    (cited in Lartz & Lestina, 1995, p. 360)

These strategies, with a natural language and methods at their base, provide the child with a smooth demonstration and nearly 100% access to all of the content presented in the stories.

ASL has been cited in the facilitation of the early language development of hearing children as well. For example, Holmes and Holmes (1981) studied the communicative behaviors of a hearing son of hearing parents who was communicated with from birth using both sign and spoken words. As a result, they hypothesized that the addition of the signed component may have been responsible for the child's early language acquisition. His first words were spoken and his first 50 words were acquired several months earlier than the average. Daniels (1993) conducted a study involving 14 hearing children who were born to Deaf parents and learned ASL as preschoolers. Results show that these bilingual youngsters scored higher than average on a language test, suggesting that knowing ASL had a positive influence on a hearing child's acquisition of English.

New evidence concerning the functioning of the human brain supports the idea that a visual system of language is closely linked with other language structures. The brain is found to be wired for systems of grammatical, gestural language, which is no surprise to those who study language development in children. Babies have been found to make complex gestures before they speak (Stokoe, 1998). A developmental psychologist, Dr. Elizabeth Bates, reported that children who make referential gestures early begin spoken language early, and those who gesture late also begin spoken language late. Dr. Bates pointed out that gesture and spoken language share a common neural substrate, which is entirely consistent with the idea that vocal language develops out of gestural language (Begley, 1999). These findings offer supporting evidence that a visual language such as ASL could facilitate later English language development.

In March 1994, the National Association of the Deaf (NAD) published a position paper supporting ASL and bilingual education. This paper proclaimed ASL to be the natural language of the American Deaf community. The authors emphasized that deaf children have the right to be educated, particularly with regard to reading and writing, in a bilingual or multicultural environment (Vernon & Daigle-King, 1999).

Literature, art, and drama entertain and inspire. They also preserve and transfer to the young the values and transitions of Deaf Culture (Vernon and Andrews, 1990). Deaf artists use vibrant colors that accent the visual aspects of their lives.

Tapestry
Created by Morris Broderson.
Black-and-white version found on page 28.

Art, No. 2
Created by Chuck Baird.

View from Washburn Art Building
Created by Mary Thornley.

Spirit
Created by Morris Broderson.

Sunset in Austin
Created by Chuck Baird.

Grant Thy Spirit
Created by Chuck Baird.
Black-and-white version found on page 156.

America
Created by Chuck Baird.

Knowledge
Created by Charles Wildbank.

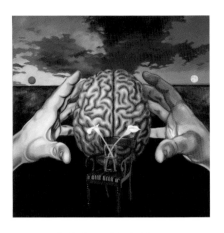

Left Brain/Right Brain
Created by Chuck Baird.
Black-and-white version found on
page 133.

Freedom
Created by Charles Wildbank.

"...I wanted to show the sign for 'prison' against the rising sun as symbolizing freedom, since one cannot obscure the light of the sun. No thing can contain enlightenment, enlightenment can contain all things."

—Charles Wildbank

FOLKLORE

Deaf literature and folklore are critical vehicles with which to transmit the culture in a visual, systematic manner. Much of a person's enculturation in this world occurs through its folklore (Rutherford, 1993). For instance, through the ages, storytelling has been valued by cultures throughout the world as entertainment, a manner of identification, and a means of promoting social conformity. In discussing folklore in Deaf Culture, Padden and Humphries (1988) viewed storytelling in Deaf Culture as instructional, extending beyond recalling the past by teaching about how one's life should be conducted and what must be valued. These stories help children learn values of their families and the heritage of their culture. Cultural values such as the importance of ASL as the language of Deaf people, the need for social togetherness and belonging, and the demonstration of Deaf pride through literature are hallmarks of storytelling in the Deaf community (Padden & Humphries, 1988). Deaf Culture uses storytelling to instruct and develop meaning about its existence (Isenberg, 1996).

ABC Stories

ABC storytelling is an example of the rich drama and folklore history within Deaf Culture. The storytelling within the ABC play occurs in ASL. The performer must be highly skilled in the language and have a strong Deaf identity. ABC stories are lauded by the Deaf audience.

The sign play of the ABC story can be seen as a mediation between the two poles of two languages—external English control and internal ASL affective expression, occurring simultaneously. Using the community's two languages, the ABC story is a form of linguistic play that manipulates the phonetics of one language with the phonological system of the other (Rutherford, 1993).

Although there are many functions that the ABC story may serve for the Deaf population, it can parallel the linguistic experiences of Deaf people. Using the manual alphabet at its base, the hearing, English order is maintained, A–Z. The Deaf actor is expected to perform the external, structured flow of the alphabet with the internal spirit, soul, art, and identity as expressed in ASL. Figure 4.2 shows an example of an ABC story in two-dimensional format.

THE CAR RACE

English Synopsis:

The cars are low and sleek racing cars. Spectators are astonished as they watch them speed past. The winning driver turns out to have a swelled head and looking at another driver, says, "I beat you." The second driver is jealous and thinks to himself: "Boy, is he big-headed. He thinks he's king of the road." The second driver reflects on what had happened before and why he did not win the race. He remembers starting the car. With hands on the steering wheel, he was ready to go. He looked at the dash gauges and noticed that something was wrong with the car. He was worried that it would not be safe and decided to put his racing plans in abeyance and not enter the race. Therefore, he did not win the race because he was not able to compete.

FIGURE 4.2   An ABC story (The Car Race). (From Rutherford, S. [1993]. pp. 39–44.)

Manual Alphabet	ASL Sign	ASL GLOSS (ALL CAPS) AND STORYLINE	Manual Alphabet	ASL Sign	ASL GLOSS (ALL CAPS) AND STORYLINE

COMPETITION. It's a Race.

"What a SWELLED HEAD!"

"M" (missing from text)

There are LOW SLEEK RACING CARS speeding around

The second driver LOOKED BACK to what had happened to him and why the other driver had won

"O" (missing from text)

Their WHEELS are vibrating

"P" (missing from text)

The STICK SHIFT is vibrating

He put the KEY in the ignition and started the car

EEEEEEEK the wheels screech

READY to go

Spectator's EYES watch the cars

Hands on the steering wheel (Both "S" and "T" represented by "A$_s$" and "A$_t$" respectively, are used in succession)

The cars GO/ZOOM past

He LOOKS AT the dash gauges

The winning driver turns to another race driver and says "I BEAT YOU!"

He's STUCK. Something is wrong with the car.

I-I-I, he displays a very large ego

WORRY (signed with "W" handshape)

The second driver is JEALOUS

His racing plans are HELD IN ABEYANCE

and says "Boy he thinks he's KING of the road."

WHY didn't he win? Because he couldn't enter the race

The informant signed "Z" while shaking head in negative fashion — meaning too bad, but couldn't go.

FIGURE 4.2 (Continued)

TECHNOLOGY

On July 26, 1990, then President Bush signed the Americans with Disabilities Act (ADA) after it was passed by Congress. This act covered the rights of a broad range of individuals, protecting them from discrimination in all of the public and private sectors of our society (Firth, 1994). The major portions of ADA have been in effect since 1992, and we are seeing their effects in such changes as establishing TTY pay phones in major metropolitan airports and offering television captioning in prominent hotels. Hotels will not only have captioned television and TTYs, but also will begin to have signaling devices such as fire alarms and flashing lights throughout their facilities and guest rooms. The ADA's major emphasis was on accessibility and safety issues; on a local level, this meant that flashing lights were finally installed in classrooms and in school bathrooms so that Deaf children could know when the fire alarm rang. It also meant that these children were able to attend programs such as those held at a state-funded museum because the provision of a sign language interpreter was required.

The ADA has increased public awareness by propelling issues about disabilities to the forefront of American public policy. Therefore, technological advances will be forthcoming as Deaf and hard of hearing people demand access to new technological services. The way our society communicates is rapidly changing. Computers, multimedia, and interactive services are promising a revolution in the way we exchange information and obtain services. The lessons of the telephone and television were invaluable to the Deaf community. Those revolutions were first inaccessible to individuals who were deaf or hard of hearing (Firth, 1994). The ADA, with its guarantees of equal access, will continue to have a huge impact on the Deaf and hard of hearing people in our society. This section examines technology as it relates to the support services available to Deaf and hard of hearing individuals and their families.

TELECOMMUNICATION DEVICES

Telecommunication devices for the deaf (TDDs) are known as teletypewriters (TTYs). These machines have the appearance of a small typewriter that can be used with regular telephone handsets to allow Deaf and hard of hearing people to communicate with each other (directly) and the hearing individuals in their lives. The TTY is made up of a typewriter-like keyboard, a telephone coupler, and some form of visual display where words are typed via TTY tones (Scheetz, 1993). The TTY can also be an interactive and immediately relevant tool in fostering the written literacy of deaf individuals, which can be introduced at early ages (Neeley as cited in Grushkin, 1998). A modern alternative for fostering literacy through interactive text is the computer. Each caller must have a TTY in order to type and read the messages printed on the display.

With the passage of ADA, relay services have been established in most major cities across the United States. A relay service involves the use of a telephone operator with a TTY which serves as a link between a deaf or hard of hearing person with a TTY and a hearing person without one (Dolnick, 1993). Relay services involve toll-free numbers at no charge to the calling party. Now a national number, 711, can be used to make relay calls. For example, hearing people who have no access to a TTY can use the Telecommunications Relay Services (TRSs) to call people who cannot use a regular telephone. A relay operator relays conversations between TTY users and those who use regular phones. The relay operator reads the TTY user's typed message to the regular phone user and then relays the voice message back to the TTY user by typing in the response.

Recently, new advancements in technology have led to the development of enhanced transmission speeds for messages typed using TTYs. In July, 2000, Hamilton Communications announced the availability of Turbo Code, which saves time and money for relay service users. Hamilton Communications reported that the use of Turbo Code makes relay calls more efficient, since neither party on the using phone or TTY has to wait for the regular (Baudot) tones to finish while transmitting. Turbo Code thus helps the relay communications to more closely achieve natural conversation rates (*DeafDigest*, 2000).

VIDEO RELAY SERVICE (VRS)

VRS is an online communication service that allows deaf and hard of hearing consumers to use sign language rather than to type their conversations. Using a webcam and a high-speed internet connection, sign language users log onto a telecommunications website and connect with a video interpreter who calls the hearing telephone user. On the website, the sign language user signs into their webcam, which appears on the screen. The video interpreter sees the sign language user signing and translates the signs into speech for the person on the other end of the line to hear. When the hearing person replies, the video interpreter translates their speech into sign language for the sign language user (AT&T Consumer, 2003; D-Link, 2003).

Also, because of ADA, hotels will have captioned television and TTYs and will begin to have signaling devices such as fire alarms with flashing lights.

HEARING AIDS

A hearing aid is an electronic device that is designed to amplify and deliver sound to the ear and consists of a microphone, amplifier, and receiver (Stach, 1997). Many people consider the use of hearing aids as vital to the education and interactions of deaf and hard of hearing individuals. However, relatives, friends, and uninformed others erroneously believe that deaf people can become hearing when they are fitted with the device (Meadow, 1980). The type of hearing loss determines which aid is best and most effective. Hearing aids come in a variety of shapes and sizes. The designs of hearing aids are improving daily. The first electric hearing aid was patented in 1901 (Harrison, 2003). The newest, digitally programmable hearing aids have been available during the past 8 years or so. Digitalization means that incoming sounds are converted to numbers, which are analyzed and manipulated by a set of rules programmed into a computerized chip in the hearing aid. Digital hearing aids are found to reduce the types of distortions that were associated with older hearing aids based on analog technology (American Academy of Audiology, n.d.).

Hearing aids do not restore hearing; they make sounds louder. Even with the best hearing aid, some people hear some speech sounds and others may not hear any speech at all (Deyo & Gelzer, 1991). Keep in mind that what information is gathered specifically from the environment by use of a hearing aid is unknown; do not assume that when you interact with a deaf person with a hearing aid, the person is able to hear each aspect of what you say.

As mentioned earlier, not all individuals benefit from hearing aids. In fact, some deaf adults may not like wearing them even if some sounds are heard. They may feel uncomfortable or amplify sounds in a way that is painful (Mahshie, 1995). Of note is that only 20% of those who need a hearing aid have one (Hard of Hearing Advocate, n.d.). Depicted in Figures 4.3 are examples of hearing aids.

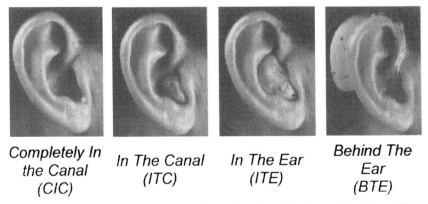

| Completely In the Canal (CIC) | In The Canal (ITC) | In The Ear (ITE) | Behind The Ear (BTE) |

FIGURE 4.3   Styles of hearing aids. (From American Academy of Audiology, 2002.) Website

COCHLEAR IMPLANTS

Cochlear implants are electronic devices that bypass the nonfunctioning inner hair cells and convert sounds to electrical impulses. Implantees must undergo a surgical procedure to receive the implant involving the placement of an internal coil under the skin behind the ear and a stimulating electrode directly within the inner ear or cochlea (Epstein, 1987). The cochlear implant has become a controversial issue in the Deaf community, especially when implantees are young children. Figure 4.4 describes the implant and its function.

At present, the statistics at the bottom of Figure 4.4 describing those who have received cochlear implants are out of date and the numbers are increasing daily. For instance, Ms. Pamela L. Carmichael, editor of NTID's *Focus* magazine, stated that the National Institutes of Health approximates that 70,000 people worldwide have now received cochlear implants, including more than 21,000 adults and children in the United States (P. L. Carmichael, personal communication, June 19, 2002).

A cochlear implant is an electronic device that helps provide a sense of sound for some deaf people. Unlike a hearing aid, a cochlear implant does not amplify sound; it allows a user to perceive sound by directly stimulating the auditory nerve.

A cochlear implant consists of components surgically inserted into the ear and components worn externally. There are several different types of cochlear implants, but in general, an implant works like this:

A microphone worn behind the ear picks up sound and converts it to an electrical signal (#1).

The signal is sent through a cord to the speech processor, which converts the electrical signal into an electrical code and sends it to the external coil (#2).

The external coil is placed on the skin behind the ear, usually held in place by a magnet or headset (#3).

The external coil sends the electrical code through the skin to the internal coil (#4).

The internal coil sends the code to electrode(s) located in the cochlea (#5 & 6).

Nerve fibers near the electrodes pick up the electrical code and send it to the brain (#7).

The brain processes and interprets the code, and the implant user becomes aware of the sound (#8).

This entire process occurs in a split second, allowing implant users to perceive sounds as they occur.

According to the National Institute of Health's National Institute on Deafness and Other Communication Disorders, approximately 25,000 people worldwide have received cochlear implants, including more than 14,000 adults and children in the United States.

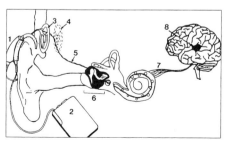

FIGURE 4.4 What is a cochlear implant, and how does it work? (From NTID's *Focus*, magazine, Fall 2000, p. 9.)

SPEAKERPHONE AND AMPLIFIERS

Some deaf and hard of hearing people can speak on the telephone with the help of amplifiers (to raise volume) or a speakerphone (so that they can speak for themselves while watching an interpreter).

FREQUENCY MODULATION (FM) SYSTEM

Used most often in an educational program, a frequency modulation (FM) system can be used with or without hearing aids. It has a microphone–transmitter (placed near the speaker) and a receiver (placed near the listener, who uses either a headset, earphone, or hearing aid with special neck loop).

INDUCTION LOOP

A special loop for students who need amplification can help the individuals to listen to the teacher's voice through the small microphone. This device will be very appealing in the future for people with cochlear implants who work in various businesses or other kind of workplaces.

Also, currently an induction loop is compatible with hearing aids. It is a length of wire circling a given area and connected to an amplifier and the speaker's microphone; the magnetic field within the loop is picked up by the "T" setting on hearing aids or by personal induction loop monitoring devices. The loop system can be used in classrooms, small seating rooms, and automobiles (Harris Communications, 2004).

SIGNALING DEVICES

Signaling devices use light (regular or strobe) or vibration to assist deaf and hard of hearing individuals to attend to different sounds in the environment such as the telephone or door bell ringing, baby crying, or smoke or fire alarms (Scheetz, 1993). Wake-up alarms, telephone or doorbell signalers, emergency warning devices, and emergency alarm devices have all been developed through the emergence of this technology.

Signalers use light or vibration to warn people when there is an important sound nearby (see Figure 4.5 for a diagram of rooms with examples of specifically placed signaling devices).

Examples of signalers:

- Telephone signalers flash a light when the telephone rings.
- Doorbell signalers flash a light when the doorbell rings (this flash of light is different from the flash for a phone ringing).

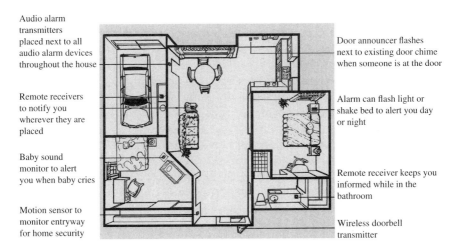

Audio alarm transmitters placed next to all audio alarm devices throughout the house

Door announcer flashes next to existing door chime when someone is at the door

Remote receivers to notify you wherever they are placed

Alarm can flash light or shake bed to alert you day or night

Baby sound monitor to alert you when baby cries

Remote receiver keeps you informed while in the bathroom

Motion sensor to monitor entryway for home security

Wireless doorbell transmitter

FIGURE 4.5   Rooms fashioned with signaling devices (Walker/Ameriphone Wireless Notification System, adapted from CSD illustrated catalog, Vol. 13, 2004, p. 34. Available from CSD, 15155 Technology Drive, Eden Prairie, MN 55344-2277).

- Wake-up alarm signalers flash a light or vibrate under a pillow.
- Pagers can receive messages from touch-tone phones, cell phones, personal computers, and TTYs.
- Safety devices include strobe lights connected to fire alarms and smoke detectors.

TELEVISION AND MOVIE CAPTIONING

For many years before closed captioning of network television programs became a reality, television was not a source of entertainment or information for most deaf and hard of hearing people. The thrill deaf and hard of hearing people get from television can be likened to the experience hearing people had when television was a novelty in the 1950s (Schragle, 1994). A television caption decoder is used for watching captioned programming. Under ADA, after 1993, all televisions were built so that the viewer could turn on the captioning without buying an external device, making this support readily available (Lightman, 1998).

In addition, some videotapes are beginning to be open captioned and do not require a decoder to view. These videotapes, however, are still expensive to process and make. At this time, deaf and hard of hearing people are gaining a greater sense of equal access to information and a greater sense of independence as they take advantage of captioning technology. The educational benefits of captioning are tremendous (Schragle & Bateman, 1994). For instance, captioned words during a television news program supplement the newspaper and can help build English vocabulary. However, the quality and readability of captioning need to improve in future years. Even though captioning enhances understanding of television programming, the complexities of written English still pose obstacles for deaf and hard of hearing viewers (Higgins & Nash, 1987). The words and sentences on the screen appear and disappear quickly. The captions are like subtitles in foreign films. Children who enjoy reading will probably benefit most from watching captioned television. Some parents of young children report that captioning encourages interest in reading (Deyo & Gelzer, 1987). The Telecommunications Act of 1996 (PL 104-104) required that virtually all video programming be captioned by some time after 2001 (Bowe, 1998).

COMPUTER ELECTRONIC MAIL (E-MAIL) AND THE INTERNET

With the advent of the computer age, many homes and offices have personal computers that have the capacity for electronic mail (e-mail). This technological advance has afforded deaf and hard of hearing individuals the opportunity to converse with each other or with hearing persons using the e-mail system. E-mail has augmented the TTY as a potential communication tool for all members of our technological society. In addition, the Internet benefits the Deaf community and its culture because it is a vehicle for dispersing information quickly. Bowe (1998) noted with fascination that hearing people have eagerly grasped the new technologies such as e-mail and the Internet to "save time" and be more efficient at gathering and imparting information. For deaf people, however, there is a caveat that may inhibit some of the same fascination and excitement experienced by their hearing counterparts; these technologies are visual, yes, but rely on the written word. In order to take advantage of the benefits of these technologies, all must possess strong reading and writing skills (Bowe, 1998). In the past, when they were cut off from sources of information and entertainment taken for granted by hearing people (radio, phonograph, telephone, television, and the cinema), the only source of interaction for Deaf people was found in the Deaf clubs. Now, Deaf people can interact on the Internet with their own special chatroom, called DeafChat (Deaf Life, 1997).

FACSIMILE (FAX) MACHINES

Detailed information and graphics can be transmitted accurately and rapidly with a fax machine. Deaf and hard of hearing people are using this technology sometimes in lieu of TTYs and e-mail because of the frequently instant response time and more detailed descriptions allowed.

PAGERS

Vibratory pagers with an alphanumeric display screen offer a new means of contact with deaf people. Some pagers can receive messages from touch-tone and cell phones, personal computers, and TYYs. Telecommunication Deaf International (TDI) provided a comparison of pagers useful for the Deaf consumer in their "The GA-SK" section (House, 2001).

COMMUNICATION SOFTWARE

Software that enables people using personal computers and modems to communicate with ASCII-compatible TTYs is available.

ASSISTIVE LISTENING SYSTEMS

Business and Personal Computer Networks

These networks allow users to make contact with one another in a variety of ways such as using e-mail. E-mail allows people to write and send letters, memos, and files to each other without handling a piece of paper. E-mail users can read and answer mail at their leisure, using their time efficiently. Deaf and hard of hearing individuals have often said that the TTY will be outdated by such network systems.

T-Mobile

The T-Mobile Sidekick connects to wireless networks and provides the deaf, hard of hearing, or hearing person with the ability to browse the Internet, exchange instant messages, and send and receive e-mail with image attachments. Other features include a full-featured phone, personal information management (PIM) applications, access to a personal Web portal, entertainment applications, and a camera accessory (T-Mobile Sidekick Reference Guide, 2002, p. 4) (see the following image of the T-Mobile Sidekick).

Wyndtell

Wynd Communications was founded in 1994 to bring simple but power-ful wireless communication solutions to its customers. A pioneer, Wynd is recognized as a respected and qualified provider of innovative wireless com-

The T-Mobile Sidekick

munication services and a company committed to serving the needs of people who are deaf or hard of hearing. Wyndtell is the only two-way wireless service designed specifically for people who are deaf or hard of hearing. It is a nationwide wireless service (Harris Communications, 2003). Wyndtell provides easy, accessible communication to all with comprehensive services such as e-mail, TTY, fax, text to speech, speech to text, alpha paging, and nationwide operation. For example, the new Wyndtell RIM 950 offers specific features such as: two-way e-mail, direct connect to AAA roadside service, and Insight cinema movies information (Harris Communication, 2004).

iCommunicator System

The new iCommunicator System allows a person who is deaf or hard of hearing to comprehend spoken language, achieve two-way communication without a human interpreter, improve reading skills, improve linguistics, and learn sign language. The iCommunicator System gives the user more independence and greater ease of communication (Harris Communications, 2002).

The iCommunicator System in real time converts:
Speech to text
Speech to sign language
Speech to computer-generated voice
Text to computer-generated voice

Talking Keyboard (Link Communication Device)

The talking keyboard is an easy-to-use communication device. A person types on the keyboard and then vocalizations are heard. The unit is lightweight and can be taken anywhere. It can connect directly to a telephone for a private conversation.

Braillephone

This device enables people who are deaf/blind to communicate either on the telephone, face to face, or via computer. It is designed to meet the needs of people who are comfortable with using a standard TTY over a phone system but can also be switched easily to allow a user to activate the home keys and space bar as a braille keyboard. Users can be kept informed of the status of the conversation while keeping their hands devoted to the tasks of typing and reading the braille display (Harris Communication, 2004).

TECHNOLOGY'S FUTURE?

Technology continues to make strides in providing language access to Deaf people and others with communication differences. At age 17, Ryan Patterson took a golf glove outfitted with sensors and created a way to translate the sign language alphabet to printed text (Figure 4.6). Patterson won the title of the world's top young scientist in 2002's Intel Science Talent Search for designing the glove (People, 2004). He met with the National Institutes of Health to discuss the merits of his invention. He is hoping that with the translator glove, hearing people with no knowledge of sign language may be able to communicate with deaf individuals by using the glove

Intel

FIGURE 4.6   The translator glove and its designer. (From Thomas, K. [2002]. Glove lends the deaf a hand. *USA Today*, January 15.)

to offer up a hand-held receiver so that both can chat through fingerspelling and translated text (Hartman, n.d.; Thomas, 2002).

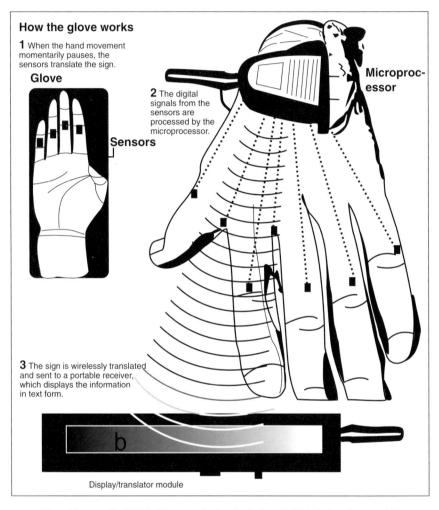

How the glove works

1 When the hand movement momentarily pauses, the sensors translate the sign.

Glove

2 The digital signals from the sensors are processed by the microprocessor.

Sensors

Microprocessor

3 The sign is wirelessly translated and sent to a portable receiver, which displays the information in text form.

b

Display/translator module

(From Thomas, K. [2002]. Glove lends the deaf a hand. *USA Today,* January 15.)

A suggestion for the future made by a Deaf person in DeafDigest, an e-mail newsletter for those in the Deaf community, was offered in jest but is interesting nonetheless:

A Deaf Vending Machine offering the following:

1. Alphabet and number reference cards
2. Pen and pad of paper (a deaf emergency kit)
3. Hearing aid batteries
4. "I Love You" jewelry
5. TTY printing tape
6. Sign language reference guide

(DeafDigest, 2001).

Future technology has a great deal of promise for bridging the void of interactions between Deaf and hearing people in our communities.

5

ISSUES FROM THE PAST
. . . ISSUES FOR THE
MILLENNIUM:
THE PROFESSIONALS'
PERSPECTIVES

WINFIELD MCCHORD

*Headmaster American School for
the Deaf, Ret.*

This chapter features resources involving a succession of fascinating and insightful interviews and written works by prominent individuals whose careers have been devoted to facets of the mystique of the deaf and hard of hearing.

There are 28 million deaf and hard of hearing Americans. Most Americans have little familiarity with deaf and hard of hearing people and not more than a moderate interest in them. Yet these people and their predecessors have affected the lives of every American, hearing or deaf or hard of hearing.

William E. Hoy, a deaf man, was an outfielder for the Cincinnati Reds and the Washington Senators. It is rumored that umpires began "signing" balls and strikes to cue him during the games.

Alexander Graham Bell's wife, Mabel Hubbard Bell, was hard of hearing. Bell dedicated himself to inventing a hearing aid for Mabel and, in the process, invented the telephone instead.

Gallaudet College was playing a football game against a well-known university in the late 19th century. The Gallaudet Bisons were trailing their opponents by a wide margin. Late in the second quarter, one of the Gallaudet players noticed the avid interest with which one of the players on the opposing team watched them as the Gallaudet Bisons discussed their next play in sign language. It occurred to the Gallaudet team that the player on the other team, while having normal hearing, probably had deaf parents and was translating their plays each time to his teammates before the ball was snapped. That afternoon, the football huddle was born.

Among the great deaf men and women who made significant contributions in their respective fields of science was Konstantin E. Tsiolkovsky, considered to be the founder of cosmonautics and human spaceflight. In his autobiography, he attributed to his deafness his increased powers of concentration, which enabled him to realize his greatest achievements. The world's first artificial satellite, *Sputnik*, was launched into space in 1957, near the centennial anniversary of Tsiolkovsky's birth.

There are many more stories and legends about deaf Americans and their contributions to our American way of life. You will meet Bernard Bragg, "literally born to miming," who was the first American to study privately under the great French mime Marcel Marceau. Bragg, the only deaf actor in the original group founding the National Theatre of the Deaf in 1967, shares his experiences in television, films, nightclubs, and theatre.

Dr. Karen Christie, a professor at the National Technical Institute for the Deaf (NTID), speaks of literacy, American Sign Language (ASL), linguistics, expression, poetry, English, and the complicated and often mystical process through which the deaf and hard of hearing develop better reading competence.

Doctors Patricia M. Chute and Mary Ellen Nevins address advances in medical technology (access to computer technologies, cochlear implants, audiometric screening of newborns) and a host of emerging medical developments that have resulted in the extension of the life span and the improvement of the quality of life for everyone.

Robert Pollard, Ph.D., a hearing psychologist whose wife is deaf, discusses mental health and deaf and hard of hearing individuals. Widely considered the leading expert in mental health and the deaf, he recognizes that there is a subpopulation of the deaf, just as there is of the hearing community, who need mental health services. He recommends that mental health providers acquire fluency in sign language skills and a working knowledge of deafness and deaf society. He recites his interesting and informative list of the hearing population's "myths" about deafness and deftly dispels them.

Pamela S. Rohring, M.S., specialist in ASL and Deaf Studies, reviews Dr. Harlan Lane's past contributions. Dr. Lane is a renowned author and spokesman on Deaf Cultural and community issues. Pamela highlights Dr. Lane's work and responds to it by pursuing the questions, Whose culture is it? Are the Deaf a minority group or are they members of a linguistic minority? Pamela's reflections on Dr. Lane's material effectively speak to issues such as the world's views on the ethics of cochlear implant surgery on children.

Catherine Morton, M.S., explores the culture and behaviors of deaf people through storytelling, humor, heritage, and communication. She examines Deaf Culture from the perspectives of hard of hearing people and individuals with cochlear implants.

As a son of deaf parents, I have been an educator of the deaf for 40 years, and for 32 of those years I have served as the chief administrative officer of the Kentucky School for the Deaf, my parents' alma mater (10 years); the American School for the Deaf, the oldest permanent school for the deaf in the New World (20 years); and St. Mary's School for the Deaf (2 years) in Buffalo, New York. I have been president of two national organizations in special education, and my schools have hosted three national conventions and four regional conventions. It has been an honor and a privilege to have collaborated with national leaders in deafness, including many of the authors who have contributed to the pages of this important and impressive chapter. So, read on and meet various professionals who will open your eyes and mind to the past, present, and future of an exciting world—the world of the deaf and hard of hearing!

Winfield McChord, Jr.

BERNARD BRAGG

Performer

The following is a summary of an interview of Mr. Bernard Bragg conducted by John W. Adams, Ph.D.

An accomplished actor, director, playwright, and lecturer, Bernard Bragg has trekked around the globe for 40 years beginning in 1956, when he studied with Marcel Marceau in Paris upon his invitation. As if that was hardly sufficient, he embarked on yet another trip to Europe in September 2001 and conducted seminars on cinematic storytelling in both Scotland and Italy. In the 1960s, he played an instrumental role during the formative years of the National Theatre of the Deaf (NTD), contributing as an NTD leading actor, administrator, and sign master for 10 years. He has written numerous articles and several books related to theatre and signed arts. Among his many national and international awards, Mr. Bragg was granted an honorary doctorate in human letters from Gallaudet University in recognition of his extraordinary service to Deaf people of the world in theatre, education, and communication. A resident of California, Mr. Bragg continues to enjoy teaching, playwriting, and directing at the California State University at Northridge.

Bernard Bragg is fond of saying that he was "literally born to miming." It's true. As the Deaf son of Deaf parents, Bragg spent all his young days trying to communicate with the outside world. How did he try to make himself understood in the hearing world? Through mime and gesturing. Bragg, who is credited as one of the first people to popularize mime in America, was the first American to ever study privately with Marcel Marceau, the great French mime. Marceau and Bragg exchanged many ideas in their work together and have continued their contact over the years.

After his return home from Paris, Bragg quickly rose to national prominence as a mime artist, starring in his own public television show, performing throughout the country, and attaining both national and worldwide recognition. During the winter of 1973, he spent 6 weeks in Russia as Artist-in-Residence with the Moscow Theatre of mimicry and gesture. Surprisingly, his performance with an all-Russian cast was the first time in more than 100 years that an American actor had appeared on stage in that country. His predecessor was a Black American actor named Richard Aldrich.

Bragg's work with mime does not begin to cover the scope of his expertise and experience. Among persons such as Edna Levine, David Hays,

Bernard Bragg: Down Memory Lane

Boyce Williams, and Mary Switzer, who have each in their own way contributed to the concept of the NTD, Bernard Bragg, one of its founders, continues to play his many unusual roles in its development. Some of Bragg's writings on the subject of theatricalized sign language were included in the grant application submitted to the U.S. Department of Health, Education, and Welfare to establish the NTD. Most importantly, Bragg was responsible for bringing to the NTD company his theatre colleagues and friends, Audree Norton, Joe M. Velez, and Charles Corey, who helped get the NTD off to a great start.

DRAMA AND THE DEAF COMMUNITY

Drama has had a major influence in the deaf community. Bernard Bragg's father was an actor and director. He had his own amateur company in New York and toured several cities in the East. His influence on young Bernard was so great that he became active in school dramatics. He graduated from the New York School for the Deaf (Fanwood). His first major job was as a teacher at the California School for the Deaf at Berkeley, but the stage was always his first love. He began his professional career as a nightclub performer in San Francisco; had a one-man weekly television show, *The Quiet Man*; studied with Marcel Marceau in Paris; and was the only professional Deaf actor in the original National Theatre of the Deaf, which he helped establish in 1967.

The almost three decades since the first rendezvous between the NTD and the Moscow Theatre in Belgrade is quite a short span of time when viewed in the context of the history of civilization. A number of Deaf theatres around the world have grown slowly and steadily toward full maturity, struggling to overcome amateurism. By exposing their work to others as well as being exposed to others' work, theatre people of the Deaf world are able to see where they stand and how they can improve their theatres. They zigzag between original and adapted works, at times interpolating Deaf Culture into classics or contemporary plays. Most Deaf theatres perform exclusively for Deaf audiences, but in a few countries they promote their theatres to the hearing public as well. That is not to say that the Deaf theatres in these countries aim to bring about social change.

Presenting Deaf theatre as an art form is their primary intent, although it may secondarily play a critical part in helping enhance the image of Deaf people. Through their dedication, Deaf theatre groups around the world have made significant and impressive contributions not only to their own Deaf communities but also to the general cultural life of the societies in which they live.

Drama and theatre are critical in the lives of deaf and hard of hearing people. Drama and theatre offer excellent entertainment and educational value for both the Deaf community and the general public. The value is broad, in both its cultural enrichment and sociological benefits for everyone, especially our young deaf children all over the country. The visual nature of drama and theatre makes them excellent sources of education for our youth.

UNIQUELY DEAF

There are certain parts of the theatre world that are uniquely related to the contributions of Deaf and hard of hearing actors: ASL (American Sign Language)! Using conversational sign in acting requires an understanding of conventional (i.e., standardized everyday) signs as well as unconventional signs. In signing for the theatre, not only do Deaf actors use conventional signs but also these signs can sometimes be enlarged, modified, or adapted, making them unconventional. Indeed, a new sign is often created in order to capture the exact meaning of a word. Unconventional sign in acting is an art inspired by words, yet it goes beyond words. The inner life of the word, or the concept behind it, is expressed through the hands and face, indeed the whole body. The rhythm and phrasing of signing, the flow and intonation of signs, with stress, emphasis, resonance, and tone color, can be suggested by the formation of signs. Variations in the pacing of signs built to a climax on the stage are an integral part of theatre in sign.

There is a signed art form, termed visual vernacular (VV), which has universal appeal to Deaf performers and audiences alike for its use of cinematic techniques. VV does not involve words and signs but rather makes use of close-up views, the long shot, the panoramic view, zooming, slow motion, fast motion cross-cuts, and cutaway views—all natural movements of the human body. It is close to our hearts, and Deaf actors with whom I have shared these techniques in my workshops are creative at expressing themselves in VV.

THE DEAF COMMUNITY
AND MAINSTREAM THEATRE

In the past, the Deaf community has not had a great deal of involvement in the mainstream theatre community with exception of some Deaf actors on television and in the movies. A Department of Education grant, totaling $4 million, has already helped Deaf West Theatre (under the able leadership of Ed Waterstreet and his staff) to present three main-stage productions a year while sending one show on a national tour. In addition, the grant fosters a professional training conservatory for Deaf theater artists. A summer-session program was held in 2001, with plans to expand gradually year-round. On-site theater programs are in place at a handful of Deaf and mainstream schools in the area, and Saturday morning storytelling workshops are held for youngsters and their parents.

Currently, Deaf West Theatre is very much involved in the mainstream theatre arts because this theatre company has garnered so many Ovation Awards and nominations from the esteemed fellow artists at Theatre Los Angeles for their productions of *A Streetcar Named Desire* and *Oliver*.

The establishment of such a professional theatre school in Los Angeles is bound to result in a growing number of Deaf actors, directors, costume and set designers, and producers all over the country. Also, it is bound to result in wider public recognition and acknowledgement of Deaf talent and creativeness and skills in the theatre arts.

There are many possibilities for hearing, hard of hearing, and deaf people to interact and enjoy the theatre contributions of all three groups. Creative interplay of signing and speaking actors is the key to the enhancement of a deaf theatre geared for the general public. Signing lends itself to cinematics—a picture that is visual, dramatic, expressive, and full of action all rolled into the one art that both deaf and hearing artists can call their own. Both signers and voicers (those voicing for Deaf actors) intertwine and become mutually involved rather than perform as two separate identities. The marriage of cinematic signing and dramatic voicing provides a double benefit for hearing and hard of hearing people in their audiences; they see and hear words at the same time. Deaf people especially enjoy colorfully visual aspects of their own language. Nothing can be more poignant than to see mixed groups of Deaf and hearing people in the same audience sharing cathartic experiences. These are opportunities for both communities to interact not only as actors but also as audience members.

DRAMA AND THEATRE AND THE YOUNG

It is important to cultivate a love of theatre and drama when deaf and hard of hearing children are young so that they learn the importance of these experiences in their culture. First of all, parents and teachers need gentle persuasion to attend Deaf theatre, where they may see and appreciate creative integration of both Deaf and hearing actors as well as the inventiveness of their dramatic works, which provide equal enjoyment for both Deaf and hearing audiences. This kind of exposure may inspire both parents and teachers to begin thinking about the implications of Deaf theatre for their deaf and hard of hearing children. They need to be given new ideas, which will do wonders for the language, culture, and theatre for these children. Start a beginning storytelling workshop for both parents and teachers and help them to improve their storytelling skills—taking their storytelling to a whole new level of dramatic performance, even taking it into theatre format: story theatre. Build up a repertoire of stories that are of interest for different ages; they can include not only folk tales, legends, and myths but also Deaf people's own stories—their own experiences. The sky is the limit.

KAREN CHRISTIE, PH.D.

National Technical Institute for the Deaf at Rochester
Institute of Technology

The following is a summary of an interview of Karen Christie, Ph.D., conducted by Pamela S. Rohring, M.S.

LANGUAGE DEVELOPMENT/LANGUAGE ISSUES AND DEAF AND HARD OF HEARING PEOPLE

Karen Christie became involved in language issues because they fascinated her. Her background includes work in linguistics, literature, laterality studies, first language acquisition, second language learning, teaching English, teaching English as a second language, and teaching ASL.

Dr. Christie believes that language is endlessly amazing and a magical part of being human. She currently teaches literature to Deaf students at the National Technical Institute for the Deaf (NTID) using literature from both English and ASL writing using a contrastive method with ASL and English. In addition, she teaches language acquisition and variation to graduate deaf and hearing students. All of Dr. Christie's current work allows her to remain involved with languages.

THE WORLD OPENED THROUGH ASL

When she was growing up, English was not easy for Karen. She struggled in elementary school, especially in reading, but at the end of her middle school years, she felt the connection that opened her to reading competence. However, as Steve Nover, a linguistics expert who is Deaf, has described, "my own language 'wholeness' did not truly occur until after learning ASL."

In learning ASL, she discovered a face-to-face language that satisfied her basic needs as a language user and helped her develop better competence in English.

She began learning ASL about the same time she became fascinated with English poetry. To Dr. Christie, poetry is the ultimate expression of how people can use language to create art. She studied under William Stafford and Vern Rustala. Later, she became a coordinator of the two National ASL Literature Conferences in Rochester. Through these experiences, she fell in love with ASL poetry and the works of people such as Ella Mae Lentz, Clayton Valli, and Peter Cook.

As an educator, she believed that learning to share English with students while still hailing ASL would be a major goal. This led to further study in linguistics and in teaching ASL. She has never had deaf or hard of hearing students tell her that learning English was not important to them.

Dr. Christie believes that all deaf people should be bilingual in ASL and English and should have the opportunity to study both languages. All deaf people should be exposed to the literatures of both languages.

LANGUAGE ACQUISITION

To acquire language is a natural human phenomenon. Elissa Newport has argued that to acquire a language it must be a natural one and accessible early in life. For children who are deaf and growing up in an environment where there is no exposure to a natural visual language, it becomes problematic. Research and practice have demonstrated that young Deaf children who are exposed to ASL acquire language in a natural language-driven manner.

Young deaf children who are exposed to spoken English naturally often do not acquire the language competently. For children with various degrees of hearing loss, one might need to ask, how much access to a natural language is enough to stimulate language acquisition? Swisher has addressed this in her discussion of access via hearing aids and lip-reading, showing, at most, that acquiring English in this manner is risky at best.

Language is what we need to acquire during interactions with others in our environment at a young age. Visual languages such as ASL, French Sign Language (FSL), or Japanese Sign Language (JSL) are fully accessible natural languages which stimulate language acquisition, and the models of these languages are Deaf people. These models would provide Deaf children not only with access to language but also with self-acceptance and learning about ways to be Deaf in a world of mostly hearing people. So for hearing parents, perhaps the necessity would be to change their view from having handicapped or disabled children to the realization that they have seeing, visual children whose access to language and information about the world and themselves will be through their eyes.

ENHANCING LANGUAGE DEVELOPMENT IN DEAF CHILDREN

The best strategy to enhance language development is to provide opportunities for Deaf or hard of hearing children and their parents to socialize with Deaf parents who have young Deaf children. This needs to occur early in life and not only when a deaf child begins his or her educational experience. The best advice comes from poet Ella Mae Lentz. In her poem, "To a Hearing Mother," she recognizes the need for a deaf child to have his hearing parent and Deaf community member work together to provide a fertile foundation in which the child can grow to his utmost potential.

> To a Hearing Mother
>
> You and I are different.
> Different worlds, languages, life experiences.
> You grew up ignorant of Deaf people though
> You may have heard of a few
> Here and there.
> I grew up in the DEAF–WORLD, all too familiar with the
> hearing and their oppressive ways.
>
> Now you give birth to a boy. He's Deaf!
> You're shocked! I'm surprised and delighted!
>
> You struggle to make the boy like you.
> However, he'll grow up to be like me.
> He has your likeness.
> However, he has my ears, soul, language, and world view.
> He's your son, but he's of my people.
> Then, who does the boy belong to? You or me?
> He's like a tree.
> Without our people
> he would wither and be left with no soul, no sense of self.
> But without you, there wouldn't be any trees.
> Our great people and language would dwindle.
> Our struggles and fighting can be like a saw
> that brings down the tree.
> We must stop it, and share, and love, and accept
> and together be the ground to nourish the tree
> so it will grow tall, proud and strong.
> And seek the heavens.
>
> Created by: Lentz, 1995
> Translated into English for *A Journey into the Deaf
> World*. Original ASL version can be found in *The Trea-
> sure: Poems by Ella Mae Lentz.*

People in the Deaf community need to reach out more to hearing parents of deaf children. It is necessary for the members of the Deaf community to learn how to better interact with and to better serve these families.

Opportunities to share information for social and educational interaction and to provide sign language courses will both be important. Parents need to know that if they are taking sign language courses or other parental education experiences, their input to establish these opportunities is invaluable. They are necessary so the child can be exposed to a variety of individuals and interaction situations involving visual communication.

EARLY INTERVENTION AND VISUAL COMMUNICATION

There is a great deal of pressure on hearing parents to provide their deaf child with exposure to sound at an early age. Of course, hearing parents generally want what is best for their child and they often think that to be able to take full advantage of all American culture has to offer, their child needs to learn to speak English like a hearing child.

Therefore, traditionally most deaf individuals in our community acquired their natural language (sign language) at a later time than their hearing peers. Despite years of education primarily focused on teaching English, most deaf students graduate from schools for the deaf as individuals with competence in ASL, which they learn in informal interactions. For example, Dr. Christie's dissertation research showed that older deaf peers, when interacting with young deaf children, modified their interactions and adjusted their signing. The older deaf children appeared to modify and adjust their signing not only in relation to the perceived linguistic limitations of the young learners but also because of the perceived cognitive immaturity of the conversational partner.

Although language and cognitive skills are somewhat related, the key is not the modality difference or which language to use, the key is having a language. The risk to deaf children occurs when communication input in any language is so sparse that stimulation of these cognitive abilities is compromised.

USE OF SIGN LANGUAGE AND ITS EFFECTS ON ENGLISH PROFICIENCY

Strong and Prinz (1997) have demonstrated that deaf children who grow up with at least one Deaf parent and are fluent in ASL have better English skills than those who do not. Clearly, having a fully developed first language, even if it is not the language of the schools, assists the learning of the second language in terms of generalizing skills. Some of Dr. Christie's research demonstrated that when taught about the structure of their first language (how to tell a story appropriately in ASL) and about the structure of the second language (how to write a narrative essay appropriately), students can learn how to adjust their narratives to match the language with which they are working. However, caution must be used when reviewing these findings because there is not enough research to determine definite recommendations in this area.

Deaf people experience pervasive literacy problems (Gallaudet Research Institute, 2001). Large numbers of deaf high school students are leaving school systems with much more limited reading skills than their hearing counterparts. The level of reading achievement barely falls within the definition of literacy offered by the National Literacy Acts of 1991 as "an individual's ability to read, write, and speak in English and compute and solve problems at levels of proficiency necessary to function on the job and in society, to achieve one's goals and to develop one's knowledge and potential."

As noted from Lane, Hoffmeister, and Bahan (1996), literacy is a misunderstood term in general education. In the education of the deaf, it is not only misunderstood but also misstated and misapplied. Many deaf people depend on American Sign Language. Reading and writing English are components of literacy. There are three types of literacy: functional, cultural, and critical. Some deaf people who are functionally literate can read a simple newspaper and possibly fill out a job application but are not able to read most books. Others are culturally literate and are able to read and understand more elevated journalism and books. Deaf people who are critically literate can write an article for a newspaper analyzing a topic in some depth.

Some deaf people are very limited in the English language because it is their second language and American Sign Language is their first, primary language. Reporting that deaf people can read and understand English at an average of third and fourth grade level is erroneous. Some have skills that are varied across levels, and others have gaps in their English language learning. Other deaf people may have difficulty writing notes or watching captioned television. However, research has shown that for children who have some grasp of language, captioning can actually help their English vocabulary development.

Personally, Dr. Christie is not sure that professionals really know how to assess the English language skills of deaf people in a way that truly provides an understanding of how English is being processed. Deaf people who have limited proficiency in written English seem to function as if trying to make a whole story out of missing parts. Of course, deaf people who have a rich background in a particular area such as car mechanics can handle much more challenging material in that area than in an area in which they do not have any background knowledge (this is true of hearing people also).

Often, watching television or movies with deaf people is a group event. There is a group effort at taking meaning from it all, so you often see deaf people signing to each other during these times. In education, at a certain point, teachers expect students to learn through reading. When there is so much focus on decoding the language, there is not enough cognitive energy left to figure out new concepts. This can also happen to people who are trying to read in their second language.

Basic functional literacy allows one to handle the newspaper, captioned television, and day-to-day communication. But, further, cultural literacy and critical literacy are needed. Deaf people need to learn how to use English to empower themselves not only to understand information. These activities are usually contexualized, and much of what will be understood has more to do with how much background information is known. Reading level per se is not as important in these situations as background knowledge. Because background knowledge varies greatly depending on the context, the effect on the individual would also vary greatly.

DEAF PEOPLE, COMMUNICATION, AND THE WORKPLACE

When hearing and deaf people work in the same environment, the best way to approach the situation would be through negotiation. They need to work out a way to interact with each other that is satisfactory. Negotiating might result in use of a pen and pencil or in using an interpreter. The deaf person would need to be able to communicate clearly his or her needs, and the same would be true of the hearing coworker or boss. Although a general workshop on Deaf Culture, ASL, teletypewriter (TTY), and pager use would be helpful, each work situation is unique and it would be best if individuals could negotiate in much the same way as people from two different cultures meet and negotiate understandings. However, when important information is being shared that people need to complete their job effectively or when professional development is provided, hiring an interpreter is most appropriate. As you will see in Chapter 6, there are techniques through which the supervisor or manager can make the work environment more Deaf and communication friendly.

Chapter 6 will provide specific communication techniques that could be incorporated in the work environment. But, in general, hearing people simply need to be open to the variety of ways in which deaf people prefer to communicate in a given situation. Communication is a two-way street, however, so both hearing and deaf people need to determine ways in which their own communication techniques work most successfully for each in a given interaction situation.

COMMUNICATION, DEAF PEOPLE, AND SERVICE PROVIDERS

A large number of Deaf people live in Rochester, New York. Because of this, many services and companies in the area have a great deal of awareness of and experience in dealing with deaf individuals. This awareness is almost an economic necessity. Use and understanding of basic signs and Deaf Culture in restaurants are common. For example, at a particular restaurant in Rochester, they do not call out the number for a deaf person's order, they bring it to the person's table. This has occurred mainly because of the great numbers of Deaf consumers and the economic power of Deaf people in this area. Also, in many businesses, salespeople are ready to provide a pen and pencil for communication. Of course, if an in-depth discussion is needed, an interpreter is warranted and will be requested beforehand. Although in many situations, deaf people need to remind business staff to request the interpreter, a number of places know how to make requests and their offices arrange the service without reminders.

Some deaf people are comfortable with written English in certain circumstances and some are not. The awareness that many people depend often on written information is growing. In airports and other places, print and visual images are being used much more frequently.

A combination of awareness and advocacy is what is needed within a community with diverse members. Community services should mean just that—services to the community. If a community includes deaf people, a shared responsibility exists so that access is not given to some people while others go underserved.

THE LAST WORD . . .

Dr. Christie believes that one of the most compelling issues related to the topic of language and deaf individuals is how best to involve, at an early age, a deaf child and his or her hearing family in a linguistically rich and accessible environment.

Another compelling issue and challenge concerns the best way to develop literacy skills in a visual language (ASL) in young children and how to transfer those skills to a language which appears in a print form (written English).

Dr. Christie strongly believes that answers exist for these and other questions if only society looks to deaf people in their functioning lives and listens closely to what they have to say.

PATRICIA M. CHUTE, ED.D.
AND MARY ELLEN NEVINS, ED.D.

Mercy College   Kean University
Dobbs Ferry, NY   Union, NJ

MEDICAL TECHNOLOGICAL ADVANCES FOR DEAF AND HARD OF HEARING PEOPLE

Technological and medical advances during the past two decades have affected the lives of all individuals regardless of age. Developments in computer technology have created a global village within which communication is instantaneous for all; developments in medical technology have resulted in the ability to extend the life span and improve the quality of life for many. Perhaps the greatest beneficiary of technological and medical advances is the population of persons with hearing loss. This group of more than 28 million Americans is growing substantially as more people are living longer and the effects of aging on the ear, known as presbycusis, are revealed. In addition, national projects that focus on universal newborn hearing screening are now available in almost half of the 50 states. These mandates require that every newborn child be screened at birth for the presence of hearing loss. However, within this large group of individuals with hearing loss, lifestyle and culture choices influence which of the technological and medical advances are accepted by any one individual with hearing loss.

For the members of the Deaf Community who primarily utilize manual communication, access to computer technologies such as e-mail, text-deliverable beeper systems, and closed captioning has provided more access to the everyday world than was ever imagined. Likewise, other technologies including digital and implantable hearing aids, sound field amplification, FM systems, and cochlear implants have provided access to sound for individuals interested in using spoken language as their primary mode of communication. Of the technologies noted, none has had more of an impact on the population of deaf individuals than the cochlear implant. The implant represents a blending of medicine and technology and has offered individuals with severe to profound hearing loss access to the hearing world in an unprecedented manner.

Cochlear Implant Evolution

Although the cochlear implant has been available on a clinical basis since the mid to late 1980s, it has been only in the past few years that the number of individuals receiving implants has grown to large proportions (Niparko, 2000). This has been a direct result of implant technology yielding better performance, implant design providing more cosmetically appealing devices, and wider distribution of information about implants overall. In addition, with the advent of newborn hearing screening programs, more children are being identified as having hearing loss earlier and therefore are eligible to receive implants at younger ages.

The cochlear implant consists of both external and internal portions (see Figure 5.1). The internal component includes the electronic packaging, an antenna, a magnet, and stimulating electrodes. The number of electrodes can be as few as 1 and as many as 22. The internal portion is surgically implanted in an area on the head known as the mastoid in a 2- to 3-hour procedure by an otologist. After cochlear implant surgery, there are no noticeable profile differences; that is, there are no wires or receivers that protrude through the skin.

The external portion of the implant consists of a microphone, speech processor, and transmitter. These are worn outside the body like a traditional hearing aid. The speech processor houses a computer chip that requires programming on a regular basis as the implant recipient's perceptions adjust to sound. The processor uses a specialized computer program to deliver the signal to the internal electrodes. These computer programs are often referred to as speech processing strategies. Manipulating speech strategies over time permits the implant user to improve speech perception ability continually. Because the internal components are driven by external software, the implant user can upgrade without additional surgery as improvements in technology occur.

Although still in its infancy, the field of implant technology has a history of rapid development. Major improvements in implant technology in recent years have included increasingly sophisticated speech processing strategies and the development of smaller, more compact external equipment. The presence of multiple implant manufacturers has encouraged research and development so that consumers have more choices available to them and a better product overall. At present, there are three companies that develop

Nucleus® 24
Cochlear Implant System

6 Internal implant converts code to electrical signals

1 Sound is received by microphone

7 Signals are sent to the electrodes to stimulate the remaining nerve fibres

Transmitter **5** sends the code across the skin to the internal impalant

8 Signals are recognized as sounds by the brain producing a hearing sensation

Cooded signals **4** are sent to the transmitter

2 Sound is send from microphone to speech processor

Speech processor **3** analyzes and digitizes the sound into coded signals

SPrint" – the body worn speech processor

ESPrfr^na – the ear level speech processor for the Nucleus 24

Cochlear

FIGURE 5.1   The cochlear implant. (From Chute, P.M. and Nevins, M.)

and manufacture implants: Cochlear Corporation, Advanced Bionics Corporation, and Med El Corporation (see Appendix C for addresses and website information). Each of these manufacturers has support systems in place for the consumer, clinical facilities that perform implantation, and teachers and therapists who assist in the rehabilitation process.

The Cochlear Implant Process

Candidacy requirements for implantation have changed substantially in recent years. A decade ago, individuals who received cochlear implants tended to represent the group of the profoundly deaf who had minimal hearing (Osberger, Robbins, Miyamoto, Berry, Myres, Kessler, & Pope, 1991). As improvements in implants have occurred, audiologic criteria for candidacy have changed to include individuals with lesser degrees of hearing loss. At the present time, implants are placed in only one ear; studies are now being developed to measure the effectiveness of these devices in both ears for adults and children.

As noted previously, the surgical procedure for cochlear implantation is performed by a trained otologist and may require an overnight hospital stay. This procedure is covered under most insurance policies and by many state-supported programs; Medicare also funds implantation. The implant procedure itself is performed under general anesthesia and is usually accomplished within 2 to 3 hours. There is a healing period of approximately 1 month before the implant recipient receives the external equipment. During this time there may be minor restrictions on the child's or adult's physical activity. After this short period of recuperation, normal activity can resume.

The postoperative follow-up for individuals who receive cochlear implants is most often determined by the age at implantation and the duration of deafness. For adults who were born with normal hearing and later lost their hearing from some external cause, the process of training is relatively short term and, in most cases, home based. For adults who are congenitally deaf or deafened at a very young age, the rehabilitation process is more extensive and requires a long-term commitment on the part of the recipient.

For children who receive implants, habilitation is continuous throughout their educational careers and is especially intensive during the early language learning years. Although a variety of educational environments can support implantation, those that incorporate speaking and listening on a daily basis yield the best outcomes. This does not preclude the use of a sign language system for children with implants; however, it stresses the importance of the use of that system with the addition of spoken language.

Cochlear Implant Performance

The performance of individuals who receive cochlear implants varies in a manner similar to the performance of the general population of hearing aid users. On average, adults who are postlinguistically deaf (deafened after the development of speech and language skills) and have a short duration of deafness achieve the best speech perception abilities (Shipp, Nedzelski, Chen, & Hanusaik, 1997). Adults who are congenitally deaf and have a long duration of deafness demonstrate improvements but not of the magnitude of their postlinguistic counterparts (Kirk, 2000). The latter group represents a very small population of implant users because most of these adults communicate with sign; their culture and lifestyle do not compel them to seek implantation.

For children who receive implants, the results can also be variable. Children who are congenitally deaf and are implanted at a very young age, 2 years or younger, demonstrate auditory, speech, and language skills commensurate with those of the same age who have normal hearing after 2 to 3 years of implant use (Robbins, Osberger, Miyamoto, & Kessler, 1994; Waltzman & Cohen, 1998). Children who are congenitally deaf and are implanted as adolescents may demonstrate performance improvements over a much longer period of time and may not reach the same level of auditory skill as the children implanted at younger ages (Nevins & Chute, 1996). Children who are postlinguistically deafened with a short duration of deafness reach maximal performance quickly and demonstrate abilities that are equal to those of their normally hearing peers in most cases (Fryauf-Bertschy, Kelsey, & Gantz, 1992; Staller, Beiter, Brimacombe, Mecklenberg, & Arndt, 1991).

CONCLUSION

The field of implant technology has experienced rapid growth. This technology yields increasingly better performance and is available to a wider range of implantees. However, there is a danger in overvaluing the importance of technological advances in our everyday lives. Seldom does any one advance fit the needs of the entire population for whom it was designed. The Deaf and hard of hearing people are a very heterogeneous group with different types and degrees of hearing loss, personal and family characteristics, educational, psychological, and social needs, and cultural perspectives. Within this heterogeneous population, an individual's choice to defer implementation of technological innovations should not call for a value judgment from others who may choose them.

The cochlear implant is one such advance that has polarized the communities of persons for whom it may be appropriate. Those who choose implantation must respect the decision of those who do not; conversely, those who do not choose implantation should respect the decision of those who do.

ROBERT POLLARD, PH.D.

MENTAL HEALTH AND DEAF AND HARD OF HEARING INDIVIDUALS

The following is based on an interview with Robert Pollard, Ph.D. conducted by John W. Adams, Ph.D.

PROFESSIONAL BACKGROUND

Robert Pollard was born and raised in Rochester, New York. He became involved with deaf and hard of hearing people in a professional way during his second year of graduate school. At this time, the Board of Directors of DePaul Mental Health Services in Rochester was considering the development of a group home serving deaf people. While the group home was in the process of being established, Dr. Pollard became aware that this population was underserved. His work concerning deafness and mental health issues was initiated because of the lack of research and other professional information available in this area and the serious lack of mental health services provided. He began taking sign language courses and doing writing in his graduate school program regarding mental health issues and the deaf population.

Dr. Pollard was hired as a member of the first staff at the DePaul group home. It was at this home that Dr. Pollard obtained sign language fluency and Deaf Culture knowledge. Keith Cagle, a Deaf man, was the home's first director. Through their shared experiences and their own intellectual curiosity, Dr. Pollard and Mr. Cagle often had long conversations about deaf and hearing culture conflicts and other matters relevant to their work with deaf consumers and deaf and hearing professionals.

In 1984, he began his first professional job working as a psychologist at The Community Center for the Deaf in Columbus, Ohio. In 1986, he accepted a position at the Center on Deafness at the University of California, San Francisco. According to Dr. Pollard, the years between 1986 and 1990 were an exciting time in which to work at the center and in the mental health and deafness fields.

His life continued to become more influenced by the Deaf community. He met a Deaf woman through a mutual friend, an interpreter. They dated long-distance, Ohio to California, for 3 years and were married in 1989. Both experienced unique challenges found in families that have mixed hearing and deaf members. Dr. Pollard characterized his wife's family as having limited knowledge concerning deaf issues even though another family member, a sibling, was also deaf. Her parents did not use sign language communication. Visiting them presented many difficult communication situations. Because his wife was often not directly included in conversations, Dr. Pollard or a hearing sibling frequently played the role of an interpreter. Unfortunately, this family scenario described by Dr. Pollard is typical of many hearing families with deaf members.

MENTAL HEALTH NEEDS AND DEAF AND HARD OF HEARING PEOPLE

There exists a subpopulation of the Deaf community, similar to that within the hearing community, who need mental health services. The limited research conducted to determine base rates of mental illness in the Deaf and hard of hearing population suggests that most mental illnesses occur at equal rates in deaf and hearing populations with some exceptions. Among the exceptions are various developmental and organic mental disorders such as mental retardation and learning disabilities. Some of the medical disorders that cause deafness can also cause other neurological problems. Neurological disorders such as mental retardation, learning disabilities, and attention deficit disorders occur at higher rates in the deaf and hard of hearing population because this group of people has already experienced a medical event that caused the hearing loss, often a neurologically significant medical event.

The second area in which mental disorder rates are higher is depression among adults who have late-onset deafness. Depression is a frequent reaction to late-onset hearing loss because adjustment is required after spending one's whole life as a hearing person and having one's life dramatically change.

Another mental health diagnostic category in which the incidence may be higher in the deaf population is personality disorders. The reason, however, is very important to understand. Deafness in and of itself would not lead to a disorder in personality. However, if the family, school, and/or community reacts poorly to the challenges posed by the hearing loss, this may lead to social and personality development problems. If these problems are not handled well, the challenges to adjustment and development could result in patterns of behavior that affect the personality in more serious, maladaptive ways.

Throughout an individual's growth from birth to later years, a series of developmental opportunities occur that aid in a forming a person's psychological and social skills and resources, such as parent–child relationships, curiosity and exploration, language and communication skills development, education, gaining a fund of information, and social experiences. Each of these areas presents an opportunity. Depending upon how these opportunities are experienced, healthy psychological growth will occur or be thwarted. If a family or a community continually responds poorly to the stimulus or challenge of the deaf youngster, such as failing to communicate effectively, or if grief or other psychological reactions interfere with the early parent and child bond, these events can have negative consequences. In later years, if a child is not allowed to go to the corner store to buy a loaf of bread even though the clerk may not understand his or her voice very well, the child misses a developmental experience that may affect subsequent independence. Personality disorders and other psychological difficulties can develop over time if a child consistently does not experience success in the hierarchy of challenges that lead to a mature view of and competence in the world. Some families, schools, and communities continue to "drop the ball" in terms of offering growth experiences, and the deaf or hard of hearing person continues to be at risk.

A critical issue affecting the diagnoses of psychiatric disorders is language use. How proficient a person is in his or her language can affect how a person is diagnosed. The vast majority of hearing persons in the world are fluent in their preferred language. Those hearing people who are less than comprehensible in their own native language are usually suffering from active psychosis, drug intoxication, severe retardation, or some other psychiatric or neurological problem. The distribution of language fluency (spoken English or sign language) in deaf people is much broader. A difference exists between the percentages of deaf versus hearing people who are proficient in their preferred language. The percentage of those with low language fluency is higher in deaf people than hearing people. This occurs because of the great variability in when deaf children are first exposed to sign language and the difficulty acquiring English through the visual sense alone. Many deaf children are not exposed to fluent sign language early enough or frequently enough to develop fluency themselves. If persons such as these enter the mental health system, psychiatrists and psychologists will have tremendous difficulty reaching diagnostic conclusions. Questions such as, Is this a psychotic deaf person? Is this a deaf person with dysphasia? Or is this a deaf person who never learned any language very well? are difficult to answer with this minority deaf group unless one is specifically trained and fluent in sign language.

BARRIERS TO EFFECTIVE
MENTAL HEALTH SERVICES

Barriers to effective services include the limited number of sign-fluent clinicians and the limited availability of sign language interpreters especially those trained to work effectively in mental health settings. Another barrier involves the knowledge and the skills of clinicians to do assessments, evaluations, diagnoses, and treatment plans in relation to the unique characteristics of a particular deaf client being served. One example of the type of knowledge needed to work within the deaf or hard of hearing population involves understanding myths about hearing loss such as the myth that "lipreading" is easy and effective or the myth that most deaf people have normal English literacy skills. Another example of the type of knowledge central to serving the deaf consumer is understanding Deaf cultural issues.

Sign Language Proficiency

Access to mental health and other healthcare services is a serious issue of concern to the Deaf community. But there are very few mental health service providers who are fluent in sign language communication. Those few mental health service providers who are accessible linguistically are often generalists providing a wide range of services because communication is key. A broad client base with a variety of mental health issues is the norm for most of these providers. For instance, a deaf couple may request marriage counseling from a sign language-fluent provider even though the provider may not specialize in this area of therapy. The number of specialists in the field will grow in time. As the pool of trained, sign-fluent service providers becomes larger, specific subspecialties will develop.

Knowledge about Deafness

In addition to sign language proficiency, providers must have knowledge about deaf issues. Knowledge about deafness and sign language fluency are critical factors when determining a diagnosis and rendering treatment. For example, distinguishing between a thought disorder and a developmentally induced language limitation requires a keen analysis of knowledge about deafness and sign language nuances.

Basic levels of education concerning knowledge about deaf issues need to include the myths about deafness which will be expanded on below.

Myths About Deafness

Dr. Pollard outlines four common myths concerning deafness. The first myth is that deaf people can read lips easily and the mistaken idea that this way to communicate is sufficient for understanding between deaf and hearing people. Lip-reading or speech reading is not efficient for any person to use to gather information. Only about 30% of English speech movements are seen on the outer mouth and the lips; hence, as an ideal estimate, the best speech reader will directly understand no more than one third of the message from this means of transmitting information. The rest is entirely guesswork, and trying guesswork at that.

A second myth involves some people's belief that sign language is similar to mime, is like English, is international, or is easy to learn. Sign language is a language in and of itself. A third myth is that deaf people are literate in English. English is essentially a second language for most deaf people. Fluency in English cannot be expected. People assume that deaf people are literate in English because the printed word is visually accessible and therefore should be readily accessible to deaf people. What most hearing people do not recognize is that hearing persons are typically fluent in (spoken) English by the time they arrive in kindergarten. Individuals in the child's home environment are fluent in that language, and in sharing this language the child becomes very knowledgeable in its use and function. Teachers then demonstrate how this shared language is written or read. This scenario must now be compared with the experiences of a typical deaf person. The deaf child arrives in kindergarten without fluency in a language because a shared language system is not available at home (unless the child is born to a Deaf mother and father, which is rare). Young deaf children do not acquire English fluency through "lipreading" Since a language foundation necessary for English literacy work does not exist when they enter school, and because of the typical language barrier between teacher and student, reading and writing become a lifelong struggle for many deaf people.

Dr. Pollard offers the medical students he teaches a fourth myth. He emphasizes that medical expertise in hearing loss does not equal expertise in deafness. Medical professionals can develop a broad understanding of deafness only if they experience interactions with a variety of deaf and hard of hearing people with different types of hearing loss, with different types of communication modes, and within a variety of positions in society. This experience will provide them with knowledge about deaf people which cannot be derived by knowing the function or dysfunction of the ear alone.

Pollard notes there is also a general perception among hearing people in society that individuals do not want to be deaf. This is largely untrue. The deaf population is different from any other disability or medical group. No other group of people who have a medical particular condition are in such disagreement with the people who treat that condition. Preventing or "curing" deafness is not prioritized or valued in the Deaf community. This phenomenon is unlike any other within a population having a disability or chronic medical condition. Within our field, deaf advocates are in disagreement with the people who are trying to cure deafness because to them, searching for a cure is a threat to a language and a culture (Deaf Culture) within our society.

Deaf Culture: Minority Versus Majority Cultural Issues

Deaf Culture involves the unique behaviors, norms, language, traditions, art, literature, and technology that help form the deaf person's identity. Critical to understanding living a life in a minority culture is to examine issues relative to those influenced by interaction within the majority culture.

Dr. Pollard often presents lectures on the topic of minority values in relation to the deaf population. He compares issues related to the Deaf community and to other minority groups. For example, one issue of comparison is autonomy and who decides what affects our lives? Hearing people are in control of many aspects of deaf people's lives. Hearing people are in control of deaf education and generally will dictate when or if deaf children will be exposed to sign language. Hearing people are in control of the training programs designed to produce teachers of the deaf. Such issues of control are of critical importance when determining the future development and the future leaders in areas influencing deaf politics, deaf education, and the overall quality of life in the Deaf community.

Self-definition is another area of comparison between the Deaf community and other minority groups. For example, in the past, the popular accepted terms for a person of African descent has changed from "colored," "Negro," to "Black," and then to "African-American." The self-definition of deaf people has also changed. Years ago, at the beginning of his career, Dr. Pollard remembers that it was polite to say "hearing impaired," and now the acceptable terms are "deaf" and "hard of hearing."

Common in any minority group is its relationship with the majority community, in this case the relationship of deaf people to hearing people. It is important to examine how a minority population is defined and portrayed within the majority community.

Group versus individual priorities are an issue. Many deaf people recalled watching television when Marlee Matlin (a deaf woman) prepared to accept her Oscar. She chose to speak her acceptance speech rather than sign it. The disappointment was seen around the Deaf world because the Deaf community thought Matlin's fluent sign language could have been portrayed to hearing people as a symbol of her pride and success and yet she displayed only her ability to speak.

The Deaf community is vital to Deaf life, and what one does to further the group's priorities is as important as what one does to further individual priorities. If Marlee Matlin wants to stand up and speak because she chooses to and is proud of her voice, she puts her individual priorities ahead of those of the group. The Deaf community reacted with disappointment concerning this missed opportunity.

The protection and enculturation of deaf children are critical concerns. Any minority group is involved in the protection and enculturation of their children. For example, a good number of Jewish people feel strongly about their children receiving a Hebrew education, marrying another Jewish person, and having a Jewish family. A priority is to perpetuate their religion and the culture associated with that religion. Similarly, Deaf people are concerned about the protection and enculturation of deaf children. This issue is paramount to the Deaf community. However, 95% of deaf children are born to hearing, not deaf, parents.

The protection of the schools for the deaf is a priority. The schools for the deaf are the primary locations where deaf children can be exposed to sign language fluency and Deaf Culture. It is much more difficult for a deaf child to acquire sign language fluency and a sense of Deaf Culture identity in mainstream educational environments.

The issue of enculturation of children is central to many minorities. Deaf young people can internalize negative beliefs about their deafness, just as persons from ethnic minority groups can internalize society's racism and think poorly of themselves. If schools for the deaf are not available to help educate deaf children and the general public about the positive aspects of sign language communication and Deaf Culture, myths about deafness and other destructive forces may reinforce negative beliefs.

A Client's Fund of Information

According to Dr. Pollard, one of the most significant issues in the lives of deaf people is how well they deal with diminished access to information. From a clinician's viewpoint, this diminished access results in fund of information deficits. A limited fund of information is apparent among many deaf individuals regardless of intelligence. Literacy is compromised in this population. There is no access to the radio, limited access (English captioning) to information on television, and no opportunity to acquire incidental information by overhearing others' conversations in families or in public.

Most of what a deaf person learns is what he or she has learned directly through reading or has been told directly in sign or through the limited avenue of speechreading. This fund of information is significantly less than that to which a hearing person is exposed. The challenge of a limited fund of information is underappreciated. Dr. Pollard provided an example of what happened at Columbine High School in Colorado to illustrate this point. When someone utters "Columbine," most hearing people know exactly what is being conveyed. If a youth walks by in a black trench coat and someone makes an offhand "Columbine" comment, hearing people would most likely know what is meant by the comment. An average deaf individual may certainly know of the news story of what occurred in Columbine, but would the word "Columbine" immediately bring up all the associations concerning the whole American tragedy? This is an example of a fund of information issue.

As seen within Dr. Pollard's clinical practice, fund of information deficits can lead to problems that fundamentally undermined a person's self-esteem and social functioning. Information concerning medical and psychological issues and services may also be limited and therefore the access to and outcomes of the services can be negative.

In conclusion, any diagnoses made and treatments conducted will involve a provider's *sign language proficiency*, and *knowledge of deafness*, such as an understanding of the myths about deafness, in depth familiarity with of Deaf Culture and critical evaluation of a client's fund of information.

Aside from the communication issues, cultural differences, and the fund of information question, the heterogeneity of the population is so critical to understand. All deaf and hard of hearing people are unique and different in terms of their degree and type of hearing loss, family background, educational experiences, and ability to use spoken English or sign language. These differences determine the manner in which the service worker would provide their services.

A WORD TO THE PROFESSIONALS OR THOSE IN TRAINING WITHIN THE MENTAL HEALTH FIELD

The National Association of the Deaf has emphasized mental health as a service priority area. And, Dr. Pollard believes that the politically active segment of the national Deaf community views mental health as important. Gallaudet University's clinical psychology program produces a number of trained professionals at the doctoral level each year. Other training programs across the country are producing better trained practitioners as well. Years ago, only 25 or so doctoral-level psychologists practiced in the deafness field. At present, there may be up to 100 of these providers in the field.

As a hearing person working in the deafness and mental health field, it is a cross-cultural endeavor. This endeavor is similar to that of a Caucasian individual wanting to work in an African American or Hispanic setting. To work with deaf individuals, you need to cross over cultural *and* linguistic lines, to gain "legitimacy." When it comes to the deafness field, legitimacy is principally gained through sign language fluency. Nothing is more key to the cross-cultural legitimacy in working with deaf people than one's sign language communication abilities. Knowing sign language alone is not enough but it is a top priority. Understanding Deaf Culture and knowledge of and interaction within the Deaf community are critical.

In Dr. Pollard's opinion, it is not possible nor necessary to acquire all of the components of cross-cultural legitimacy, mental health knowledge, language fluency, Deaf Culture understanding, and community interactions, all at the same place or at the same time. You can obtain language fluency at one place, deaf cultural knowledge elsewhere, and clinical experience somewhere else. The bottom line is that you will have to earn your cross-cultural stripes in the community in which you live and work no matter where you gained your knowledge, skills, and experience. Dr. Pollard's article in *American Psychologist* on the emergence of the discipline presents information related to deafness and mental health and on cross-cultural legitimacy (Pollard, 1996).

THE FUTURE: ACCESSING MENTAL HEALTH SERVICES

Dr. Pollard predicts that because the availability of specialized services for the deaf is still sparse, the next wave of service provision will be video conference-based.

Service innovations have been conducted in South Carolina. A psychiatrist fluent in sign language holds clinics in over 20 remote sites via video conferencing. This psychiatrist is located at one end of a video conference unit and interviews deaf patients via sign language in a variety of other sites. Providing service over video conferencing is one means of service provision to broaden future accessibility.

A separate means of service provision is being pioneered by Dr. Pollard in his use of video conferencing to provide interpreter services to remote locations. His project primarily involves emergency medical services in health centers. In the future, this project could be expanded to include mental health services. An interpreter is positioned at the University of Rochester Medical Center and interprets the information exchanged between a deaf person and a hearing health care provider who are in a remote setting. Specifically, video conference units have been set up in remote hospital emergency rooms. When a deaf patient walks into that remote hospital emergency room and the staff is unable to communicate with that person, they activate their video conference unit which accesses a sign language interpreter from the University of Rochester Medical Center's "Strong Connections" service. Through this technology, communication is facilitated at distant sites providing accessibility to these services that would not otherwise be available. More information can be accessed by contacting their website at www.urmc.rochester.edu/strongconnections.

The need is great but training specialist clinicians is a slow process. Dr. Pollard may seek funding to place video conference units in state hospitals and in large state psychiatric facilities so whenever a deaf patient arrived, the psychology staff of Dr. Pollard's Deaf Wellness Center (www.urmc.rochester.edu/dwc) can consult with them directly in sign language communication. The effectiveness of such a treatment modality is an empirical question. A greater number of telepsychiatry and telepsychology services are being created. Time and research will determine the success and effectiveness of such services.

MENTAL WELLNESS: SUGGESTIONS FOR COMMUNITY SERVICE PROVIDERS

Similar to professionals in the mental health field, most employers and employees have limited knowledge about deaf and hard of hearing people. A healthy work environment for deaf and hard of hearing people would start with a strong foundation. Key hearing people who are educated about deafness and trained to be sensitive to deaf issues need to be in the work setting. For example, if a deaf clinician is hired by a hospital emergency room, one or more of the hearing supervisors should become well-versed in deaf issues. Along with the deaf employee, this key supervisor would be responsible for orchestrating communication plans and a deaf-friendly environment—acting like a foreman. It is often more feasible and effective to have one person be the expert rather than to try to teach the whole work group simultaneously. One supervisor who is very knowledgeable can have a major impact working in partnership with the deaf employee.

When a hearing person is knowledgeable and skilled in deaf issues, the burden of orchestration of communication and support services does not rest solely on the deaf employee or sign language interpreters. For instance, in most work settings, there is rarely one conversation occurring at a time. The central person will help others to understand that the deaf employee or interpreter can attend only to one conversation at a time.

The hearing "foreman" would take better control over group meetings. This coordinator could help determine whether the deaf person is having full access to the communication situation or whether immediate actions are necessary to make the situation more accessible.

Preparation for supervisory staff is important for placement success. A consultant coming in as an expert can be only so effective. The deaf employee's own comfort in educating others is critical. It is best when the deaf person is comfortable with the teaching role. He or she usually functions as an ambassador between the deaf and hearing workplace world. The better ambassadors they are the better and more accessible the workplace will be.

In any work site, not every "hearing student" is going to learn what he or she needs to learn. Individuals who really have a good understanding of deafness need to be models. For example, suppose a deaf clinician is scheduled to care for a hearing patient. The workplace coordinator must model being comfortable with the established therapeutic arrangement. The more the coordinator can model sensitivity and skills in the employment setting, the more understanding will be fostered among the employees. As the experiences continue, more employees will contribute to the deaf-friendly environment, and the setting will be preestablished for success.

Interpreters also can be viewed as professionals to help establish a deaf-friendly and a communication-accessible work site. They can help provide information to adapt the workplace for accessibility. Frequently, it is the interpreter who can understand both hearing and deaf perspectives and needs and this person should be included along with the deaf employee in the communication management decisions. Unfortunately, interpreters are often viewed only as communication translators.

Deaf workers and their interpreters need to be involved in a dynamic relationship in which they determine what is best for the work environment. This is especially the case when a deaf individual is in a professional position. A different scenario exists when an assembly line employee is deaf and has an occasional relationship with the interpreter as compared with a deaf executive who has an ongoing working relationship with the interpreter. In a typical situation, for example, an interpreter may be hired for a large group workplace meeting or for a small employee evaluation session. In these circumstances, the interpreter cannot meet ongoing communication needs because he or she is present only on occasion.

The environment needs to be deaf friendly yet nonthreatening to hearing people who are afraid of learning a new language, sign language. Many employees may not be motivated to take on sign language classes and may not learn much from formal courses. Taking small steps to make the environment more accessible is very effective (see Chapter 6 for effective communication strategies and how to set up a deaf friendly environment). You can provide sign language videotapes and dictionaries in the office. Teach the staff to use writing techniques and some finger spelling to communicate basic messages. Place a box in the secretary's office with sets of sign language flash cards. The staff can take a set to practice in their spare time. Assistive devices such as TTYs, flashing smoke detectors and fire alarms, and captioned television should be prominent. It is also suggested to provide written materials about deafness, deaf culture, and about how to communicate with deaf people in advance so that people have some basic knowledge about their coworker(s). Of course, recruiting more individuals who are deaf is most beneficial.

Deaf employees may vary concerning their preference for social integration in the workplace. For example, Dr. Pollard's training program has included many deaf trainees, some of whom shared a limited desire to be a part the hearing trainees' program. Other deaf trainees' social activities were more concerned about that matter and wanted to be deeply integrated into the hearing trainees' social groups and planned activities.

Employers and employees who are educated about the issues that affect the lives of deaf and hard of hearing people would be ideal. Professional development workshops and inservices focused on awareness and basic communication techniques are additional ways to instill how to show respect and how to use skills when interacting with the deaf employee.

Education about the deaf and hard of hearing population is the key element and a stepping stone to offering accessibility to services in the mental health area or in the majority community. Dr. Pollard strongly encourages all service providers to learn more about this underserved population—a unique people, culture, and language.

WHOSE CULTURE IS IT ANYWAY?

Dr. Lane is a renowned authority on issues related to the Deaf Community, its Culture and its struggle within a hearing society. Highlights from Dr. Lane's work (primarily taken from the book he co-authored, *A Journey into the Deaf-World*, and his articles, "Constructions of Deafness" and "The Cochlear Implant Controversy") are presented below. Each of Dr. Lane's major viewpoints is followed by commentary (in italics) made by Ms. Pamela Rohring.

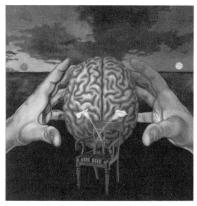

"Left Brain/Right Brain"
Created by: Chuck Baird

It matters greatly whether you see a person who is deaf as primarily a member of a disability group or as a member of a linguistic minority. Numerous organizations are associated with each of the prominent constructions of deafness. When reviewing the numbers, the national organizations primarily associated with deafness as a disability included the A. G. Bell Association (4500 members), the American Speech-Language Hearing Association (40,000), the American Association of Late-Deafened Adults (1300), Self Help for the Hard of Hearing (13,000), the American Academy of Otolaryngology, Head and Neck Surgery (5600), and the National Hearing Aid Society (4000). Contrarily, national organizations associated primarily with the construction of Deaf individuals as a linguistic minority included the National Association of the Deaf (20,000), the Registry of Interpreters for the Deaf (2700), and the National Fraternal Society of the Deaf (13,000) (Burek, 1993; Van Cleve, 1987).

Each construction has a core client group. No one disputes the claim of the hearing adult who becomes deaf from an illness or aging that he or she has a disability and is not a member of Deaf Culture. Nor, on the other hand, has anyone yet criticized Deaf parents for insisting that their Deaf child has a distinct linguistic and cultural heritage. The two constructions have persisted across the centuries in part because there is no simple criterion for identifying most childhood candidates as clients of one position or the other. The population of deaf and hard of hearing people is so heterogeneous that no specific guidelines can exist that would clearly separate one group from the other.

In an ideal world, I suppose it may be beneficial if specific guidelines were clearly developed to help determine whether a person was culturally Deaf, deaf, or hard of hearing. Of course, I assume that these guidelines and criteria would be used to clarify a person's identity if clarification

*was needed. Fortunately, our lives in the Deaf World are not that defini-
tive. Many of our identities are in constant flux within the process of enculturation. This enculturation changes as we see ourselves "fit in" the Deaf
and Hearing worlds when we interact with our hearing and deaf counterparts in different ways and in a variety of associations.*

*In my opinion, there is more benefit in taking advantage of the diver-
sity in both worlds rather than clearly separating one from the other.*

In general, most people knowledgeable about deaf issues would agree
that late deafening and moderate hearing loss tend to be associated with
the disability construction of deafness whereas prelingual deafness and profound deafness involve an entire organization of the person's language,
culture, and thought around vision and tend to be associated with the
linguistic minority construction.

One Deaf woman's perspective:

> Deaf people believe that this is a battle waged between the medical
> and the Deaf communities. The medical establishment, as well as
> its allies in the professional community (e.g., audiologists, speech
> pathologists) view deafness from their own perspective, a defi-
> ciency perspective. This model suggests that deafness is the
> "absence of hearing" derived from abnormalities in the function of
> the ear. It is a condition that needs to be diagnosed, treated (with
> devices) through prescriptions, and a plan of rehabilitation to be
> implemented. Contrast this with the Deaf person's view of deaf
> perspective, "being deaf," as opposed to the medical view of "deaf-
> ness." The cultural views being deaf as living deaf. This previous
> statement sets the stage of the difference as not a deficit. To a Deaf
> person, being deaf is a normal part of life full of a rich language
> and a beautiful culture, not as a pathological condition that needs
> to be "fixed."

In general, we identify children as members of a language minority when
their native language is not the language of the majority. Ninety percent of
Deaf children, however, have hearing parents who are unable to model the
spoken language effectively for most of them (Marschark, 1997). Advocates
of the disability construction contend that these are hearing-impaired children whose language and culture (although they may have acquired little
of either) are in principle those of their parents. Advocates of the linguistic minority construction contend that the children's native language, in the
sense of primary language, must use visual communication techniques such
as manual language and that their life experiences will eventually guide
them into the circle of Deaf Culture.

*As a member of the Deaf community representing its Culture, I, like
many of my fellow Deaf, believe that it is the most natural, comfortable,
and identifiable group to which to belong. Unfortunately for many of us,
we discover our culture only after some separation has occurred between*

us and our families. Most hearing parents discover their child is deaf when that child is at a young age. Most diagnoses of hearing loss still occur between the ages of 1 and 3. The audiologist or another hearing medical professional may suggest a narrow viewpoint of alternative ways for a quick solution or "cure" (e.g., cochlear implants) or a strictly oral approach to "fit in" with the hearing family. Unfortunately, most hearing parents do not understand deafness and are looking for answers provided by these hearing professionals. Because this is a very vulnerable time for the parents, many of whom are grief stricken, the hearing professionals help engage them in a process of denial which often continues throughout a good portion of the child's life, further delaying the child's introduction into the Deaf community.

Individuals who take on the medical and disability perspective view hearing loss as a gravely disabling condition. Proponents of the cultural, linguistic minority perspective vehemently disagree. U.S. Deaf scholar Tom Humphries best describes the opposition as follows: "There is no room within the culture of Deaf people for an ideology that all Deaf people are deficient. It simply does not compute. There is no handicap to overcome. Deaf people have a vision of integration that is different from what hearing people envision for them. Deaf people see a grounding in culture and sign language of the Deaf community in which they live as the most important factors in their lives. Integration comes more easily and more readily from these roots" (Humphries, 1993).

The majority (hearing people) naively take the position of wanting to find a "cure" for a "disability" where the minority (Deaf people) see no disability. The potential benefits of medical and surgical procedures that proclaim success in transforming hearing loss into hearing potential loom large as a potential yet misleading hope. Suppose one viewed children born deaf as exhibiting merely another form of human variation, such as small stature; then the reactions are of adaptation rather than of cure.

The opposing perspectives on Deaf people were nicely drawn by the founder of Gallaudet University, Edward Miner Gallaudet, and Alexander Graham Bell at a professional conference over 200 years ago. Gallaudet stated that education had transformed being Deaf from a calamity to "little more than a serious inconvenience." Bell, on the other hand, when challenged on the importance of speech to the Deaf, replied: "I am astonished. I am pained. To ask the value of speech? It is like asking the value of life!"

Now these lines were drawn between cultures long ago. Today the agendas have not changed. The hearing agenda for Deaf people is constructed on the principle that members of the Deaf World have a disability, and because our society seeks to reduce the numbers of people with disabilities through preventive measures, hearing people have long sought ways to reduce the numbers of Deaf people, ultimately eliminating this form of human variation and with it the Deaf World.

In a 1993 interview with the *New York Times*, Bell's words of 200 years ago were echoed by the chairman of a National Institutes of Health planning group. He stated, "I am dedicated to curing deafness. That puts me on a collision course with those who are culturally Deaf" (cited in Lane, Hoffmeister, & Bahan, 1996).

How do we resolve the issues that divide the members of the Deaf World and many hearing professionals and parents on their desire to best meet the Deaf child's needs? Unfortunately, the child is a minor and the Deaf perspective is treated in the same way. The majority are hearing parents and hearing professionals. Hearing parents have the rights and hearing professionals have the knowledge and the positions of influence. Most of the time, Deaf people and their views are of no concern. For instance, although there is wide agreement that most implanted children will remain severely limited in their hearing and will continue to rely on manual and visual means of communication, none of the past childhood cochlear implant conferences in the United States has had a single Deaf speaker (Lane, 1994). A more practical, everyday example exists in the lives of children who are Deaf and hard of hearing. Typically, hearing parents of D/HOH children first meet hearing professionals such as medical doctors and audiologists when confirming the hearing loss. These people become their support and information resources. Rarely do these parents meet professionals or parents who are deaf and hard of hearing themselves until the child is much older, if at all.

Our future depends on hearing professionals who hold these views to develop an understanding of our culture. The leaders in our community not only must take stands politically for activism (which is always needed) but also must provide outreach to these professionals who have the most intricate influence on the lives and the future of deaf children.

Unfortunately, concerning advances in technology, sometimes profits and professional interests have been the most important driving forces from early on (Enerstvedt, 1999). For example, hearing parents who can afford a cochlear implant see it as an answer to their dreams, to have their child "hear" and perhaps learn how to speak. Most of the parents who choose implantation have heard or read about successful cases and some testimonials about an individual's sudden abilities to hear and speak more readily, and these stories are both moving and convincing. Sadly, these stories and the encouragement to implant occur at a very fragile time for many of the parents—after discovering their child has a newly diagnosed hearing loss. These practices involve serious *ethical* concerns that must be addressed and confronted by the medical community and implantation supporters. In our culture, with its strong interests in pathology and profit, a freely made choice may be difficult for those oriented toward what is best for the child (Enerstvedt, 1999).

One such ethical concern involves the child's future development and functioning, which could be at stake because the children may be caught between both cultures, the hearing and the Deaf, with little in common with either.

In my experience as a Deaf person and professional, most doctors and audiologists are not the only or even true experts on hearing loss. They must provide parents with viewpoints and perspectives based on medical and cultural information. They often lack the cultural understanding. If they do not offer referrals or contacts within the Deaf community, then hearing parents will make choices based on a narrow fund of information at a critical juncture in the life of their deaf child. There is no excuse in the age of the new millennium for hearing professionals such as medical doctors, audiologists, and speech therapists to be ill informed about Deaf Culture information. It is my strong opinion that the practice of supplying parents with limited information is unethical because any decision that a parent may make quickly would not be an informed one.

When I teach Deaf Studies to hearing parents and professionals, I often like to use the following example to illustrate how we, in our society, frequently do not consider future consequences of our decisions.

One student responded proudly during a Deaf Studies lesson, "I can hear the phone ring! Too bad, you can't hear the phone ring." This statement was made by a 16-year-old deaf student with a cochlear implant. It may not only demonstrate a lack of sensitivity to a Deaf person but, sadly, may also indicate the few benefits that this device may give this particular student. He may be disappointed if this becomes the primary benefit of a device that is costly and may have helped separate him from his culture.

I often wonder why our newest generation of deaf children wants to choose something different from those from our current generation. Clearly, I understand that cochlear implantation is a new form of technology; however, often these children do not think toward their future. A sense of identity is very critical to the life of any child. A sense of identity is at the core of every mentally healthy Deaf person. If using a cochlear implant precludes interactions with and within the Deaf community, it can result in the stunted growth of their identity. If an informed teenager or an adult chooses implantation on the basis of an informed view, then it is a choice based on their own decision-making process, which has included weighing the consequences. For example, Heather Whitestone, a deaf adult and former Miss America, has decided to receive an implant because she wants to hear her child when crying and portions of her child's voice. This is her choice based on her life's needs.

Some parents report that they believe deafness to be a disability and not a culture and that they want their children to function normally. These

parents and the professionals who agree with them are terribly misinformed
if they believe that an implant will change the child's condition to function
as hearing. Many implanted youth will still be *deaf* and will still need to
learn sign language to communicate with their peers and learn about many
of their counterparts' culture.

*History will be written to demonstrate that the Deaf community has a
new subgroup, deaf and hard of hearing individuals who have cochlear
implants.*

*Again, I believe that hearing parents do not receive comprehensive
information about other options or what the future may bring. Informed
parents may still elect implantation or may allow the child to make his
or her own choice in later years. Informed parents, however, will not consider the cochlear implant a "miracle" and will not ignore the important,
positive influence the Deaf community or its language, sign communication, can have on their child's life. If the parents make uninformed decisions, it is likely that in later years, when their children or young adults
choose sign language, the natural visual language available to them, the
parents will be alienated from their own children. They will not share an
even basic level of the language that the majority of their children will be
choosing to use.*

Hearing parents and others need to be educated that their child can live
in the world as a deaf person and can still cherish both cultures. If deaf children are alienated from their hearing loss early, adjustment problems can
result in later years when differences between them and their peers become
more apparent. All who are involved in raising a healthy deaf individual
need to use the tools for a "middle road" approach to this issue, to give the
child the opportunity to cross between the hearing and the Deaf communities. An individual can certainly have a cochlear implant and still maintain his or her Deaf cultural identity at the same time. When a child becomes
older he or she may choose to belong to or immerse into the Deaf community, perhaps for reasons of communication, socialization, or identification. One does not preclude the other. In the past, some rejected hearing
aids, believing that wearing them made them less "Deaf." Cochlear implants
are devices to enable deaf individuals to obtain more information from
their environment and are nothing more than that. If they were viewed in
this manner, hearing parents and others would not be searching for unanswered dreams but would realistically see them as a tool that can help them
to continue to raise their child to become a healthy, deaf person.

A potential roadblock to this view is the disadvantage that there is little
built-in cultural transmission of beliefs of a bicultural perspective. The most
persuasive advocates for Deaf children, their parents, must be taught generation after generation the counterintuitive linguistic minority construction because most are not Deaf themselves, nor did they have Deaf parents.

Some want to blame the zealots of the medical view because the acceptance of a linguistic minority perspective is long in coming. However, some

of the gravest obstacles to broader acceptance of the linguistic minority model come from members of the minority itself. Many members of the minority were socialized in part by professionals (and parents) to adopt a disabled role. Some Deaf people openly embrace the disability construction and thus undercut the efforts of other Deaf people to discredit it. Worse yet, many opportunities are provided to Deaf people (e.g., funds for access to interpreters, money received from Supplemental Security Income [SSI]) on the condition that they adopt the alien disability construction. This double bind—accept our construction of your life or give up your access to equal citizenship—is, in the eyes of many Deaf people, a powerful form of oppression.

Deaf and severely hard of hearing people who receive SSI or SSD (Social Security Disability) often do not understand that if they are healthy enough to work full time and garnish a good wage, they are in opposition to the tenets of the Deaf community and in opposition to our culture. Many of us believe that these supportive monies to help those in need can become forms of "welfare" and can inhibit healthy independence. A Catch-22 exists, however, in that many young deaf adults may need federal funds to supplement income when employment opportunities or upward movement in their current positions is limited due to communication differences within a hearing community.

Another example of this double bind of disability-or else-phenomenon occurred after 1990. Many members of the Deaf World enthusiastically endorsed the Americans with Disabilities Act with its provisions for deaf people, all the while believing they are not disabled but lending credence to the claim that they are. A related example of the double bind also occurred in 1990. Dr. Larry Stewart, a professor at Gallaudet University, presented a talk about cultural and societal issues to a crowd of professionals from the Deaf community at the National Technical Institute for the Deaf (NTID) in Rochester, New York. He stunned the audience by stating that the proponents of the cultural perspective need to be careful because they may doing unexpected harm to Deaf children. He warned that if the government representing our society accepts the cultural perspective, Deaf people will no longer be considered disabled.

The government provides funding for disability groups to help with costs of accessibility. For example, SSI funds are provided to certain families so that they can buy medical supplies, assistive devices, or needed additional care to offer support for the disabled child. These funds are used to help individuals who are deaf or hard of hearing afford the costly devices that the hearing person would not need (e.g., hearing aids, TTYs). These funds could be removed because D/HOH people would be considered nondisabled.

A Deaf child grows up and is potentially influenced by two cultures. How does one decide about the major issues and decisions such as communication mode used in the family, educational placement, or even, when the ultimate decision surfaces, implant surgery? Specifically, what does one do when an ethical dispute arises on whether a child needs to be "fixed" when two cultures disagree on the wisdom of a surgical procedure, such as a cochlear implant, because of fundamentally opposed values? Under certain restricted conditions, it does seem possible for one culture to overrule the other ethically.

Members of one culture might intercede when horrendous acts occur in another culture, to prevent torture or murder, for example. Is American culture thereby justified in interceding in Deaf Culture? If the young Deaf child has not yet had an opportunity to acquire the language and values of Deaf Culture, do the values of Deaf Culture have import in this matter? A child born Deaf is as surely a member of the Deaf cultural minority as a child born Black is a member of the Black cultural minority. That is, their life trajectories can be deflected, but the potential they have to enter into their respective cultures travels with them.

Implants are not a life or death matter. Nor are Deaf children caused suffering by the failure to provide them with implants. No one claims that Deaf parents are guilty of neglect of their Deaf children by refusing them implants. Because these special conditions do not apply, shouldn't the parents and medical personnel respect the values of Deaf culture as they demand that the members of the Deaf World respect their values? If so, how can they justify implant surgery on their born-deaf child? One physiologist from the University of California, San Fransico, Michael M. Merzenich, Ph.D., stated his justification clearly. He believes that the condition of deafness is a medical one and in need of a cure, and if the culture can be reliably wiped out, it would be a good thing (Clay, 1997).

This perspective offered by Dr. Merzenich is frightening to me as a Deaf person and offensive to me as a Deaf professional. It is beyond my comprehension why any hearing person would long to destroy diversity in our society. The idea that deafness is strictly a medical issue is ignoring the fact that over 2 million Americans embrace a culture with its own values, traditions, and language that stemmed from this "medical issue." Statements made by Dr. Merzenich advocate a form of genocide and are aimed primarily at the youngest, most vulnerable, in our Deaf community.

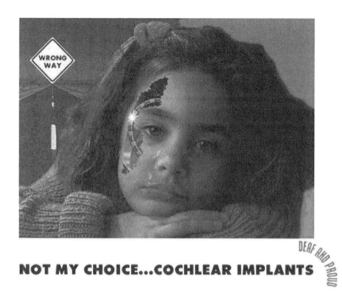

NOT MY CHOICE...COCHLEAR IMPLANTS

Wrong Way: Deaf artist Elizabeth Morris' rendition of the DEAF-WORLD perspective on childhood cochlear implants.

The decision to perform implant surgery on the Deaf child is made *for* the child, who, as a minor, is considered temporarily incompetent to make that decision. Some advocates for cochlear implants, particularly in Europe, would like to see cochlear implant surgery conducted much earlier than age 2. They argue that the auditory area of the brain degenerates as long as the infant is Deaf, but early stimulation, such as an implant could provide, would slow or reverse that degeneration so that the child with an early implant would have greater capacity to learn spoken language by ear. However, this is all speculation. It is based on research with neonatal mice, rats, and gerbils; destroying their hearing reduces neuron number and size in the auditory pathway and area of their brains, and stimulating their hearing with implants slows or reverses degeneration somewhat. However, this has not been demonstrated in humans, nor do we know whether the modest reductions in neuron numbers and size really matter for hearing.

There is evidence that, in people who grow up Deaf, some brain tissue used for hearing in hearing people has been reallocated for visual information processing. A little auditory stimulation might block this reorganization of the brain without providing usable hearing, so the child would not acquire spoken language and would be hampered in acquiring signed language. In light of all this uncertainty and speculation by the experts on when to implant Deaf children—if at all—it is perhaps clearer why the World Federation of the Deaf (WFD) was moved to condemn "experimentation on Deaf children." A WFD representative gave five reasons to question the ethics of cochlear implant surgery on children:

1. The people who know the most about living as a Deaf person do not want it for themselves or for their own Deaf children.
2. Deaf children are more vulnerable than hearing peers because their hearing parents face more obstacles to being the best advocates for the child since they cannot communicate with the child in enough depth about the procedures or the possible results.
3. Parents cannot give informed consent about the procedure and its effects on the hearing loss or the Deaf person because often they know no Deaf adults and do not understand what it is like growing up Deaf.
4. It is unethical to perform surgery on a child to change a child to fit into a majority group rather than become a member of a minority group.
5. Because the surgeon cannot predict what the outcome of the surgery will be for the child, the procedure is experimental. It is an unparalleled event in medical history for organizations of adults to raise such an outcry against a medical intervention for children like themselves.

It is critical to note that recent events have demonstrated the physical risks and dangers of implantation on young children too clearly. Some children have developed spinal meningitis (infection in their brain) when implanted with a certain type of implant (Associated Press, 2002). Although officials have not identified the source of the infections, Advanced Bionics Corporation has stopped selling its version of the product with the concern that a positioning wedge, called the Clarion, which sits in the inner ear, may be a harbor for bacteria.

Recently, implants with ceramic linings to house a receiver coil in the cochlea have been found to cause infections in implanted children because of reactions to the ceramic material. Due to this situation, some audiologists have recommended that parents of children who in the past would have been candidates for implantation consider pursuing the use of the most recently developed digital hearing aids.

Also, some deaf people with an implant have complained of severe headache related to an allergic reaction to the metal used for the device. A personal account was provided by an older Deaf adult who experienced dizziness and headache. Much later, a small tumor was discovered near the implanted area. It is important to know that deaf people who have serious health concerns cannot benefit from receiving an MRI (magnetic resonance imaging) because of the effects of the magnetic field. How many more stories of personal tragedy will our Community endure before the true medical risks are realized?

Apart from the risks associated with surgery and anesthesia, cochlear implantation of children poses several primary risks: The combination of implant surgery and postsurgical oral–aural rehabilitation may leave the implanted child substantially languageless for several years. Because individuals who are Deaf and hard of hearing will always rely mostly on a visual means of communication, parents and professionals must remember that, cochlear implant or not, manual communication will continue to be of benefit. Even parents decided on implantation for their child might be wise to follow this strategy, thus avoiding long periods of time during the formative years when a lack of exposure to language structure occurs or when little or no communication exists. There is reason to believe that children who are given rich exposure to sign language, while implanted or not, will have advantages while learning and experiencing language growth.

When it comes to potential benefit, there is considerable consensus that, with children born Deaf, acquisition of spoken language is the significant benefit desired. However, results are good for postlingual children, those who lost hearing after they acquired speech. Results are less clear for those who became deaf prelingually, before acquiring spoken language. It seems that those born deaf and those who have prelingual deafness show less promise for acquiring speech production and comprehension of spoken language (Enerstvedt, 1999).

There is a grave concern that doctors are supportive of this procedure for a variety of deaf and hard of hearing children regardless of the circumstances. Prelingual deafness is sometimes of the least concern. Children or young adults are still considered candidates for implantation even if emotional, behavioral, and/or psychiatric or developmental conditions such as mental illness or mental retardation exist. It has been my experience that for some children, the "criteria" used to recommend a cochlear implant have been loosely applied.

An important force in the growing practice of surgically implanting Deaf children as young as possible is the belief that the ability to acquire language wanes rapidly with age. Research has shown that children who begin learning ASL in infancy achieve greater mastery than those who begin at school age. Deaf teenagers and adults who were born Deaf are no longer implanted in many medical centers because the results have been so disappointing. They are able to learn ASL; they are apparently unable to learn to recognize a significant number of spoken words using the implant. The discouraging results also obtained with children who are born Deaf and implanted at school age have led many audiologists to speculate that the critical period is over by then and to implant as early as allowed by the Food and Drug Administration (age 2).

Now that these experimental implant procedures are conducted on very young children, researchers have an ethical duty to answer the question about the specific benefits versus risks involved. Before any more deaf or hard of hearing toddlers are implanted, we need to investigate the risks that have been brought to attention in recent months concerning the physical dangers of these procedures. Additionally, the risks to the children's educational, social, and psychological development must be determined and evaluated for each child.

Let us look at a specific benefit proposed by the proponents of implantation. Improvements in children's speech perception and production are often reported. The language and educational outcomes associated with childhood implants are not well known, but oral language development remains slow and training intensive. Why is this so? It is reasonable to assume that most parents and professionals want children to be implanted to ease communication with family, friends, and within their local schools. However, these past studies have never looked at language acquisition or conversational language functioning levels. They look at speech production of various words. Counting the number of practiced and recognized words does not measure whether the semantics, syntax, and structure of language will be used and improved effectively. These studies focused on only a small part of language with less than useful results. This practice is evaluation of reading comprehension at a certain grade level by having the child recognize a few words in isolation.

There is no conclusive evidence yet of significant benefit, and if it exists, we are unable to predict which children will receive it. Consequently, although an increasing number of children have been implanted, the treatment remains highly experimental. If experimental medical treatments of children can be justified ethically at all, it is only in the setting of a small, highly controlled long-term study.

As implants are perfected and more research is conducted, the risk/benefit ratio seems likely to improve. And, while more research and better implants are accomplished, the parties of disagreement may come closer together; however, what will remain is the profound difference in the way Deaf and hearing cultures construe hearing loss and, therefore, how they both view the ethical dilemmas presented.

Adults deafened before learning spoken language show little improvement. Deaf teenagers and adults who were born Deaf are no longer implanted in many medical centers because the results have been so disappointing. In fact, many teenagers and adults who have chosen the implant technology often do not use their implants later when long-term hopes are encouraged and promises made remained short-term gains.

In the United States, a medical conference in 1988 aimed at creating a consensus on cochlear implant surgery (no Deaf people participated) concluded that the usual implant candidate is a healthy adult who lost hearing after learning spoken language and who does not receive any benefit in lipreading from a hearing aid. The conference participants concluded that the most common benefit of cochlear implants is some improvement in lip-reading. It found, furthermore, that it is not possible to predict who will benefit from an implant and that patients with implants must avoid contact sports, MRIs, and some other medical procedures. The conference experts recommended that children should receive implants only after a 6-month trial of hearing aids with no success. And it cautioned that "children with implants still must be regarded as hearing-impaired [and] will continue to require educational, audiological, and speech and language support services for long periods of time."

The 1989 position statement of the American Academy of Otolaryngology–Head and Neck Surgery finds "implants an acceptable procedure in prelingual children when approved [by regulatory agencies]." (A prelingual child is one who lost hearing before mastering oral language.) A leading implant surgeon has defended to his colleagues the ethics of cochlear implant surgery on children. His article in the January 1994 issue of the *American Journal of Otology* finds childhood implants ethical because (1) to be deaf is to have "a handicap and a disability," (2) the question of their effectiveness "should no longer be asked," and (3) deaf children of hearing parents are not members of the Deaf community. How can this be defended when it is only perspective, conjecture, and opinion?

What is even more alarming is not this one man's opinion but how the media has elevated cochlear implants to the status of the "miracle" to cure deafness. For example, one in a long list of recent headlines in newspapers read, "New Hope for Deaf Children"; "Cochlear Implants: Opening Up a Whole New World"; "High-Tech Ear Implants Offer New Hope to Profoundly Deaf", (Guttman, 1998); and "Breakthrough for Deaf Children: Doctors Have Perfected a Quick and Relatively Straight-forward Way to Restore Hearing to Profoundly Deaf Children", (BBC News, 2001); and "Implant Restores Deaf Firefighter's Hearing (O'Brien, 2003). Also, as recently as December 21, 2001, Katie Couric on the Today Show announced that conservative talk show host, Rush Limbaugh, would have his hearing restored in weeks because of implant surgery just con-ducted (Zucker, 2001). This one statement offers false hope and several inaccurate implications. First, hearing is never restored because damage to nerve cells and bone tissue produces a condition that cannot be reversed. Second, as mentioned in Chapter 1, the hair cells in the cochlea transmit sound waves to the nerves. The cells that are remaining in the cochlea that are involved in the implant are destroyed because the implant stimulates nerve cells directly. Third, the intensive mapping procedures and auditory training needed could take years, if helpful at all, and not involve a short period of time as indicated in this statement.

The implant is not considered a "cure" for deafness, and benefits vary from one individual to another. Implantation does not restore "normal" hearing. It bypasses damaged cells in the cochlea, in the inner ear, which ordinarily generate the electric current that travels to the auditory nerve to the brain, registering as the sensation of sound.

In other countries, the opposition to implantation has been more dramatic. In January 1994, representatives of the Deaf community of Ontario, Canada demonstrated at entrances to legislative and hospital buildings to protest a recent government decision to launch a $1.7 million childhood cochlear implant program. They called for an end to cochlear implant surgery on children and the establishment of a commission of inquiry. The Canadian Association of the Deaf, calling for a moratorium on cochlear implants for Deaf children, sponsored rallies in several cities in May 1994. A *Toronto Star* headline the next day read, "People Born Deaf Have Right to Keep their 'Silent but Rich' Culture."

A position paper of the German Deaf Association stated that they would allow implantation of individuals beyond the age of 18 as they can give adult consent. It concluded, "[We] reject cochlear implantation of Deaf children when this procedure leads to separating the implanted children from other Deaf children and is associated with an exclusively oral language orientation." The British Deaf Association "does not accept the negative model of deafness as a pathological defect to be cured or eradicated"; it calls for extended research on the consequences of childhood implants and is "unable to recommend" them for children.

The World Federation of the Deaf resolved at its 1995 World Congress that "the congress does not recommend cochlear implant operations for Deaf children because cochlear implants will not help the language acquisition of a Deaf child and can harm the emotional/psychological personality development and physical development. We believe that since there is no proof that implants improve the educational achievement or the English language development of Deaf children, it does not justify the emotional, physical, and psychological suffering that the implanted child could undergo years before he/she recognizes and accepts his/her identity as a member of the Deaf community. We believe that being Deaf is more than okay. Being culturally Deaf and having a Deaf identity as a Deaf person is actually a positive, healthy option."

CATHERINE MORTON, M.S.

Mental Health Specialist
St. Mary's School for the Deaf
Buffalo, New York

DEAF CULTURE AND DIVERSITY

The Culture and the Behaviors of Deaf People

Hearing loss sets the stage for a very heterogeneous population. Some people are born deaf as a result of genetic or other conditions. They may use sign language (perhaps ASL) as their primary form of communication. Many of these individuals are members of Deaf Culture. Others are born hearing and may become deaf later in life. Many of these individuals have a spoken language base and must adapt to their condition through the use of hearing aids, visual forms of communication, lip-reading, and so forth. They are called late-deafened adults (LDAs). Still others may grow up with or may acquire a mild to moderately severe loss and are considered hard of hearing. They may or may not use sign language, depending on their interactions with deaf individuals, but will most probably use hearing aids, oral techniques, and various visual methods to supplement their understanding of the spoken word. And, even within the hard of hearing group, some individuals experience tinnitus (a ringing or noise in the ear). This condition can have accompanying emotional effects such as anxiety, depression, and sleep disturbances given the assault of the constant noise on the human condition and can present additional strains on their communications and interactions with others (Sandlin & Olsson, 2000).

Understanding Diversity within Our Population

Identifying yourself as a deaf, hard of hearing, or LDA person involves a process that includes many influencing factors, of which hearing loss is but one. Figure 5.2 contains a comprehensive list of issues within the area of Deaf Studies. Individuals who "reside" in the diverse Deaf community population include deaf individuals, those who are culturally deaf, LDAs, hard

DEAF STUDIES

DEAF CULTURE
- Identity
- Social Characteristics
- Behavior & Norms
- Values
- Traditions/Events

DEAF COMMUNITY
- Members (11 specific groups)
- Affinity Groups
- Regional Communities
- Clubs/Organizations

DEAF HISTORY
Global/National/Local Views of:
- Education
- Evolution of Sign Languages
- Communities
- Biographies
- Media (theatre, television, films)
- Technology
- International Deaf

DEAF LITERATURE (Written form)
- Art
- Books (fiction & non-fiction)
- Humor (jokes, cartoons & anecdotes)
- Poetry
- Publications

ENTERTAINMENT
- Television Movies/Shows
- Films
- Drama-Theatre
- Biographies

ASL LITERATURE
- ABC Stories
- Number Stories
- Poems
- Folklore
- Humor
- Personifications
- Children's Stories
- Adaptations
- Original Narratives

SIGN LANGUAGE STUDIES
- Teaching of ASL
- ASL Linguistics
- Language Use
- Sign Systems
- Foreign Sign languages
- Sign Language Research
- Interpreting
- Sign Language Illustrators
- ASL Programs-Schools
- Resources

DEAF EDUCATION
- Schools for the Deaf
- Colleges/Universities
- Degree Programs

TECHNOLOGY
- Communication Devices and Services
- Alerting Devices
- Auditory Devices
- Companies (assistive technology and community resources)

SPORTS
- Athletes
- Sport Teams
- Clubs/Organizations

DEAF & THE LAW
- Family
- Public
- Police
- Courts
- Lawyers
- Interpreter Resources

SOCIAL SERVICES
- Medicine
- Mental Health
- Vocational Rehabilitation
- SSD (Social Security Disability)
- SSI (Supplemental Security Income)

FIGURE 5.2 Topics in Deaf Studies. (Adapted from: Lee Dray, 2001.)

of hearing people, and individuals with cochlear implants. These individuals have determined or are in the process of determining where they fit in this kaleidoscope of the population with a hearing loss.

As can be seen from the figure, many factors influence the lives of Deaf and hard of hearing people. For example, a Deaf individual is considered a member of Deaf culture if the individual displays an enjoyment of and motivation to experience the life of a culturally Deaf person. When a person is culturally Deaf, he or she embraces ASL as a visually based natural, independent language with its own grammatical structure. Because it is a validated language, it is seen as the primary entry way into Deaf Culture (Brueggemann, 1999).

For the LDA person, the late onset of hearing loss occurs when an individual progressively loses his or her hearing after the age of 18. Many become profoundly deaf with no residual hearing. The LDA's language functioning is often supplemented with hearing aids and lip-reading techniques before the person becomes deaf. However, the learning of sign language for these people is likened to learning a foreign language. Therefore, many LDAs do not learn sign language through personal choice due to years of trying and adapting to their loss with the use of oral techniques such as lip-reading, writing, and other verbal means of communication. Often LDA individuals believe that they do not "fit" into the deaf group. Those who identify with deaf groups go to clubs or events and use their primary language, ASL. Often the LDA individual feels shocked when first experiencing this aspect of Deaf Culture. Because the LDA person may have relied solely on auditory means and some visual resources when communicating, it may take several years for the individual to adjust to experiences within Deaf Culture.

A hard of hearing person may grow up in primarily hearing environments and go to mainstream schools with limited services for the deaf. Rarely do these individuals receive the full range of benefits provided in a setting established with visual support services and staff knowledgeable about hearing loss. In fact, a study conducted in 1991 demonstrated that approximately 80% of hard of hearing students do not receive the support services required for communication accessibility (Hallahan & Kaufmann, 1997). Often, hard of hearing individuals do not receive the same additional services that could result in better mental health. Specifically, Adams (1997) reported that those who display mild to moderate losses were found to demonstrate more social and emotional difficulties such as perceived behavior problems. One explanation for this finding could be that hearing adults make assumptions and form expectations about what these individuals can and cannot hear, adding to confusion and misinterpretation within daily interactions. The differences in behaviors noted are probably due to the frustrations stemming from misinterpretations and miscommunications between hearing adults and these individuals with hearing loss.

Another explanation for the higher incidence of social and emotional problems involves hard of hearing people's lack of a sense of belonging to a certain identifiable group. They may not feel as though they "fit" in either the hearing or the deaf world and therefore may demonstrate more social and emotional difficulties because of identity and self-image issues. An additional explanation with more serious consequences over time is the lack of mental health services available to the Deaf community in general and to the hard of hearing in particular.

My experience living as a hard of hearing person up to the age of 13 and having two hard of hearing children supports the points made by Adams and others. For example, as a hard of hearing child, speech therapy was the only service provided to me in my school. At the age of 13, I became profoundly deaf. It was not until the middle of my senior year in high school that a teacher asked questions about other programming in the country offered specifically for the deaf. Within a program such as this I could have received support services such as sign language, notetaking, and an FM system to amplify sound in the classroom. Six years had passed before any additional services were recommended. Access to communication was impeded at a critical time in my youth. No one will really know what impact those "missing years" of support services had on my learning and my life.

Individuals who have cochlear implants may find the technology beneficial in helping form the bridge from the deaf to the hearing world. Others may experience being shunned by their deaf counterparts because many culturally Deaf people believe that the implant is controversial. They may believe that the implant is a surgical technique that helps hearing parents adjust to their child's loss. Others who are culturally Deaf support the implant when people can make the decisions for themselves. Others want to believe that the technology is a "cure for deafness." I have had some of the benefits of a cochlear implant for several years, but the implant had to be removed due to an infection. In my case, the removal of the implant was likened to becoming deaf twice. The benefits of the cochlear implant and its influence on the Deaf community will be examined and evaluated in time through solid research and practice.

As discussed in previous pages, one view held by some hearing and deaf individuals is that people with hearing loss are a disabled population with barriers and limitations who need support in order to become as "normal" as possible. They often consider being deaf as a physical disability. A second view held by many in the deaf community and their advocates is that a segment of the deaf population is a separate cultural group with behaviors, values, and language that define that group. A Deaf person with this perspective would say a resounding "no!" if asked if he or she was disabled. The deaf person prides him- or herself in giving confidence and encouragement to other deaf community members to make it as an independent person in the hearing world and not dependent on those within it. They believe their issue with the hearing world is one of communication, not one of a disability association. Given the same educational and linguistic opportunities, a deaf individual will function as well as anyone else.

I am a Deaf woman, a deaf professional, who uniquely experienced being hard of hearing, deaf, and having a cochlear implant. I have been deaf the majority of my life. It is my belief that Deaf Culture includes a rich heritage and promotes pride concerning the ability to overcome adversity as an individual or a group. Because many deaf people do not use a spoken language, they seek out other Deaf community members to communicate with and treasure these communication opportunities. This community shares with each other and with their young a common sense of pride in their culture and language. They share in a rich heritage and pride in the ability to overcome adversity as individuals or as a group.

The view held by each individual or each professional or advocate will determine his or her basic association within the Deaf community. Of course, with deaf people, this view will form the foundation of identity. The perspective of the individual will also determine his or her knowledge about and ultimately access to services in the community.

ACCESSING SERVICES

In our world, the Deaf World, what we experience is separate and distinct from that experienced by hearing people. Being deaf is a way of life, a process of becoming. For those who interact and provide services within the segment of the Deaf community that embraces Deaf Culture, it is important to become more knowledgeable about the culture as well as the foundation of that culture, sign language. Being knowledgeable means not only that the professionals have skills in sign language, particularly American Sign Language, but also that they use this language in the community whenever present with individuals who are deaf. However, if you are a professional training to work with the Deaf and hard of hearing or one who may service these populations in the future, you need to be very aware of the diversity within the Deaf community, of which the culturally Deaf is one segment.

To strengthen their knowledge base, professionals are encouraged to become members of an association that focuses on deaf needs, such as the National Association for the Deaf (NAD) or the American Deaf and Rehabilitation Association (ADARA). Memberships in these types of organizations demonstrate commitment to and support of the Deaf community. These organizations and their contacts, along with a listing of many others, can be found in Chapter 7.

Many Deaf people who are members of Deaf Culture often become aware of the community services around them because they are often in the communication "loop." Their Deaf group shares information about services more readily than others who are not part of the culture. On the other hand, individuals such as the LDA may be unaware of the more comprehensive services and may request the services for the disabled because their expressive and receptive spoken language is now limited and impaired. And other individuals with hearing loss may believe they do not "fit" into a deaf group. These people may often feel awkward because of visual language limitations. Others who are hard of hearing or have a cochlear implant may feel ostracized from Deaf groups and therefore do not interact with their members. Due to the lack of involvement with the mainstream Deaf, they are unaware of all the services available to them such as doctors, lawyers, and mental health professionals who are more "Deaf aware" or professionals who can converse in sign language and use visual communication techniques.

A person who has been deaf since birth or childhood and uses sign language may consider support services such as interpreting his or her rights and will request this service when needed. However, individuals who are LDAs, mild to severely hard of hearing, or those implanted may not be aware of their rights to services or may not know how to obtain them. These individuals may not be aware of the different technologies available to them such as live time captioning, oral interpreters, notetakers in classrooms or business meetings, as well as telephone relay services. They may consistently see themselves as disabled individuals in need.

WHAT IS COMMONLY SHARED

The culturally Deaf use ASL as their primary language, and these people practice the traditions enhanced by ASL such as attending ASL plays, using ASL humor, telling ABC stories, and reading ASL literature. Attending theatrical plays for the deaf gives culturally Deaf individuals a significant expressive release and attachment to the visual excitement of the language's ease on the hands and the eyes. For example, the theatrical production of *Sign Me Alice* by Gil Eastman imparts the values of the culture where Deaf people tell their famous "success stories" following the struggles and adversity faced in their lives. Deaf, hard of hearing, LDAs, and those with a cochlear implant can all celebrate the visual dynamics of plays and productions that are performed by Deaf and hard of hearing individuals because these experiences are visually based, relevant and beneficial to all in the Deaf community.

Humor and folklore, which are critical parts of the Deaf World, can be enjoyed by all with a visual sense. Following is a joke using deaf humor that, when told by a culturally Deaf person, would incorporate ASL. Deaf humor is frequently about oppression, giving the life experiences of a cultural minority. Readers who are hearing may have a hard time grasping the extent of the humor within the joke, whereas a deaf person may consider it "one of the best" passed along:

Three people are on a train: One Russian, one Cuban, and one Deaf person. The Russian is drinking from a bottle of vodka. She drinks about half the bottle, then throws it out the window. The Deaf person looks at her, surprised, "Why did you throw out a bottle that was half full?" The Russian replies, "Oh, in my country we have plenty of vodka." Meanwhile, the Cuban, who is smoking a rich aromatic cigar, abruptly tosses it out the window. The Deaf person is surprised again and asks, "Why did you throw out a half-smoked cigar?" The Cuban replies, "Oh? In my country we have plenty of cigars." The Deaf person nods with interest. A little while later a hearing person walks down the aisle. The Deaf person grabs the hearing person and throws him out the window. The Russian and the Cuban look up in amazement. The Deaf person shrugs, "In my country we have plenty of hearing people."

(Lane *et al.*, 1996, p. 157)

On the other hand, a "hearing" joke can be difficult to understand for most deaf people. The use of idioms common in spoken language is confusing because of the irony in the English language used in many of these jokes. These jokes are difficult to translate into ASL because the idioms are a play on words often confusing when presented visually. For example, the expression, "throwing your money away" would be seen as foolish when signed to a Deaf person. Hearing people would understand what this statement meant—that a person is spending money recklessly and not that a person is putting money in the trash and therefore throwing it away. Naturally, a good interpreter would not sign it in the English manner presented. A skilled interpreter would sign a statement similar to "buy, buy, buy, waste money, worthless." Visually, this interpretation would explain the meaning of this idiom.

Another example is "people in glass houses should not throw stones." Can you imagine the response if an interpreter signed this as expressed in spoken English? The natural reaction would be, "Of course you cannot throw stones in this house, broken glass would be everywhere!"

ASL in storytelling is also highly valued in Deaf Culture (Isenberg, 1996). In ASL literature, one generation passes on its wisdom, values, and pride to the next. These are the bonds that unite a younger Deaf generation. Deaf children need to read to learn about their history and their values, which lead to a sense of value of self. Mastery of ASL and skillful storytelling offer prestige among Deaf viewers. The Deaf seek each other out for social interaction and emotional support. LDAs, hard of hearing people, and those with a cochlear implant may not experience ASL storytelling to the same degree as the culturally Deaf person; however, all members of the Deaf community could appreciate the creative, entertaining, and beautiful visual images presented.

Deaf clubs are located in major cities around the United States. These clubs often have weekly gatherings that promote various activities such as socializing, card games, fundraising events, and holiday gatherings. Deaf clubs do not discriminate among the people who want to attend events or frequent the club itself, but it is generally understood who is culturally accepted within the group. The choice may be different for an individual who has been mainstreamed and primarily "orally" educated as a child but as an adult chooses to attend these events and takes time to adjust to the language and other cultural experiences. The Deaf community may accept hearing, hard of hearing, and deaf members who protect and use the common language and demonstrate their interest by attending fundraising and special events. However, many who remained in the mainstream, primarily hard of hearing or LDA individuals, are probably not aware of the available deaf social activities.

It is important to note that some individuals who are hard of hearing may consider themselves functionally deaf due to their social upbringing in the Deaf community. Perhaps their parents were deaf or good friends are associated strongly with the community. These people can function in both worlds and often move easily between them.

COMMUNICATION BEHAVIORS AND
THE DEAF AND HARD OF HEARING

Overall, hearing people and people with a hearing loss experience the world very differently. It is not natural for deaf or hard of hearing individuals to focus on a hearing perception of the world rather than their visual interpretations during their communications or interactions. Whether it is merely waking up in the morning, visiting the doctor, or ordering a pizza, deaf and hard of hearing people must often find ways to accomplish these tasks that hearing people take for granted. Our world is filled with vibrating alarms, flashing lights, interpreters, text telephones, captioning, and a beautiful visual language, which provides us with access to the same things as our hearing neighbors but in a unique and different way (Wentzel & Livadas, 1995).

Specific to their language experiences and needs, deaf and some hard of hearing people use devices called telephone typewriters (TTYs). A TTY is a small teletypewriter, which resembles a mini word processor and is used to "talk" to others in the same way as other people chat on a computer. Also, acoustic technology has allowed the hard of hearing, LDA, and some of those implanted to experience increased amplification on their telephones while at the same time reducing interference noise. Expanding technology has shaped the life and the behavior of deaf and hard of hearing people around the world. It opens the doors of freedom and independence and contributes to positive self-esteem in the population.

Telephone conversations and face-to-face interactions have evolved into specific cultural behaviors out of their everyday routines. For example, when a call arrives for a deaf person, a lamp flashes on the TTY itself or in the room to let the user know of an incoming call. Sometimes callers need to let the phone ring several times to give the deaf person an opportunity to receive the blinking light in their field of vision. On a light note, following a conversation, many deaf and hearing people working with the deaf measure the conversation by "feet" of paper if a printer is used rather than the length of time they have talked.

During face-to-face interactions a hearing person will indicate turn-taking by dropping the inflection in his or her voice. A deaf person will establish eye contact, decrease the signing speed, and drop his or her hands to a resting place to indicate "yielding the floor" (Glickman & Harvey, 1996).

Sharing information is an important norm in the Deaf community. When there is a change in the routine or expectation, an explanation is strongly needed. Deaf people in their everyday conversation share a great deal of information about their day-to-day lives while talking about family, friends, community news and events, and what they have been doing. The quest for information is vital because few individuals can communicate in their required mode. For example, during a conversation, if you want to leave a room at a party or during a meeting, you should explain why you are leaving to not only one person but also to most people within your communication range. Another example involves being late for class. You should give an explanation about why you are late. This explanation is not to be viewed as providing an excuse but rather perceived as a way to offer information to a group of individuals who do not readily receive whole communications from their environment because of using one channel for getting information and because few people have knowledge of sign language.

Deaf individuals use a variety of visual means to communicate. Also keep in mind that hard of hearing people should not just be considered "less deaf" (Wilson, 2003). Hard of hearing people also rely on visual communication and visual cues during their interactions and communications. For example, when trying to get someone's attention, D/HOH individuals may wave in the direction of the person or if closer, lightly tap the person's shoulder. At other times, they may tap on a table to get another deaf individual's attention from the vibration made by the tabletop. If two deaf people are walking down a path or a hallway, the one who is not communicating through sign at the time looks out for barriers to walking and moving forward because the communication partner is using eye contact and attention to the person while signing. And, two people who are using sign communication may stop in a small area to talk and someone wants to pass. It is more important for the sign communication to continue without interruption than for the person who is making his or her way through the area to excuse him- or herself or to make the two people move. Walking through is less of a visual distraction to the signing partners than the interruptions caused by delaying the conversation. These communication behaviors come naturally to many deaf and hard of hearing people. These are but a few of the cultural behaviors that indicate some differences between the Deaf and hearing worlds.

Each Deaf person is unique with different experiences and opinions because of the type of hearing loss, use of hearing aid or cochlear implant, parents' hearing status, use of ASL, family communication, Deaf social interactions, and so forth. The D/HH group of individuals is so heterogeneous in composition that the criterion for membership in this population may only be having a hearing loss. However, belonging to Deaf Culture is related to a pattern of attitude, values, behavior, and interaction indicating strong ties to the Deaf community. It is important that the Deaf community does not define the culture within too narrowly or we will exclude the beauty and wonder of its diversity. Deaf Culture is presented in more depth in Chapter 4; however, the details make up a wide perspective on life as a proud Deaf or hard of hearing person. The best way to know about the community and its diversity is to experience it—communicate and share information, open yourself to the celebration of differences!

"Grant Thy Spirit"
Created by: Chuck Baird

6

BEST PRACTICES WHEN COMMUNICATING WITH DEAF AND HARD OF HEARING PEOPLE

Approximately a decade after the passage of the Americans with Disabilities Act, deaf and hard of hearing people and others with specific disability conditions, remain the most significantly unemployed and under-employed segments of the U.S. population (Geballe, 1999).

Communication is often seen as *the* barrier to employment and service accessibility.

The following recommendations have been adapted from a variety of sources (specifically, Cornell University, 2000; Daiss, 1987; Iacelli, 1992; Myers, 1992; National Association of the Deaf, 1997–1998; Rochester Institute of Technology, 2003; Recruitability, n.d.), including recommendations from individuals who are deaf or hard of hearing or work with these individuals in the community. These are only guidelines that could be used as a checklist for helping those in the community to offer accessibility to service. Even though these guidelines will give you an idea of how to offer a Deaf-friendly environment, and how to respond to deaf or hard of hearing people, it is important to ask the individual or group of individuals if the communication accessibility is adequate or how it could be improved (see Appendix D for a comprehensive communication accessibility checklist).

What exactly is a Deaf-friendly environment? Aetna Financial Services designed a new program, introduced in Hartford, Connecticut, to meet the needs of deaf and hard of hearing employees and customers. It was reported that this company's administration and staff displayed a very positive attitude concerning deaf individuals. The company also visibly recruited deaf employees and interns. Aetna provided interpreters and Deaf Culture and sign language classes for their hearing staff. Aetna employs 12 deaf workers in Hartford and one in Phoenix, Arizona (Gallaudet Today, 2000).

Some questions you may ask to make your organization or office "deaf-friendly" or D/HOH accessible are, Does your company have and advertise a TTY phone number so deaf and hard of hearing customers can directly conduct business with you by phone? If so, does your staff know how to recognize a TTY call when it comes in and can the staff use proper TTY etiquette when answering the call? When a deaf customer walks into your establishment, does the staff make that individual feel welcome? (Adapted from Geballe, 1999). Also, if your company employs one or more deaf employees and a social event is held, do you offer these employees communication accommodations such as an interpreter for this event? (iCan, 2001).

Answers to these questions will help determine how "deaf aware" or "deaf friendly" your company has become. Besides the established accommodations, staff attitudes and skills, and administration support, the environment can be arranged to offer a "deaf friendly" atmosphere and provide maximum accessibility.

SETTING UP THE ENVIRONMENT

Environmental accommodations for deaf people are those that improve visibility and reduce vibrations and distracting noises. Each service area requires different physical adjustments depending on deaf employees' or consumers' tasks and/or communication preferences. See Figure 6.1 regarding how to set up a "Deaf-friendly" environment.

❑ Natural light is preferable.

❑ Backlight (both from windows and artificial light sources) on speakers and interpreters is very tiring and denies the deaf/hard of hearing person complete information.

❑ Specific, adjustable lighting for instructors, interpreters, blackboards, and visual displays are essential. Ball-and-socket mounted spotlights are recommended because of their versatility.

❑ Proper placement, shielding, or diffusion of light sources including windows can control glare, light-blocking curtains (or shades, blinds) should be provided, and room surfaces should be selected to avoid glare.

❑ Adjustable room lighting helps. Switches that are in a location that permits lecturers to control lights easily and with minimal distraction and interruption are ideal.

❑ Consider placing the D/HH worker in a quieter environment if environmental noise could interfere with communication.

❑ Arrange the workstation in a way that the D/HOH worker can readily see when someone enters their office or work site.

❑ If your work environment has a television, keep the closed captioning on regularly.

❑ Have an ASL dictionary available for public and staff use.

❑ Keep deaf literature and publications around the office for public use. For example, have on hand information about how to reach an interpreter and/or a list of phone numbers that offer services for the Deaf and hard of hearing.

❑ Be familiar with the use of relay service (711) and TTY equipment. *GA to SK Etiquette* is one resource for using a TTY (Cagle & Cagle, 1990).

❑ Request a TTY directory and have it visible in the office.

(See Appendix E for a shopping guide for employers of deaf and hard of hearing people).

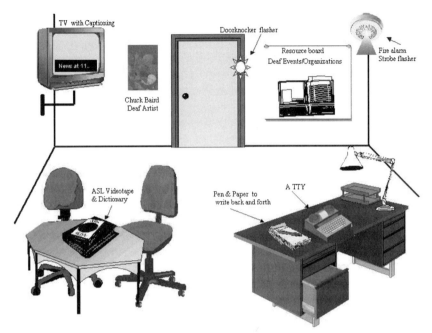

FIGURE 6.1   Setting Up a "Deaf-Friendly" Environment
Source: Developed by: Lee Dray, 2002.

JOB INTERVIEWS

When a deaf person has a job interview at a workplace, the potential employer needs to provide an interpreter. Deaf individuals must have the same access to communication with the interviewer as does their hearing counterparts. Ask the deaf applicants if they would like an interpreter, what type of communication do they use, and whom do they recommend to be their interpreter? The deaf applicant could provide the employer a name of the interpreter, which could ease the search for one.

❑ Provide organizational literature for deaf applicants to review before the interview.
❑ Provide a written itinerary if applicants will be interviewed by more than one person.
❑ Inform your receptionist or secretary beforehand that you are expecting a deaf applicant for an interview.
❑ Ask deaf applicants if they would like an interpreter.

(Source: Rochester Institute of Technology (2003). *Employers: How to work with a deaf person.* Retrieved November, 2003, from www.ntid.rit.edu/nce/emp_work.asp.

HOW TO REQUEST AN INTERPRETER

It is important to plan in advance for the need of interpreting services. You can contact your local deaf adult service agency and provide the information below. Oftentimes it is a good idea to ask the deaf person for the name of an interpreter he/she prefers. In doing so, you can hire a freelance interpreter who knows the communication style of the deaf person and may be more reliable than an agency interpreter who is in frequent demand. Whether you call a freelance interpreter or one who works for an agency, it is good to secure the services approximately one week in advance. Interpreter fees are determined by certification level and are to be paid by the service provider. It is important to locate a certified interpreter when possible who indicates level of skill, ethical standing, and professionalism.

Obtain:

❑ Date services are needed.
❑ Time services are needed.
❑ Location.
❑ Name and phone number of requestor.
❑ Name and phone number of contact person, if different from requestor.
❑ Name of deaf individual(s).
❑ Description of situation.
❑ Language preference of deaf person.
❑ Billing information: name and address of department/individual responsible for processing the invoice.
❑ If the meeting, class, or lecture will take longer than an hour and a half, two interpreters should be retained to relieve each other. Scheduled breaks are helpful due to fatigue and to prevent repetitive motion injury.

WORKING WITH INTERPRETERS

❑ Interpreters are professionals (see Figure 6.2 on how to set up the environment to work with an interpreter).

Plan to meet with interpreters about 15 minutes before the meeting, program, or other event to explain what will be covered.

❑ Provide a straight-back chair for comfort and positioning.

❑ Interpreters should be introduced before the program begins. This is an important courtesy extended within the Deaf community.

❑ The speaker should speak directly to the deaf employees or the deaf person, not to the interpreter. The thoughts and the information conveyed are those of the deaf participant, not those of the interpreter.

FIGURE 6.2 Working With an Interpreter
Source: Developed by: Lee Dray, 2002.

FIGURE 6.3   Working With an Interpreter in a Small Group Setting
Source: Developed by: Lee Dray, 2002.

❑ Good lighting is an integral part of effective interpreting. A neutral or dark background behind the interpreter improves a deaf person's ability to see clearly.

❑ If using a slide show, film, or theatrical production, provide a small light to illuminate the interpreters (see Figure 6.3 for working with an interpreter in a small group setting).

❑ The interpreter can serve as a liaison and provide information to the deaf person, employer, presenter, etc., regarding ways that most benefit the flow of communication and how to provide the best access to information. During the group discussion, only one person should speak at a time; it is difficult for an interpreter to follow several people speaking at once. Brief pauses between speakers permit the interpreter to finish before the next speaker begins. This technique also ensures that the deaf person can follow the communication turn-taking.

❑ The interpreters are at the site to translate the spoken word to sign language and sign language to the spoken word. They cannot and should not join the conversation or the meeting activities as a participant. This is unethical, since he/she is used for communication purposes only. Participation would compromise professionalism and confuse boundaries.

❑ As a courtesy, the interpreters should be thanked at the end of the session.

GETTING ATTENTION/
COMMUNICATING ONE-TO-ONE

❑ Do not place all of the responsibility of communication on the deaf or hard of hearing person. Many deaf and hard of hearing people are excellent communicators because they always have to communicate in and negotiate through a largely hearing world (iCan, 2001). Meet D/HOH individuals halfway on the two-way street of communication.

❑ Get the person's attention before speaking. A light touch on the shoulder, a wave, or other visual signals will help.

❑ Consider flashing the room lights and tapping the desk or floor instead of using your voice.

❑ Install a light on the telephone to signal incoming calls.

❑ Be sure not to ignore the deaf person when you carry on a conversation with someone else while he/she waits. Briefly explain the reason for the interruption. Tell the deaf person if the telephone rings or if there is an interruption. He/she should have access to this information, which is common knowledge to a hearing person.

❑ Ask deaf people about their communication preferences. It is not polite to ask them if they read lips.

❑ Maintain eye contact. This is a part of Deaf Culture, demonstrating your interest and providing meaning to your words.

❑ Make sure the lighting makes your face clearly visible. If a glare occurs, adjust the blinds or move the furniture to accommodate so the glare does not interfere with the visual communication.

❑ Look directly at the person when signing/speaking, even when an interpreter is present.

❑ Use facial expressions and body language to support your communications.

❑ Make sure that the deaf person knows the topic of the conversation, and inform the individual if the topic changes.

❑ Speak clearly without shouting, and be careful not to exaggerate or overemphasize lip movements.

❑ Be aware that gum chewing, cigarette smoking, pencil biting, and similar visual distractions and obstructions of the mouth area will lessen the effectiveness of your communication.

❑ If you have a beard or mustache, consider the fact that facial hair can interfere with a person's ability to speech read, making this difficult process even more difficult.

❑ Specifically, keep your hands away from your face and mouth while speaking.

❑ Be sure to let the deaf individual know if the conversation is not clear. Also, check frequently for feedback to ensure the clarity of your message.

❑ Keep in mind that when communicating with a deaf or hard of hearing person, the length of conversation may be more lengthy than compared to those using spoken language only. Your patience helps ensure clear and effective communication.

❑ Have a pencil and paper available and use them if they are needed. You could use your computer's word processing program to convey messages as well. E-mail networks can be invaluable to communication throughout the office for all, including the D/HOH employee. Always keep in mind a person's English literacy level.

❑ Vibrating papers or beepers in text format can alert the D/HOH employees of important messages or announcements.

❑ Fax machines can be used for D/HOH staff and/or D/HOH customer communication.

❑ Take a sign language course and encourage co-workers to do the same. Sign language courses are offered in most communities at local colleges, universities, and agencies. Area schools for the deaf also offer classes in sign language communication.

❑ It is a good idea to ask deaf employees if they are willing to demonstrate some basic sign language and fingerspelling to their co-workers.

MEETINGS AND GROUP COMMUNICATION

❏ Ask deaf employees if they prefer an interpreter.
❏ Be sure to let deaf employees determine the best seating arrangement in order for them to see the speaker and interpreter in an optimal way (see Figure 6.4 for working with an interpreter in a large-group setting).
❏ Set up the best place for the interpreter and seat for the deaf person in order to provide good communication.
❏ Install an assistive listening system for *some* hard of hearing people.
❏ Inform deaf employees of important public address announcements by pagers.

FIGURE 6.4 Working with Interpreters in a Large-Group Setting. (Developed by Lee Dray, 2002.)

❑ If the group is a smaller one, set up chairs in a semicircle to optimize a deaf person's visual field and provide ease of communication. Or, use a round table to open sightlines for people who may want to lip read and to provide a clear view of facial expressions and body language.

❑ Let deaf people know who is speaking during the group communication. It is a good idea to have people raise their hand when responding to give enough time for the deaf person attending the group session to be able to orient to the speaker and to give adequate time for the interpreter to reposition him/herself if needed.

❑ Keep eye on and watch for the signals concerning deaf employees who wish to contribute.

❑ *It is important that only one person speaks at a time.*

❑ Speak clearly and slowly for an interpreter.

❑ Set up visual aids, flip charts, written agendas, and handouts in presentations.

❑ Use Computer Assisted Note-taking (CAN). CAN involves using a personal computer and possibly a projector to aid in access to communication. Clerical staff sits in on a group session, typing summaries of the communications occurring. The deaf or hard of hearing person can watch the projected work or a personal computer monitor. It must be noted that the communications seen are only summarizations.

❑ It is important not to talk while your back is turned to the audience while writing on the blackboard or flip chart or while referring to a projected image.

❑ Give enough time for deaf people to read the minutes or notes.

❑ It is normal and a natural part of Deaf Culture and behavior for Deaf people to talk to each other and at times the interpreter during group sessions. This behavior may seem rude but it is a necessary part of the Deaf person's repertoire to clarify issues or content concerning the group activity or presentation.

COMMUNICATION TIPS: GUIDELINES FOR CLASSROOM COMMUNICATION AMONG DEAF, HARD OF HEARING, AND HEARING PARTICIPANTS

❑ Visual line of communication is critical. Be sure the deaf or hard of hearing person is sitting in a place that can optimize communication and participation. While it is believed that front of room placement is optimal, it must be understood that if placed in the front and center of the room, the deaf student will not be able to receive information about what is happening in the majority of the class.

❑ Be sure the students are following the flow of the communications and that they are attending to the speakers.

❑ Speak at a normal pace and check with the interpreter if it appears that he/she needs you to wait for the interpreter to catch up.

❑ Set up some guidelines how you will acknowledge and recognize speakers in the class so the deaf or hard of hearing members can follow class participation.

FIGURE 6.5   Working with an Interpreter in the Classroom. (Source: Developed by: Lee Dray, 2002.)

ROLE OF THE INTERPRETER (CLASSROOM)

❑ Be aware of school policies and procedures.
❑ Prepare for interpreting assignments by talking with the teacher and by studying the content area, lesson plans, and outlines ahead of time.
❑ Keep all interpreting assignments-related information strictly confidential within the members of the educational team.
❑ Arrive promptly for interpreting assignments.
❑ The teacher needs to position him/herself so the student can see him/her or the speaker (or screen) and the interpreter simultaneously (see Figure 6.5 about how to set up interpreting interaction in a classroom environment).
❑ Interpret what is being said and voice what is being signed.
❑ Render the message faithfully, always conveying the content and spirit of the message intended by the speaker.
❑ Ask the teacher or speaker for clarification should information be misunderstood or unclear.
❑ Report any concerns related to the student to the appropriate supervisor.
❑ Strive to acquire further knowledge and skills through participation in workshops and professional meetings.

COMMUNITY SERVICE HELPERS

❑ Determine if the person coming to see you for service is deaf or hard of hearing and ask them their communication needs.

❑ Provide a pencil/pen and paper for a deaf person to write if appropriate (keeping in mind literacy issues since English is the second language).

❑ Keep written information short and simple.

❑ If the deaf or hard of hearing person uses sign language as his/her primary communication mode, you are struggling with communication, and it is futile trying to converse with the person, schedule another, future appointment and get an interpreter for ease of communication and to prevent a communication barrier from occurring. Sometimes deaf, hard of hearing, and/or hearing people smile knowingly to each other while interacting but they really have no idea what has been said. For a sign language user, an interpreter is the smart choice to be sure the communications are accessible and accurate (see page 158 on how to request an interpreter).

❑ When talking with a deaf or hard of hearing person, always be aware of the effect of glare from a light source that can impede visual communication. For example, when a police officer discovers that he/she has pulled over a deaf or hard of hearing person, he/she should not shine the flashlight directly into the person's face. Deaf and hard of hearing people will not see you well because of glare and sensitivity to the light.

❑ Take basic sign language classes. And watch sign language videotapes to acquire survival sign language communication skills. As a person with survival sign language abilities in your profession, you may be of great help to our deaf and hard of hearing children, adolescents, and adults who may use your services.

RESTAURANT

❏ If you and the deaf or hard of hearing person are struggling to communicate when given a menu, provide a pen and paper to the person to write down his/her choices or other needs.

❏ If a "specials" menu exists, write it down ahead of time on your notepad so you can use this while all are ordering instead of having a hearing companion explain or speak for the deaf or hard of hearing person. Keep in mind that the best lip reader can only receive a small portion of the meaning of information by lipreading. Do not assume that deaf people can lipread well.

❏ Use a special menu to demonstrate all foods in picture form (see Figure 6.6 to view types of special menus used in foreign countries or for those with visual language needs). These menus can be helpful to all limited English users.

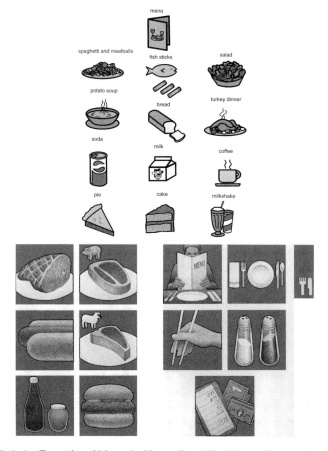

FIGURE 6.6   Examples of Menus in Picture Form. The Picture Communication Symbols are copyright © 1981–2003, Mayer-Johnson, Inc. Used with permission. The lower pictures are from Drolet, C. (1982). *Unipix: Universal language of pictures*. Los Angeles, CA. Imaginart Press.

GOING TO THE BANK

A bank teller needs to be aware of the following:

❏ Maintain eye contact
❏ If you know how to communicate with a deaf person who uses visual communication, utilize your basic sign language or fingerspelling skills and knowledge.
❏ Provide a pen and paper for a deaf person to write information down.
❏ Keep communications simple and short.
❏ Provide information for internet banking if this method would be easier for the deaf or hard of hearing individual.
❏ If the transaction is a complicated one, determine with the deaf person if an interpreter is needed, then reschedule. *Do not* ask family members or friends to interpret for a deaf person due to the privacy of banking. There may exist a conflict of interest between the deaf person and a family member.

GOING TO THE DOCTOR'S OFFICE OR HOSPITAL

When a deaf or hard of hearing person has an appointment with a doctor, the communication about health issues is critical. These communications are confidential, personal, and vital to functioning. Not only does the deaf or hard of hearing person need to know his/her health status, but the details must be clearly understood. If the person needs an interpreter, to ensure effective communication, the doctor is *required by law* to provide one. For example, when a deaf person has an appointment and a lengthy discussion, including a medical history, is taken, he/she must have an interpreter in the doctor's office since it is the best way to ensure communication access and accurate information.

A ROUTINE VISIT TO THE DOCTOR

❑ The room should be stocked with a paper and pen so the patient, nurse, and doctor can communicate in brief statements during the visit.

❑ Write short notes back and forth (if the appointment is brief, not serious or complicated, such as a routine check-up or brief physical. (Also, please follow the guidelines on page 159 on how to set up a deaf-friendly environment and page 160 on how to communicate with a deaf or hard of hearing person one on one.)

A MORE SERIOUS OR MORE COMPLICATED VISIT TO THE DOCTOR'S OFFICE OR HOSPITAL

❑ A deaf patient with sign language needs will need an interpreter to communicate with a doctor or specialist during important or lengthy discussions. Interpreters are critical during the important portions of the hospital stay or clinic visit. Intake and discharge procedures are important, critical times of care and require an interpreter's services.

❑ Request an interpreter in advance. If it is an emergency, call the local deaf adult services to attempt to provide emergency interpreting services. *It is not appropriate* to ask his/her friends or family to interpret for the deaf person. Their role is to be at the hospital for support for their loved one, not to be a communication liaison.

❑ If the patient requires a hospital stay, provide assistive devices (Chapter 4) such as a TTY, flashing light for phone, closed caption on the television, clock with an alarm (flashing light or shake awake), and fire alarm with a light strobe. If the hospital or outpatient clinic provides televisions in five or more rooms, a means for decoding captions must be given on request (National Association of the Deaf, 2000).

WHEN DEALING WITH SAFETY
ISSUES IN THE WORKPLACE

A supervisor needs to prepare the deaf, hard of hearing, and hearing staff for an emergency situation. The supervisor needs to consider the setup for assistance devices, such as pagers, flashing alarms, etc. (see Chapter 4, pages 93–94 for descriptions of various signaling devices).

❑ Install flashing lights to work in conjunction with auditory alarms.
❑ Develop a buddy system.
❑ Review safety procedures, including exits, alarms, buddy system, extinguishers, and hazards.
❑ Encourage deaf and some hard of hearing employees to have pagers. Use the pagers like you would use an intercom/announcement system for your hearing employees. Some employers use their network e-mail system to provide general information about upcoming events or drills.
❑ If an audio system is used or if a staff member enters a room to inform all staff of a current situation, the hearing staff members must inform the deaf or hard of hearing people immediately so that they have access to the needed information.
❑ If a local, regional, national, or international emergency or crisis occurs, turn on the television with captioning. Contact interpreting services (if needed) as soon as possible for an emergency request. If no interpreter is available or needed, then be sure a hearing person is designated to keep the deaf or hard of hearing staff member informed about the progress of the situation.

ACCESSIBILITY, ADA, AND YOU

Many people who do not know any deaf and hard of hearing individuals often make false assumptions about their abilities based on negative stereotypes or lack of experience. Some employers may resist hiring Deaf people because they are concerned that needed accommodations will cost too much or cause legal problems. The Equal Employment Opportunity Commission (EEOC), which handles employment complaints based on Title I of the ADA, reports that indeed the most common complaints filed by the deaf and hard of hearing work population is about the failure to provide reasonable accommodations (Shellabarger, 2000).

While meeting reasonable accommodations is a concern of some employees or service providers, the biggest obstacle to accessibility still is in attitude and acceptance. Deaf, hard of hearing, and hearing people are often able to work out communication difficulties at work sites and other accessibility issues at the companies where they coexist. And, if the intern or the potential employee has attended one of the three well-known Deaf college programs (Gallaudet University, the National Center of Deafness at California State University, Northridge, and the National Technical Institute of the Deaf [NTID] at Rochester Institute of Technology [RIT] in Rochester, New York), they have access to employment services and internship opportunities designed to accommodate deaf and hard of hearing people. Additionally, if placed in large agencies or government offices, these programs often provide Deaf Awareness Training, interpreters, and other support services. Specifically, NTID offers employers short-term assistive equipment loans, and Gallaudet University has published a supervisor's manual for employers with tips on working with the Deaf employee (Shellabarger, 2000).

7

RESOURCES

Within various communities across our country, deaf adult service agencies, speech and language centers, and local schools for the deaf can be of assistance to hearing individuals who seek more information, training development activities, or involvement in social events to gain access to a beautiful language, culture, and a people rich in history, endurance, and tradition. In Chapter 7, we offer a comprehensive listing of organizations, resources, and references to provide additional support to aid you in this process and journey. It is our hope that this book has helped you take a step toward accessibility for all individuals, hearing and non-hearing alike.

AMERICANS WITH DISABILITIES ACT AND OTHER LEGAL ISSUES

BOOKS, HANDBOOKS, AND JOURNAL ARTICLES

ADA Compliance Guide. (2003). Washington, DC: Thompson Publishing Group.

ADA—It's Everybody's Business. Northeast Disability and Business Technical Assistance Center. 354 South Broad Street. Trenton, NJ 08608.

ADACAP: Health Care Providers, Q and A. (1992). National Center for Law and Deafness. 800 Florida Avenue, N.E. Washington, DC, 20008.

Advocacy Handbook. (1995). Washington, DC: Alexander Graham Bell Association for the Deaf and Hard of Hearing.

Americans with Disabilities Act Handbook. (October, 1991). U.S. Equal Opportunity Commission, National Office. 1801 L Street, NW, Washington, DC 20507. (AD0010440).

The Americans with Disabilities Act: Questions and Answers. La Ley Para Personas con Impedimentos Preguntas y Respuestas. (1992). U.S. Department of Justice. U.S. Government Printing Office. (AD0010226). P.O. Box 371954, Pittsburgh, PA 15250.

Andrews, J.F., & Martin, G. (1998). Hopwood, affirmative action, and deaf education. *American Annals of the Deaf, 143,* 305–313.

Baldridge, D.C., & Veiga, J.F. (2001). Toward a greater understanding of the willingness to request an accommodation: Can requesters' beliefs disable the Americans With Disabilities Act? *Academy of Management Review, 26,* 85–99.

Bateman, N. (1995). *Advocacy skills: A handbook for human service professionals.* UK: Ashgate Publishing, Limited.

Bienenstock, M.A., & Vernon, M. (1994). Classification by the States of deaf and hard of hearing students: It's not how much you hear, but where you live. *American Annals of the Deaf, 139,* 128–131.

Burgdorf, R. (1991). Equal member of the community: The Public accommodations provisions of the Americans with Disabilities Act. *Temple Law Review, 64,* 499.

Busby, H.R., & Danek, M.M. (1999). *Tranisition planning and programming: Empowerment through partnership.* Washington, DC: Gallaudet University Press.

Caccamise, F., Mitchell, M., & Reeves, J., Burch. (1998). *Signs for legal and social work terminology.* Rochester, NY: Rochester Institute of Technology, National Technical Institute for the Deaf.

Corker, M. (1998). *Deaf and disabled, or deafness disabled? Towards a human rights perspective.* Buckingham: Open University Press.

Corrado, C. (1995). The IEP: Once more, with meaning. *Perspectives in Education and Deafness, 13,* 22.

Council for Exceptional Children. (1999). *Section 504 and ADA: Promoting student access: A guide for educators.* Reston, VA.

Fasman, Z.D., Dollarhide, M.C., Hahn, J.M. (1991). *What business must know about the Americans With Disabilities Act.* Washington, DC: U.S. Chamber of Commerce.

Hoschegang, J. (2000). Title II of ADA under scrutiny by court. *Silent News, 32 (November),* 1.

Johnson, C. (2000, December). *How the Individuals With Disabilities Act (IDEA) applies to deaf and hard of hearing students.* [Kids World Deaf Newspaper]. Washington, DC. Gallaudet University, Laurent Clerc National Deaf Education Center, Available from: The Kids World Deaf Net Web Site.

Lucas, C. (2003). Language and the law in Deaf Communities. Washington DC: Gallaudet University Press.

Maatman, M.E. (1996). Listening to Deaf Culture: A reconceptualization of difference analysis under Title VII. *Hofstra Labor Law Journal, 13, (Spring),* 269–344.

McCrone, W.P. (1990). A summary of the Americans with Disabilities Act and its specific implications for hearing impaired people. *JADARA, 23,* 60–63.

McCrone, W.P. (1990). Equality under the law. *Gallaudet Today*, 14–18.

National Association of the Deaf Law Center. (n.d.) *Attorneys, deaf clients, and the Americans with Disabilities Act.* Retrieved November 29, 2001, from http://nad.org/infocenter/infotogo/legal/ada3lawyer.html.

People with Hearing Loss and the Workplace: A Guide for Employers to Comply with the American With Disabilities. (1993). Self Help for Hard of Hearing People, Inc. 7800 Wisconsin Avenue, Bethesda, MD 20814.

Rawlinson, S.J. (1998). The Americans with Disabilities Act: Applications in postsecondary education of students who are deaf/hard of hearing. *Journal of Deaf Studies and Deaf Education*, 3, 339–340.

Resource Directory for the Americans with Disabilities Act. (1992). U.S. Equal Employment Opportunities Commission, National Office. Warren Gorham Lamont, 1 Penn Plaza, 42nd Floor, New York, New York. 10019. (AD0011732).

The rights of individuals with handicaps under Federal law. (1998). US Department of Education, Office of Civil Rights, Washington, D.C. 20202–1328.

Schneider, J. (1999/2000). A model employer. *Careers & the disabled, Winter, 1999/2000*, 2–5.

Sheridan, B. (1995). Accommodations for the hearing impaired in State Courts. *Michigan Bar Journal, 74 (May)*, 396.

Simon, J. (1993/1994). The use of interpreters for the Deaf and the legal community's obligation to comply with the ADA. *Journal of Law and Health, 8*, 155–199.

Turner, G.H. (1993). Access to justice and applied sign Linguistics. *Signpost, 63*, 57–62.

What you need to know about ADA. (1992). Commerce Clearing House. Chicago, IL.

ORGANIZATIONS

Disabilities Rights Education-Defense Fund
2212 Sixth Street
Berkeley, CA 94710
(800) 466-4232

Law Center
National Association of the Deaf
814 Thayer Avenue
Silver Spring, MD 20901-4500
(301) 587-7730

Legal Rights Kit
Alexander Graham Bell Association for the Deaf
3417 Volta Place, NW
Washington, DC 20007

President's Committee on Employment
of People with Disabilities
1331 F Street, NW,
Washington, DC 20004
(202) 376-6200

INTERNET

www.deaflawyers.org

This website promotes the professional advancement of deaf and hard of
hearing attorneys and advances the causes of the general deaf and hard
of hearing population.

www.deaflibrary.com

A privately-maintained listing of telecommunication and ADA links and
other resources.

www.edlaw.net

Provides a list of attorneys who represent parents of children with disabilities and other law resources.

www.nod.org

The National Organization on Disability offers information updates on
issues related to ADA.

www.usdoj.gov/crt/ada

This website involves the Americans with Disabilities Act. It is a government portal to various issues relating to accessibility.

COMMUNICATION

BOOKS AND JOURNAL ARTICLES

Bahan, B., & Dannis, J. (1990). *Signs for me: Basic sign vocabulary for
children, parents, & teachers.* San Diego, CA: Dawn Sign Press.
Bodner-Johnson, B. (1988). Conversation begins at home—around
the table. *Perspectives for Teachers of the Hearing Impaired,* Novem-
ber/December, 13–15.

Bodner-Johnson, B. (1991). Family conversation style: Its effects on the deaf child's participation. *Exceptional Children, 57*, 502–508.

Butterworth, R.R., & Flodin, M. (1991). *Perigee visual dictionary of signing.* New York: Berkeley Publications.

The Canadian Hearing Society (2003). *Breaking the sound barriers: Communication Tips* Retrieved November 3, 2003, from www.chs.ca.

Collins, H.S. (1993). *Caring for young children: Signing for day care providers and sitters.* Eugene, OR: Garlic Press.

Conference of Executives of American Schools for the Deaf. (1976). Total communication definition adopted. *American Annals of the Deaf, 121*, 358.

Costello, E. (1994). *American Sign Language dictionary.* New York: Random House.

Fant, L. (1994). *The American Sign Language phrase book.* Chicago, IL: Contemporary Books, Inc.

Fletcher, L. (1989). *Ben's story: A deaf child's right to sign.* Washington, DC: Gallaudet University Press.

Flodin, M. (1991). *Signing forbids* Ny, NY. Perique.

Flodin, M. Books. (1995). Signing is fun: A child's introduction to the basics of sign language. NY, NY: Perizce Books.

Frishberg, N. (1990). *Interpreting: An introduction.* (Rev. Ed.). Silver Spring, MD: Registry of Interpreters for the Deaf.

Froude, J. (2003). *Making sense in sign: A lifeline for a deaf child.* Toronto, Canada: University of Toronto Press.

Gatty, J. (1987). The oral approach: A professional point Of view. In S. Schwartz (Ed.), *Choices in deafness: A parents' guide* (pp. 57–64). Kensington, MD: Woodbine House.

Hafer, J.C., & Wilson, R.M. 1996. *Come Sign With Us.* Washington, DC: Gallaudet Press.

Hawkins, L., & Baker-Hawkins, S. (1990). Perspectives on deafness: Hearing parents of deaf children. In M.D. Garretson (Ed.), Communication issues among Deaf people (pp. 63–65). *A Deaf American Monograph.* Silver Springs, MD: National Association of the Deaf.

Humphrey, J.H., & Alcorn, B.J. (2001). So you want to be an interpreter? An Introduction to sign language interpreter.

Humphries, T., Padden, C., & O'Rourke, T. (1991). *Un Curco Basico De Lenguaje American. (A Basic Course in American Sign Language).* Silver Spring, MD: T.J. Publishers.

Kemp, M. (1998). Why is learning American Sign Language a challenge? *American Annals of the Deaf, 143*, 255–259.

Kwikpoint. (2000). *International translator.* Alexandria, VA: GAIA Communications.

Mahshie, S. (1997). *A first language: Whose choice is it?* Washington, DC: Pre-College National Mission Program, Gallaudet University.

Matos, A.L. (1990). *Aprende senas conmigo Lenguaje de nas en Espanol-Ingles. (Learn Signs with Me—Sign Language in Spanish-English)*. San Juan, Puerto Rico: Editorial Raices.

McCoy, J.V. (1992). Communicating with your deaf client. *Wisconsin Lawyer, 65 (November)*, 16.

McIntosh, A. (2000). When the deaf and hearing interact: Communication features, relationships, and disability issues. In D.O. Braithwaite, T.L. Thompson (Eds.). *Handbook of communication and people with disabilities: Research and application*. LEA's communication series (pp. 353–368). Mahwah, NJ: Lawrence Erlbaum Associates.

Metzger, M., Collons, S., Dively, V., & Shaw, R. (2003). From topic boundaries to omission. Washington, DC: Gallaudet University Press.

Moxham, T. (1996). How to use a sign language interpreter: A guide for business. Kent, OH: Kent State University.

Penilla, A.R., & Taylor, A.L. (2003). Signing for dummies. Indianapolis, IW: John Wiley & Sons, Inc.

Pizzo, R. (2001). Growing up Deaf: Issues of Communication in a hearing world. Philadelphia, PA: Xlibris Corp.

Pollard, R.Q., Miner, I.D., & Cioffi, J. (2000). Hearing and vision loss. In T.R. Elliott, & R.J. Frank (Eds.), *Handbook of rehabilitation psychology*, (pp. 205–234). Washington, DC: American Psychological Association.

Roots, J. (2001). *The politics of visual language: Deafness, Language choice, and political socialization*. Montreal, Quebec: McGill-Queen's University Press.

Ruben, B.D. (1988). Communication and human behavior. New York: Macmillan Publishing Co.

Schick, B., & Williams, K. (2001). Evaluating interpreters who work with children. *Odyssey, Winter/Spring*, 12–14.

Schwartz, S. (1996). 2nd ed. *Choices in deafness: A parents' guide*. Kensington, MD: Woodbine House.

Stewart, D.A., & Luetke-Stahlman, B. (1998). *The signing family: What every parent should know about sign communication*. Washington, DC: Gallaudet University Press.

ORGANIZATIONS

Materials and Information about classes for
Cued Speech available from:

Gallaudet University
Audiology Department
800 Florida Avenue, NE
Washington, DC 20002
Mainstreaming Kit

Alexander Graham Bell Association for the Deaf
3417 Volta Place, NW
Washington, DC 20007

National Information Center for Children and Youth with Disabilities
  (NICHCY)
P.O. Box 1492
Washington, DC 20013
(800) 695-0285 TTY/Voice
(202) 884-8200 TTY/Voice
(202) 884-8441 FAX

National Institute on Deafness and
Other Communication Disorders
1 Communication Avenue
Bethesda, MD 20892-3456

The Rights of Parents
The National Committee for Citizens in Education
10840 Little Patuxent Parkway, Suite 301
Columbia, MD 21044

Sign Media, Inc.
4020 Blackburn Lane
Burtonville, MD 20866
(301) 421-0268 TTY/Voice

Strong Connections
University of Rochester Medical Center
601 Elmwood Avenue, Box 602
Rochester, NY 14642
(585) 275-9200

INTERNET

www.auditechusa.com

TTYs and assistive devices for deaf and hard of hearing people. Excellent
  rating for starting a communication system in the home.

www.bloomu.edu/signlanguage.html

Introduction to sign language: A CD-ROM Approach (2001). Fingerspelling,
  vocabulary, and sentences used. Clear 3-dimensional representation.

www.c-s-d.org

An online catalogue of a variety of communication assistive equipment and materials for the deaf and hard of hearing.

www.deafbiz.com

Extensive resource center for and about Deaf and hard of hearing people. Deaf-owned businesses and services are listed.

www.deafe.org/links/categories/asl.htm

American Sign Language resources, including on-line dictionaries.

www.deafness.about.com

A news site for and about Deaf and hard of hearing people.

www.kwikpoint.com

Point to pictures and Communication instantly worldwide when obtaining the International Translator—a picture dictionary.

www.library.thinkquest.org/10202/asl_dictionary_text.html?tgsl

Sign language communication center, including American Sign Language dictionary.

www.resourcesforlife.com/groups/silentcommunications/resources.htm

Silent communications resource group

www.soundclarity.com

Products for clearer hearing, speech, and communication

www.urmc.rochester.edu/Strongconnections

e-mail: Strongconnections@urmc.rochester.edu

Strong Connections provides expert, cost-effective, remote sign language interpreting services for medical settings.

DEAF CULTURE

BOOK AND JOURNAL ARTICLES

Bienvenu, M.J. (1991). Perspectives on the word "deafness". *The Bicultural Center News*, *35*, 8.

Bienvenu, M.J. (1992). *An introduction to American Deaf Culture*. (5 video-tapes and 5 workbooks). Available from: Burtonsville, MD: Sign Media/Linstok Press, Inc.

Bragg, B. (1994). Culture, language, and deafness (collectivism or individualism). In M. D. Garretson (Ed.), *Deafness: Life and culture: A Deaf American monograph*, (Vol. *44*, pp. 15–16). Silver Spring, MD: National Association of the Deaf.

Branson, J., & Miller, D. (2002). *Damned for their difference: The cultural construction of deaf people as disabled*. Washington, DC: Gallaudet University Press.

Bull, T. (1998). *On the edge of Deaf Culture: Hearing children/Deaf parents*. Alexandria, VA: Deaf Family Research Press.

Cohen, L.H. (1994). *Train go, sorry: Inside a Deaf world*. New York: Random House.

Cohen, O.P., Fischgrund, J.E., & Redding, R. (1990). Deaf children from ethnic, linguistic, and racial minority backgrounds. An overview. *American Annals of the Deaf*, *135*, (2).

Colon, A. (1996). Speaking the language of the Deaf Culture. *Buffalo News*. *February 26*, 1996, A7–A8.

The Deaf American. (Available from the National Association of the Deaf, 814 Thayer Avenue, Silver Spring, MD 20910). *Deaf Rochester News*. Rochester, New York.

Dolnick, E. (1993). Deafness as culture. *The Atlantic Monthly*, *September*, 37–53.

The Endeavor. American Society of Deaf Children, 1820 Tribute Road, Suite A, Sacramento, CA, 95815–4307.

Erting, C.J., Johnson, R.C., Smith, D.L., & Snider, B.W. (Eds.). (1994). *Deaf way: The international celebration of the language, culture, history, and arts of Deaf people*. Washington, DC: Gallaudet Press.

Gallaudet Today. (2000). William Stokoe: Rebel with a cause. *Gallaudet Today*, *Fall*, 18–20.

Gannon, J.R. (1981). *Deaf heritage: A narrative history of deaf America*. Silver Spring, MD: National Association of the Deaf.

Gannon, J.R. (1993). Shaping of Deaf America. *Gallaudet Today*, *23*, 6–13.

Gerner de Garcia, B.A. (1995). ESL applications for Hispanic deaf students. Bilingual *Research Journal*, *19*, 453–467.

Glickman, K. (1999). Deaf proverbs: A proverbial professor's points to ponder. Silver Spring, MD: DEAFinitely yours studio.

Grant, N.C. & Lewis, C. 1993. Weavings: Multicultural families with deaf/hearing impaired children. *Social Work Perspectives*, pp. 12–16.

Grosjean, F. (1996). Living with two languages and two Cultures. In I. Parasnis (Ed.), *Cultural and language diversity: Reflections on the Deaf experience.* (pp. 20–37). Cambridge: Cambridge University Press.

Hairston, E., & Smith L. (1983). Black and Deaf in America! Are that different? Terrace J.

Higgins, P. (1980). *Outsiders in a hearing world.* New York: Sage Publications.

Holcomb, R.K. (1997). The development of a deaf bicultural identity. *American Annals of the Deaf, 142,* 89–93.

Holcomb, R.K. (1986). *Hazards of deafness.* Acton, CA: Joyce Media Publishing.

Holcomb, R., Holcomb, S., & Holcomb, T. (1995). *Deaf Culture, our way.* San Diego, CA: Dawn Sign Press.

Jankowski, K.A. (1997). Deaf Employer and Employee, struggle and Rhetoric. Washington, DC: Gallaudet University Press.

Kaplan, H. (1996). The nature of Deaf Culture: Implications for speech and hearing professionals. *Journal of the Academy of Rehabilitative Audiology, 29,* 71–83.

Keast, M. (2001). One play: Our view. Frederich, MD: Webbynation.

Lane, H. (1990). Cultural and infirmity models of Deaf Americans. *Journal of the Academy of Rehabilitative Audiology, 23,* 11–26.

Lane, H. (1999). *The mask of benevolence: Disability and the Deaf Community.* San Diego, CA: DawnSignPress.

Leigh, I.W., Marcus, A.L., Dobosh, P.K., & Allen, T.E. (1998). Deaf/Hearing cultural identity paradigms: Modifications of the Deaf Identity Developmental Scale. *Journal of Deaf Studies and Deaf Education, 3,* 329–338.

Manning, A. (1996). From roots of protest, deaf power thrives. *USA Today, (March, 6, 1996, Section D),* 1–2.

McKay-Cody, M. (1998/1999). The "well-hidden people" in the Deaf and Native communities. *A Deaf American Monograph, 1998/1999,* 49–51.

Menzano, S., & Johnson, R.C. (2000). Deaf/Hearing cultural tension in a family. *Research at Gallaudet, Winter, 1,* 3–5.

Metzger, M. (2000). Bilingualism and identity in Deaf Communities. Washington, DC: Gallaudet University Press.

Monaghan, L., Nakamura, K., Schmalding, C., & Turner, G.H. (2003). *Many ways to be deaf: International variations in deaf communities.* Washington, DC: Gallaudet Univeristy Press.

Neisser, A. (1990). *The other side of silence: sign Language and the Deaf community in America.* Washington, DC: Gallaudet University Press.

Padden, C., & Ramsey, C. (1991). Deaf Culture and literacy. *American Annals of the Deaf, 138,* 96–99.

Panara, R., & Panara, J. (1983). *Great deaf Americans*. Silver Spring, MD: T. J. Publishers.

Rigney, M. (2003). Deaf side story: Deaf sharks, hearing Jets and a classic American musical. Washington, DC: Gallaudet University Press.

Robinette, D. (1990). *Hometown heroes: Successful deaf youth in America*. Washington, DC: Gallaudet University Press.

Rothwell, J. (1999). ASL access. *The Endeavor,* Silver Spring, MD: National Association of the Deaf.

Rutherford, S. (1987). *A study of American Deaf folklore*. Unpublished doctoral dissertation, University of California, Berkeley.

Sacks, O. (1989). *Seeing voices: A journey into the world of the Deaf*. New York: Harper Collins.

Sass-Lehrer, M., Gerner de Garcia, B., & Rovins, M. (1995). Creating a multicultural climate for deaf children and their families. *Perspectives, 14*, 2–7.

Schein, J.D. (1989). *At home among strangers: Exploring the Deaf community in the United States*. Washington, DC: Gallaudet University Press.

Stokoe, W.C. (1995). Deaf Culture working. *Sign Language Studies, 86*, 81–94.

Stuart, P., & Gilchrist, A. (1990). A sense of identity: Deaf minorities still struggle for acceptance of their heritage. *Gallaudet Today, 21*, 2–6, 8–10, 12–13.

Van Cleve, J. (Ed.). (1993). *Deaf history unveiled: Interpretations from the new scholarship*. Washington, DC: Gallaudet University Press.

Van Cleve, J. (1986). *Gallaudet encyclopedia of Deaf people and deafness*. New York: McGraw-Hill.

Van Cleve, J., & Grouch, B.A. (2002). A place of their own: Creating the Deaf Community in America. Washington, DC: Gallaudet University Press.

Who Speaks for the Deaf Community? (1997). A Deaf American Monograph, *47*, Silver Spring, MD: National Association of the Deaf.

Wilcox, S. (Ed.) (1989). *American Deaf Culture: An anthology*. Silver Spring, MD: Linstok Press.

Winefield, R. (1987). *Never the Twain shall meet: Bell, Gallaudet and the communications debate*. Washington, DC: Gallaudet University Press.

ORGANIZATIONS

The Bicultural Center (TBC)
5506 Kenilworth Avenue, Suite 105
Riverdale, MD 20737-3106
(301) 277-3944 TTY
(301) 277-3945 Voice
(301) 277-5226 Fax

Communications Unlimited
9618 Oregano Circle
Houston, TX 77036
(713) 271-7818 TTY
(832) 289-6309 Voice
(713) 271-8709 FAX

Lists deaf-owned business and sells books, equipment, videos, and software.

Deafpride, Inc.
1350 Potomac Avenue, SE
Washington, DC 20003
(202) 6756700 TTY/Voice

Hand Expressions, Inc.
31 Riverside Drive
Suffern, NY 10901
Email: *Sale@Handexpressions.com*
www.handexpressions.com
Custom Clothing, Novelties, Jewelry.

Junior National Association of the Deaf
814 Thayer Avenue
Silver Spring, MD 20901-4500
(301) 587-1789 TTY
(301) 587-1788 Voice
(301) 587-1791 FAX
nadyouth@nad.org Email

National Association of the Deaf
Exec. Director: Nancy J. Bloch
814 Thayer Ave.
Silver Spring, MD 20910-4500
(301) 587-1789 TTY
(301) 587-1788 Voice
(301) 587-1791 FAX

National Theatre of the Deaf
Hazel E. Stark Center
Chester, CT 06512
(203) 5264974 TTY
(203) 5264971 Voice

World Federation of the Deaf
Iilantie 4, PO Box 65
Helsinki SF-00401
+358 0 58031 Voice

INTERNET

www.asljewelry.com

Link to ASL and Deaf Culture jewelry to wear with pride.

www.colorado.edu/journals/standards/

Standards is an international journal for multicultural studies on the Web.

www.concentric.net/~tlshell/deaf.html

This website includes Deaf Community and Deaf Culture resources. It includes links and resources that may be useful to Deaf, hard of hearing people, and their families. Deaf-related businesses are also listed.

www.deafbase.com

Extensive directory of resources for deaf and hard of hearing issues. Deaf news and Deaf Community news on-line, search posts, most recent published articles, deaf-related books, friend search are available.

www.deafbuy.com

Online store for a variety of products including technology sales.

www.deafdigest.org

Deaf Digest is a newsletter sent by e-mail to all those who are Deaf, hard of hearing, and those interested in news from the Deaf community.
Those interested in subscription: *Barry@deafdigest.com*

www.deafdirectory.com

Directory of businesses and individuals involved in the Deaf community.

www.deafdude.com

A comprehensive guide to links related to a Deaf people.

www.deafkids.com

Link designed for deaf and hard of hearing children and youth with chat room.

www.deaflibrary.com

Includes reference materials and links on Japan and USA deaf cultures.

www.deaflife.com

A magazine for the Deaf Community.

www.deaftoday.com

Deaf Today brings news from A to Z around the world.

www.deafvid.com

A variety of resources for the Deaf community including deaf news and telecommunication devices.

www.dhhig.org

An organization that promotes the advancement of deaf and hard of hearing professionals. The organization's newsletter, DHHIG's Eagle Monthly Newsletter, is used for updating deaf and hard of hearing people's professional development and the professional development of those who work with the deaf and hard of hearing population.

http://hem.passagen.se/sdd/deafwebring/dwr.htm

A webring for the Deaf and hard of hearing

www.nad.org

Website for the National Association for the Deaf.

www.tomatochef.com

A website developed by a chef who is deaf, Chef Jeffrey T. Perri.

www.webbynation.com

Web by Nations Communications Corporation reports itself to be the leading company in the nation serving the needs of the general population and the niche of D/HOH persons.

EDUCATION ISSUES

BOOKS AND JOURNAL ARTICLES

Ahlgren, I., & Hyltenstam, K. (Eds.). (1994). Bilingualism in deaf education. *International Studies on Sign Language and Communication of the Deaf*, 27.

Allen, T., & Karchmer, M. (1990). Communication in classrooms for deaf students: Student, teacher, and program characteristics. In H. Bornstein (Ed.). *Manual communication in America* (pp. 45–80). Washington, DC: Gallaudet University Press.

Andrews, J.F., Winograd, P., & DeVille, G. (1994). Deaf children reading fables: Using ASL summaries to improve reading comprehension. *American Annals of the Deaf*. 139, 378–386.

College of Continuing Education, Gallaudet University. (Ed.). (1993), *ASL in the schools: Policies and curriculum*. Conference Proceedings, October 28–30, 1992. Washington, DC: Gallaudet University Press.

Barnum, M. (1984). In support of bilingual/bicultural Education for deaf children. *American Annals of the Deaf*, 129, 404–408.

Christensen, K.M. (1989). ASL/ESL: A bilingual approach to the education of children who are deaf. *Teaching English to Deaf and Second Language Students*, 7, 9–14.

Christie, K., Wilkins, D.M., McDonald, B.H., & Neuroth-Gimbrone, C. (1998). Get to the point: Academic bilingualism and discourse in American Sign Language and written English. In E.A. Winston, (Ed.). Storytelling and conversation: Discourse in deaf communities. *Sociolinguistics in Deaf Communities*, 5, 162–189. Washington, DC: Gallaudet University Press.

Cokely, D. (1990). The effectiveness of three means of communication in the college classroom. *Sign Language Studies*, 69, 415–443.

Cornett, R.O. & Daisey M.E. (2001). The Cued Speech Resource Book! For parents of deaf children Raleigh, NC: National Cued Speech Association.

Daniels, M. (1993). ASL as a factor in acquiring English. In W. Stoke (Ed.). *Sign Language Studies*, 78, 23–29. *Deafness and education international*. (2000). *Vol.2*, London: Whurr Publishers, Ltd.

Fernandes, J.K. (1997). *Deaf education today: A State of Emergency*. Washington, DC: Pre-college National Mission Programs, Gallaudet University.

Flexer, C., Wray, D., Leavitt, R., & Flexer, R.W. (1996). (2nd ed.) *How the student with hearing loss can succeed in college: A handbook for students, families and professionals*. Washington, DC: Alexander Graham Bell Association.

Focus. National Technical Institute for the Deaf magazine, Rochester Institute of Technology, Rochester, NY.

Hawkins, L., & Brawner, J. (1997). *Educating children who are deaf or hard of hearing: Total communication.* Reston, VA: ERIC Clearinghouse on Disabilities and Gifted Education.

Hayes, P.L. (1993). Clarifying the role of classroom interpreters. *Perspectives in Education and Deafness, 11,* 8–10, 14.

Higgins, P.C. (1990). *The challenge of educating together youth: Making mainstreaming work.* Springfield, IL: Charles C. Thomas.

Hoffmeister, R.J. (1996). Cross cultural misinformation: What does special education say about Deaf people? *Disability & Society, 11,* 171– 189.

Holcomb, T.K., & Foster, S. (1992). Communication in mainstream classrooms. *Perspectives in Education and Deafness, 11,* 10–11.

Jankowski, K.A. (1999). *Student life in the new millennium: Empowering education for deaf students.* Washington, DC: Laurent Clerc National Deaf Education Center, Gallaudet University.

Johnson, R.E., & Erting, C. (1989). Unlocking the curriculum: Principles for achieving access in Deaf education. *Gallaudet Research Institute Working/Occasional Paper Series,* 89–3, Washington, DC: Gallaudet Research Institute.

Kluwin, T.N., & Stewart, D. (2001). Interpreting in the Schools. *Odyssey, Winter/Spring,* 15–17.

Knoors, H., & Renting, B. (2000). Measuring the quality of education: The involvement of bilingually educated Deaf children. *American Annals of the Deaf, 145,* 268–274.

Luetke Stahlman, B. (1996). Communication tips for general educators teaching children who are deaf or hard of hearing. *CAEDHH Journal, 22,* 9–17.

Luetke Stahlman, B., & Hayes, P.L. (1994). *Parent advocacy* for the nonexclusion of students who are Deaf or hard of hearing. *Preventing School Failure, 39,* 41–46.

Lytle, R.R., & Rovins, M.R. (1997). Reforming deaf education: A paradigm shift from how to teach to what to teach. *American Annals of the Deaf, 142,* 7–15.

Mahshie, S. (1994). *A look at "sim com" through new eyes.* Presentation at a workshop entitled, Especially for Parents: Everything You Always Wanted to Know About Bilingual/Bicultural Education but were Afraid to Ask. Gallaudet University, October 26, 1994.

Mason, D., & Ewolt, C. (1996). Whole language and deaf bilingual-bicultural education—naturally! *American Annals of the Deaf, 141,* 293–298.

Metzger, M. (1999). *Sign language interpreting: Deconstructing the myth of neutrality.* Washington, DC: Galluadet University Press.

Musselman, C. (2000). How do children who can't hear learn to read an alphabetic script? A review of the literature on reading. *Journal of Deaf Studies and Deaf Education, 5,* 9–31.

Padden, C., & Ramsey, C. (1998). Reading ability in signing Deaf children. *Topics in Language Disorders, August, 1998, 30*–46.

Paul, P. (1991). ASL to English. *A Deaf American Monograph*, 107–113.

Paul, P.V., & Quigley, S. (1987). Using American Sign Language to teach English. *Language Hearing Practices With Deaf Children*. San Diego, CA: College Hill/Little, Brown.

Philip, M. (1995). Classroom strategies for developing literacy in ASL and English. Paper presented at the NTID ASL and English Literacy Series, February 10, Rochester, NY.

Prinz, P.M., & Strong, M. (1998). ASL proficiency and English literacy within a bilingual deaf education model of instruction. *Topics in Language Disorders, 18*, 47–60.

Ramsey, C.L. (1997). *Deaf children in public schools: Placements, context, and consequences.* Washington, DC: Gallaudet University Press.

Redding, R.L. (1997). Changing times, changing society: Implications for professionals in deaf education. *American Annals of the Deaf, 142*, 83–85.

Roberson, J.L., & Serwatka, T.S. (2000). Student perceptions and instructional effectiveness of deaf and hearing teachers. *American Annals of the Deaf, 145*, 256–262.

Schick, B., & Gale, E. (1995). Preschool deaf and hard of hearing students' interactions during ASL and English storytelling. *American Annals of the Deaf, 140*, 363–369.

Schick, B., & Wiliams, K. (2001). Evaluating interpreters who work with children. *Odyssey, Winter/Spring*, 12–14.

Snider, B.D. (Ed.). (1995). *Conference Proceedings: Inclusion? Defining quality education for deaf and hard of hearing students*. College of Continuing Education, Gallaudet University, 800 Florida Avenue, NE, Washington, DC, 20002.

Stewart, D.A., Akamatsu, C.T., & Becker, B. (1995). Aiming for consistency in the way teachers sign. *American Annals of the Deaf, 140*, 314–323.

Strong, M. (1995). A review of bilingual/bicultural programs for Deaf children in North America. *American Annals of the Deaf, 140*, 84–94.

Strong, M., & Charlson, E.S. (1987). Simultaneous communication: Are teachers attempting an impossible task? *American Annals of the Deaf, December*, 376–382.

Walker, L.A. (1994). *Hand, heart, and mind: The story of the education of America's Deaf people.* New York: Dial Press.

Wathum-Ocama, J.C. (1992). A survey of the appropriateness of instructional language materials used with deaf students. *American Annals of the Deaf, 137*, 420–424.

Winzer, M.A., & Mazurch, K. (2002). Special education in the 21st century. Washington, DC: Gallaudet University Press.

ORGANIZATIONS

Alexander Graham Bell Association for the Deaf, Inc.
3417 Volta Place NW
Washington, DC 20007
(202) 337-5221 TTY
(202) 337-5220 Voice
(202) 337-8314 FAX

American Organization for the Education
of the Hearing Impaired
3417 Volta Place, NW
Washington, DC 20007
(202) 337-5220 TTY/Voice

Coalition for Equal Education of
Deaf Students (CEEDS)
5569 Gloucester Street
Churchton, MD 20733

The Conference of Educational
Administrators Serving the Deaf (CEASD)
The American School for the Deaf
139 N. Main Street
West Hartford, CT 06107
(203) 727-1300 TTY/Voice

The Convention of American Instructors
of the Deaf (CAISD)
P.O. Box 2163
Columbia, MD 21045
(301) 461-9988 TTY/Voice

Council on Education of the Deaf (CED)
Box 68
Ida, MI 48140
(313) 269-3875

The Council for Exceptional Children (CEC)
1920 Association Drive
Reston, VA 22091
(800) 336-3728 TTY/Voice
(703) 620-3660

Department of Educational Resources
Rochester Institute of Technology
National Institute for the Deaf
Lyndon Baines Johnson Building
Rochester, NY 14623-5604
(716) 475-6500 TTY/Voice
(716) 475-6500 FAX
ASKCRTL@rit.edu Email

National Cued Speech Association
PO Box 31345
Raleigh, NC 27662
(919) 828-1218 TTY/Voice

National Technical Institute for the Deaf
Rochester Institute of Technology
One Lomb Memorial Drive
PO Box 9887
Rochester, NY 14623
(716) 475-2181 TTY
(716) 475-6400 Voice

Registry of Interpreters for the Deaf, Inc. (RID)
8719 Colesville Road, Suite 310
Silver Spring, MD 20910
(301) 608-0500

See Center for the Advancement of Deaf Children
PO Box 1181
Los Alamitos, CA 90720
(310) 430-1467 TTY/Voice

Sign Instructors Guidance Network (SIGN)
National Association of the Deaf
814 Thayer Avenue
Silver Spring, MD 20910
(301) 587-1788

John Tracy Clinic
806 West Adams Boulevard
Los Angeles, CA 90007
(213) 747-2924 TTY
(213) 748-5481 Voice
(800) 522-4582

United States Department of Education
Captioning and Adaptation Branch
Division of Educational Service—
Special Education Programs
400 Maryland Avenue, SW
Switzer Building
Washington, DC 20202
(202) 732-1177 TTY/Voice

Odyssey: New Directions in Deaf Education
Laurent Clerc National Deaf Education Center
Gallaudet Univesity
800 Florida, NE
Washington, DC 20002-3695
(800) 526-9105 TTY/Voice
(202) 651-5340 TTY/Voice
(202) 651-5708 FAX

Odyssey is published four times a year.

INTERNET

www.captions.org

A site that provides updated news and resources on Captioning.

www.clerccenter.gallaudet.edu/

Laurent Clerc National Deaf Education Center

www.deafed.net

A resource for the field of deaf education. It features on-line collaborative opportunities, a deaf education job bank, instructional activities, professional development, opportunities, technology news, and announcements of new web site postings.

www.deaflibrary.org

EDUDEAF

This listserv is designed for teachers, staff, administrators, parents, and others concerned with education of deaf students.
To subscribe send an email to: *listserv@ukcc.uky.edu*; in the e-mail, type subscribe EDUDEAFYourfirstnameYourlastname (for example: Joesmith).

www.franklin.com

Franklin Learning Resources. Electronic Book for Learning. Mr. Holly, NJ: Franklin Learning Resources. (Hand held computer that offer a variety of learning modules in Spanish and English.)

www.hearingexchange.com

Links and resources educating the public about hearing loss.

www.icdri.org

The International Center for Disability Resources on the Internet: Large international disability related internet links.

www.nichcy.org

National Information Center for Children and Youth with Disabilities (NICHCY)

OUTREACH

This listserv is designed to facilitate information exchange among people involved in the education of deaf and hard of hearing students and who have outreach as all or part of their job responsibilities.
To subscribe: send email to: *listserv@gallux.gallaudet.edu*; then type: subscribe OUTREACH Yourfirstname Yourlastname.

www.rit.edu/~490www/

The website for the Department of Educational Resources at the Rochester Institute of Technology. It includes many of the research papers available from the National Institute for the Deaf.

www.specialeducationconnection.com

Free access to LRP publications that offer special education e-news (brief e-mail newsletters that provide significant case decisions and important developments in the special education community.

www.stolaf.edu/network/iecc

Intercultural e-mail classroom connections

LANGUAGE ISSUES

BOOKS AND JOURNAL ARTICLES

Akamatsu, C.T., & Armour, V., Developing written literacy in deaf children through analyzing sign language. *American Annals of the Deaf, March 1987*, 46–51.

Akamatsu, C.T., & Stewart, D.A. (1998). Constructing simultaneous communication: The contributions of natural sign language. *Journal of Deaf Studies and Deaf Education, 3,* 302–319.

Andrews, J.F., Winograd, P., & DeVille, G. (1994). Deaf children reading fables: Using ASL summaries to improve reading compreshension. *American Annals of the Deaf, 139,* 378–386.

Armstrong, D.F. (1999). *Original signs: Gesture, sign, and the sources of language.* Washington, DC: Gallaudet University Press.

Cokley, D., & Baker Shenk, C. (1991). *American sign language.* Washington, DC: Gallaudet University Press.

Costello, E. (1994). *Random House American Sign Language dictionary.* Random House.

Daniels, M. (2001). Dancing with words: Signing for hearing children's literacy. Westport, CT: Bergin & Garvey.

Drasgow, E. (1998). American Sign Language as a pathway to linguistic competence, *Exceptional Children, 64,* 329–342.

Eastman, G.L. (1989). *From mime to sign.* Silver Spring, MD: T.J. Publications.

Engen, E.A. (1990). *English language acquisition in deaf children.* (Final Report: Grant from National Institute on Disability and Rehabilitation Research) Rhode Island School for the Deaf, Providence, RI, 02908.

Evans, L. (1992). Total Communication: Structure and Strategy. Washington, DC: Gallaudet University Press.

Fahey, K.R., & Reid, D.K. (2000). *Language, development, differences, and disorders.* Austin, TX: Pro-Ed.

Gibbs, K.W. (1989). Individual differences in cognitive skills related to reading ability in the deaf. *Visible Language, 134,* 214–218.

Gibbons, P. (1991). *Learning to learn a second language.* Portsmouth, NH: Heinemann.

Graney, S. (1998). *Where does speech fit in? Spoken English in a bilingual context.* Pre-College National Missions Programs, Gallaudet University, Washington, DC.

Grushkin, D.A. (1998). Why shouldn't Sam read? Toward a new paradigm for literacy and the Deaf. *Journal of Deaf Studies and Deaf Education, 3,* 179–204.

Henfer, J., & Wilson, R. (1990). *Come sign with us: Sign language activities for children.* Washington, DC: Gallaudet University Press.

Hoemann, H.W. (1986). *Introduction to American Sign Language.* Bowling Green, OH: Bowling Green Press.

Hoffman, C.M. (1990). *Sign language comprehensive reference manual.* Springfield, IL: Charles C. Thomas.

Introduction to sign language: A CD-Rom approach. (2001). Available from: Bloomsburg University, Graduate School Box 01, Bloomsburg, PA 17815.

Jeanes, R.C., Nienhuys, T.G.W.M., & Richards, F.W. (2000). The pragmatic skills of profoundly deaf children. *Journal of Deaf Studies and Deaf Education, 5*, 237–247.

Johnson, R.E. (1994). Possible influences on bilingualism. *Teaching English to Deaf and Second Language Students, 10*, 9–17.

Kannapell, B. (1993). *Language choice—identity choice.* Burtonsville, MD: Linstok Press, Inc.

Kemp, M. (1998). Why is learning American Sign Language a challenge? *American Annals of the Deaf, 143*, 255–259.

Kipila, E., & William Scott, B. (1990). Cued Speech: A response to "controversy within sign language." In M.D. Garretson (Ed.), Communication issues among Deaf people (71–74). *Deaf American Monograph.* Silver Springs, MD: National Association of the Deaf.

Kuntze, M. (1998). Literacy and deaf children: The language question. *Topics in Language Disorders, 18*, 1–15.

Leybaert, J., & Charlier, B. (1996). Visual speech in the head: The effect Cued Speech has on rhyming, remembering, and spelling. *Journal of Deaf Studies and Deaf Education, 3*, 80–134.

Lucas, C. (1998). Pinky Extension and Eye gaze. *Language use in Deaf Communities.* Washington, DC: Gallaudet University Press.

Lucas, C. (1995). *Sociolinguistics in Deaf Communities.* Washington DC: Gallaudet University Press

Lucas, C., Barkey, R. & Valei, C. (2003). What's your sign for PIZZA? Washington, DC: Gallaudet University Press.

Luetke Stahlman, B. (1993). Basic interpreting strategies for parents. *Perspectives in Education and Deafness, 12*, 12–14.

Lupton, L. (1998). Fluency in American Sign Language. *Journal of Deaf Studies and Deaf Education, 3*, 320–328.

Martin, L.A. (1994). *American sign language dictionary—revised.* New York: Harper Collins.

Meier, R.P., & Newport, E.L. (1990). Out of the hands of babes: On a possible sign advantage in language acquisition. *Language, 66*, 1–23.

Miller, D.(1999). ASL access brings sign language resources to local. *SDAD News, 14*, 40.

Nichols, M. (1993). Family communication and the right to sign. *Perspectives in education and Deafness, 12*, 18–21.

Padden, C., & Ramsey, C. (1993). Deaf Culture and literacy. *American Annals of the Deaf, 138*, 96–99.

Parasnis, I. (Ed.). (1998). *Cultural and language diversity and the deaf experience.* Cambridge, England: Cambridge University.

Peters, C. (2000). Deaf American literature. Washington, DC: Gallaudet University Press.

Pollard, R.Q. (1998). *Mental health interpreting: A mentored curriculum.* (139 page text with accompanying 32 minute videotape of interpreting vignettes) Rochester, NY: University of Rochester.

Power, D., & Leigh, G.R. (2000). Principles and practices of literacy development for deaf learners: A historical overview. *Journal of Deaf Studies and Deaf Education*, *5*, 3–8.

Ree, J. (2000). *I see a voice: Deafness, language, and the senses: A philosophical history*. New York, NY: Henry Holt & Company, Inc.

Rice, M.L. (1989). Children's language acquisition. *American Psychologist*, *44, February*, 149–156.

Rothwell, J. (1999). ASL access. *The Endeavor*, Silver Spring, MD: National Association of the Deaf.

Schein, J.D. (1995). Spanish signs in the Americas. *ACEHI-Journal*, *21*, 109–116.

Schirmer, B.R., Bailey, J., & Fitzgerald, S.M. (1999). *Exceptional Children*, *65*, 383–397.

Shroyer, E.H., & Shroyer, S.P. (2002). Signs across America. Washington, DC: Gallaudet University Press.

Sign language coloring books. San Diego, CA: DawnSign Press.

Stewart, D.A. (1990). Rationale and strategies for American Sign Language intervention. *American Annals of the Deaf*, *135*, 205–210.

Stewart, D.A. & Clarke, B.R. (2003). Literacy and your deaf child. Washington, DC: Gallaudet University Press.

Stohoe, W.C. (2002). *Language in hand*: Why sign came before speech. Washington, DC: Gallaudet University Press.

Strong, M, & Prinz, P. (1997). A study of the relationship between American Sign Language and English literacy. *Journal of Deaf Studies and Deaf Education*, *2*, 37–46.

Valli, C. & Lucas, C. (1995). *Linguistics of American Sign Language: An Introduction*. Washington, DC: Gallaudet University Press.

Volterra, V., & Erting, C.J. (1994). *From gesture to language in hearing and deaf children*. Washington, DC: Gallaudet University Press.

White, L. (1992). The language house: Building family communication. *Perspectives in education and Deafness*, *10*, 6–8.

Wilcox, P.P. (2002). Metaphor in American Sign Language. Washington, DC: Gallaudet University Press.

Wilcox, S., & Peyton, J.K. (1999). *American Sign Language as a foreign language*. Washington, DC: ERIC Clearinghouse on Language and Linguistics.

Wilcox, S., & Wilcox, P. (1991). *Learning to see: American Sign Language as a second language*. Englewood Cliffs, NJ: Prentice Hall.

Wilbur, R.B. (2000). The use of ASL to support the development of English and literacy. *Journal of Deaf Studies and Deaf Education*, *5*, 81–104.

Winston, E. (1999). Storytelling and conversation: Discourse in Deaf Communities. Washington, DC: Gallaudet University Press.

Woloshin, S., Bickell, N.A., Schwartz, L.M., Gary, F., & Welch, H.G. (1995). Language barriers in medicine in the United States. *Journal of the American Medicine Association, 273*, 724–728.

Woosley, M.L. (1998). *Target practice: Student games and activities.* Silver Spring, MD: TJ Publishers, Inc.

ORGANIZATIONS

American Speech and Hearing Association (ASHA)
10801 Rockville Pike
Rockville, MD 20852
HELPLINE: (800) 498-2071 TTY/Voice
(301) 897-5700 TTY
(301) 571-0457 FAX

ASL Access
4217 Adrienne Drive
Alexandria, VA 22309
(703) 799-4896 TTY
(703) 799-8733 Voice
Email: *ASLAccess@aol.com*

Center for Bicultural Studies, Inc.
5506 Kenilworth Avenue, Suite 100
Riverdale, MD 20737
(301) 277-3944 TTY
(301) 277-3945 Voice
(301) 699-5226 FAX
Publication: *TBC News*

Promotes public education on interaction of deaf and hearing cultures and fosters public acceptance, understanding, and the use of ASL and other natural signed languages.

Cued Speech Center
304 E. Jones Street
Raleigh, NC 27601
(919) 828-1218
National Association for Hearing and Speech Action
10801 Rockville Pike
Rockville, MD 20852
(301) 8978682 TTY/Voice
(800) 638TALK TTY/Voice

National Association of School Psychologists
Interest Group on Deaf and Hard of Hearing Students and
their Families
Interest Group Coordinators: Steven Hardy Braz,
William Kachman
4340 East West Highway, Suite 402
Bethesda, MD 20814
(301) 657-4155 TTY
(301) 657-0270 Voice
(301) 657-0275 FAX

The National Clearinghouse for
Bilingual Education (NCBE)
1118 22nd Street, NW
Washington, DC 20037
(202) 467-0867
(800) 321 NCBE

National Cued Speech Association
304 E. Jones Street
Raleigh, NC 27622
(919) 828-1218

Sign on Video
1768 Oak Crest Ct.
Tucker, GA 30084
(404) 978-3362

Visually Cued Language Cards by R. Foster and
J.J. Giddan Consulting Psychologists Press
577 College Avenue Palo Alto, CA 94306

INTERNET

www.42explore.com/signlang.htm

Offers American Sign Language practice.

www.asha.org/

Information for professionals working in audiology from the American
Speech Language Hearing Association.

www.aslaccess.org

Comprehensive site involving ASL resources; provides ASL videos.

www.aslinfo.com

Information and resources related to ASL, interpreting, and Deaf Culture.

www.commtechlab.msu.edu/sites/aslweb/browser.htm

ASL browser with an on-line video ASL dictionary.

www.cuedspeech.com

Offers comprehensive information on Cued Speech

www.funbrain.com/signs/

Fun games to review and practice ASL fingerspelling recognition skills.

www.georgetown.edu/research/i2/asl/

An overview of poetry in ASL.

www.handspeak.com

An online video ASL dictionary.

www.hearmyhands.org

A non-profit organization dedicated to providing film and video projects in ASL.

www.iaynet.net/~ggwiz/boggle/bogglefs.htm

Word boggles to practice fingerspelling.

www.iaynet.net/~ggwiz/asl/

Additional word games to practice fingerspelling.

www.nidcd.nih.gov

National Institute on Deafness and Other Communication Disorders
Fact sheet concerning deafness and communication disorders
Instituto Nacional de Sordera y Otros Trastornos de la Communcacion Centero de Distribucion.

www.oraldeafed.org

Comprehensive listing of oral deaf schools in the US and Canada. Extensive information and resources listed.

www.signmedia.com

ASL history, Deaf Culture, and interpreting topics.

www.where.com/scott.net/asl/

Interactive fingerspelling program.

MENTAL HEALTH

BOOKS AND JOURNAL ARTICLES

Broesterhuizen, M. (1990, July–August). *The prediction of social-emotional problems in deaf children.* Paper presented at the meeting of the XVIII International Conference on the Education of the Deaf, Rochester, NY, USA.

Calderon, R. (1998). Learning disability, neuropsychology, and deaf youth: Theory, research, and practice. *Journal of Deaf Studies and Deaf Education, 3,* 1–3.

Calderon, R., & Greenberg, M.T. (1993). Considerations in the adaptation of families with school-aged deaf children. In M. Marschark & M. Clark (Eds.), *Psychological perspectives on deafness.* Hillsdale, NJ: Lawrence Erlbaum Assoc.

Chovaz, C.J. (1998). Cultural aspects of deafness. In S.S. Kazarian, & D.R. Evans (Eds.), *Cultural clinical psychology: Theory, research, and practice.* (pp. 377–400). New York: Oxford University Press.

Clark, J.G., & Martin, F.N. (1994). *Effective counseling in audiology: Perspectives and practice.* Upper Saddle River, NJ: Prentice Hall.

Clay, R. (1997). Do hearing devices impair deaf children? *APA Monitor, 28,* 1, 29–30.

Corker, M. (1994). *Counseling—the deaf challenge.* Bristol, PA: Jessica Kingsley.

Courtin, C. (2000). The impact of sign language on the cognitive development of Deaf children: The case of theories of mind. *Journal of Deaf Studies and Deaf Education, 5,* 266–277.

Dean, R.K., & Pollard, R.Q. (2001). Application of demand-control theory to sign language interpreting: Implications for stress and interpreter training. *Journal of Deaf Studies and Deaf Education, 6,* 1–14.

du Feu, M. (2000). Mental health services for deaf people: Are they appropriate? *Deafness and Education International, 2,* 180–182.

Glickman, N.S., & Harvey, M.A. (1996). *Culturally affirmative psychotherapy with Deaf persons.* Mahwah, NJ: Lawrence Erlbaum Associates.

Greenberg, M., & Kusche, C.A. (1993). *Promoting social and emotional development in deaf children: The PATHS Project.* Seattle, WA: University of Washington Press.

Gregory, S. (1995). *Deaf children and their families.* Cambridge: University Press.

Harvey, M. (1992). Dear mom and dad: If you only had known. *SHHH Journal, September/October,* 4–9.

Harvey, M. (2001). *Listen with the heart: Relationships and hearing loss.* San Diego, CA: DawnSignPress.

Hindly, P., & Kitson, N. (2000). *Mental health and deafness.* Philadelphia, PA: Whurr Publishers.

Jamieson, J. (1994). Teaching as transaction: Vytgotskian perspectives on deafness and mother-child interaction. *Exceptional Children, 60,* 434–449.

Johnson, R.E., & Erting, C. (1989). Ethnicity and socialization in a classroom for deaf children. In C. Lucas (Ed.). *The sociolinguistics of the Deaf community.* New York: Academic Press.

Leigh, I.W. (ed.) (1999). *Psychotherapy with deaf clients from diverse groups.* Washington, DC: Gallaudet University Press.

Lundy, J.E.B. (1998). Theory of mind: Development in Deaf children. *Perspectives on Education and Deafness, 18,* 3–5.

Marschark, M., & Clark, M.D. (Eds.). (1993). *Psychological perspectives on deafness.* Hillsdale, NJ: Lawrence Erlbaum Assoc.

McEntee, M.K. (1993). Accessibility of mental health services and crisis intervention to the deaf. *American Annals of the Deaf, 128,* 26–30.

Meadow-Orlans, K.P. (1994). Stress, support, and deafness: Perceptions of infants' mothers and fathers. *Journal of Early Intervention, 18,* 91–102.

Meadow-Orlans, K.P., & Steinberg, A.G. (1993). Effects of infant hearing loss and maternal support on mother-child interactions at eighteen months. *Journal of Applied Developmental Psychology, 14,* 407–426.

Melik, A., & Herbert, J.T. (1995). Rehabilitation counseling with the deaf: Considerations for counselors with general caseloads. *Journal of Applied Rehabilitation Counseling, 26,* 3–8.

Menzano, S., & Johnson, R.C. (2000). Deaf/hearing cultural tension in a family. *Research at Gallaudet, Winter, 1,* 3–5.

Moore, B. (1997). *An introduction to the psychology of hearing.* New York, New York: Academic Press.

Moore, M.S., & Levitan, L. (1993). *For hearing people only.* Rochester, NY: MSM Productions, LTD (Deaf Life Press).

Morgan-Jones, R.A. (2001). *Hearing differently: The impact of hearing impairment on family life.* Philadelphia, PA: Whurr Publishers.

Nowell, R.C., & Marshark, L.E. (Eds.). (1994). *Understanding deafness and the rehabilitation process.* Boston, MA: Allyn & Bacon.

Parasnis, I., Samar, V., J., & Berent, G., P. (2001). Evaluating ADHD in the Deaf population: Challenges to validity. *NTID Research Bulletin, 6,* 1,3.

Peterson, C.C., & Siegal, M. (2000) Insights into theory of mind from deafness and autism. *Mind and Language, 15,* 123–145.

Pollard, R.Q. (1993). 100 years in psychology and deafness: A centennial retrospective. *Journal of the American Deafness and Rehabilitation Association, 26,* 32–46.

Pollard, R.Q. (1996). Professional psychology and Deaf people: Emergence of a discipline. *American Psychologist, 51,* 389–396.

Pollard, R.Q. (1994). Public mental health service and diagnostic trends regarding individuals who are Deaf or hard of hearing. *Rehabilitation Psychology, 39,* 147–159.

Pollard, R.Q. (1998). Psychopathology. In M. Marschark D. Clark (Eds.). *Psychological perspectives on deafness*, 2, (pp. 171–197). Mahwah, NJ: Lawrence Erlbaum, Inc.

Powers, A.R., Elliot, R.N., Patterrson, D., Shaw, S. Taylor, C. (1995). Family environment and deaf and hard of hearing students with mild additional disabilities. *Journal of Communication Disorders*, *17*, 15–19.

Russell, P.A., Hosie, J.A., Gray, C.D., Scott, E., Hunts, N., Banks, J.S., & Macauly, B.C. (1998). The development of theory of mind in Deaf children. *Journal of Child Psychology and Psychiatry*, *39*, 903–910.

Souza, P.E., & Hoyer, W.J. (1996). Age-related hearing loss: Implications for counseling. *Journal of Counseling and Development*, *74*, 652–655.

Steinberg, A.G., Sullivan, V.J., & Montoya, L.A. (1999). Loneliness and social isolation in the workplace for Deaf individuals during the transition years: A preliminary investigation. *Journal of Applied Rehabilitation Counseling*, *30*, 22–30.

Thomas, P.D., Hunt, W.C., Gary, P.J., Hood, R.B., Goodwin, J.M., & Goodwin, J.S. (1983). Hearing acuity in a healthy elderly population: Effects on emotional, cognitive, and social status. *Journal of Gerontology*, *38*, 321–325.

Trumbetta, S.L., Bonvillian, J.D., Siedlecki, T., & Haskins, B.G. (2000). Language-related symptoms in persons with schizophrenia and how deaf persons may manifest these symptoms. *Sign Language Studies*, 228–253.

Vernon, M. (1995). An historical perspective on psychology and deafness. *JDARA*, *29*, 8–13.

Vernon, M. (1995). Psychology and deafness: Past and prologue. *Gallaudet Today, Spring, 1995*, 12–17.

Vernon, M., & Andrews, J.F. (1990). *The psychology of deafness*. New York: Longman.

Vernon, M., & Daigle, K.B. (1999). Historical overview of inpatient care of mental patients who are deaf. *American Annals of the Deaf*, *144*, 51–61.

Watson, S.M., Henggeler, S.W., & Whelan, J.P. (1990). Family functioning and the social adaptation of hearing-impaired youth. *Journal of Abnormal Child Psychology*, *18*, 143–163.

Woodcock, K., & Aguayo, M. (2000). Deafened People: Adjustment and Support. Toronto, Ontario: University of Toronto Press.

ORGANIZATIONS

Advocacy Services for Abused Deaf Victims, Inc.
P.O. 20023
Rochester, NY 14602-0023

ASADV's mission is to provide support for Deaf adults and their children who are or have been victims of sexual assault and/or domestic violence.

American Psychological Association
Special Interest Section on Deafness, Division 22
Contact: Bob Pollard, SISD Chair
(716) 275-3544 TTY/Voice
Robert_Pollard@urmc.rochester.edu

Covenant House Nineline

(800)999-9915 TTY
(800)999-9999 Voice

A 24 hour hotline for families and youth available to the deaf and hard of hearing

Deaf Counseling, Advocacy, and Referral
Agency (DCARA) Bookstore
Town Fair Shopping Center
39138 State Street
Fremont, CA 94538
(415) 796-7661 TTY
(415) 796-7660 Voice

The National Association of School Psychologists
Interest Group on Children who are Deaf or Hard of Hearing

Contact: William Kachman, Ph.D., NCSP
Mental Health Center
Gallaudet University
800 Florida Avenue, NE
Washington, DC 20002
(202) 651-6080 TTY/Voice

National Crisis Center for the Deaf
Provides 24-hour TTY access to emergency services
for deaf persons in case of sudden illness, injury, poisoning, or fire.

University of Virginia Medical Center, Box 484
Charlottesville, VA 22908
(800) 446-9876 TTY

Parent to Parent
256 South Lake Street
Los Angeles, CA 90057
(213) 484-2642 TTY
(213) 483-4431 Voice

Rehabilitation Services Administration
Deafness and Communicative Disorder Branch
Switzer Building, Room 3414
330 C Street, SW
Washington, DC 20202
(202) 732-1398 TTY/Voice

Self-Help for Hard-of-Hearing People, Inc. (SHHH)
7800 Wisconsin Avenue
Bethesda, MD 20814
(301) 657-2249 TTY
(301) 657-2248 Voice

Substance and Alcohol Intervention
Services for the Deaf (SAISD)
August Center
115 Lomb Memorial Drive
Rochester, NY 14623-5608
(716) 475-4978 TTY/Voice
(716) 475-7375 FAX

Publishes *The National Directory of Alcohol and Other Drugs Prevention and Treatment Programs Accessible to the Deaf* available on their website: www.rit.edu/sa/coun/saisd.

Tripod
Burbank Unified School District
2901 N. Keystone Street
Burbank, CA 91504
(818) 972-2080 TTY/Voice
National Helpline: The Grapevine
California: (800) 346-8888
Outside California: (800) 352-8888

INTERNET

www.hem.passagen.se/sdd/deafwebring/dwr.htm

This website is sponsored by the Internship and post-doctoral fellowship opportunities in mental health and the Deaf population program at the University of Rochester, Rochester, New York.

www.listen-up.org

Extensive information for families of deaf and hard of hearing children. Offers a supportive email discussion group for parents.

www.nasponline.org/services/members/deaf.htm

The National Association of School Psychologists' Special Interest Group on Children Who are Deaf and Hard of Hearing developed this website which includes recommended readings, resources, and links.

www.nationaldeafacademy.com

Website for a mental health facility and resources for Deaf and hard of hearing people.

www.nationaldeafservices.com

The National Deaf Services provides a range of comprehensive mental health services for deaf people and their families in the UK.

www.rit.edu/sa/coun/saisd

Website of the Substance and Alcohol Intervention Services for the Deaf (SAISD).

www.saywhatclub.com

The SayWhatClub is an on-line group of around 400 late-deafened, hard-of-hearing, Deaf people, and other interested people who provide support and encouragement to each other through e-mail.

www.urmc.rochester.edu/dwc/

Website for the Deaf Wellness Center (DWC), a program of the Department of Psychiatry at Strong Memorial Hospital (Strong Behavioral Health). The DWC provides counseling and psychotherapy, psychological testing and evaluation services, as well as consultation services, to courts and governments on topics such as deafness, mental health, and healthcare.

www.wright.edu/sopp/mhdp/mhdp.html

Website for professional psychologists who work with deaf clients.

TECHNOLOGY

BOOKS AND JOURNAL ARTICLES

Biderman, B. (1998). *Wired for sound: A journey into hearing*. Toronto: Trifolium.

Byrd, T. (1999). Cochlear implants: Where do you stand? *Gallaudet Today, Fall, 1999*, 16–25.

Cagle, K., & Cagle, S. (1990). *GA to SK etiquette*. Bowling Green, OH: Bowling Green Press.

Carmen, R. (2004). The consumer handbook on hearing loss and hearing aids: A bridge to hearing. Chicago, IL: Independent publishers Group.

Carroll, C. (1995). Cochlear implants: More? And better? *Perspectives in Education and Deafness, 14*, 18–20.

Cherney, J.L. Deaf Culture and the cochlear implant debate: Cyborg politics and the identity of people with disabilities. *Argumentation and Advocacy. Summer, 1999, 36*, 22–34.

Christingsen, J.B., & Leign, I.W. (2002). *Cochlear implants in children: Ethics and choices*. Washington, DC: Gallaudet University Press.

Clymer, E.W., & McKee, B.G. (1997). The promise of the World Wide Web and other telecommunication technologies within deaf education. *American Annals of the Deaf, 142*, 104–106.

Estabrooks, W. (Ed.). (1998). *Cochlear implants for kids*. Washington, DC: Alexander Graham Bell Association for the Deaf.

Farley, C. (2002). Bridge to sound with a "bionic" ear. Wayzatra, MW: Reriscore Press.

Fernandes, J.K. (2000). Integrating cochlear implant technology. *Odyssey, Winter, 2000*, 17–19.

Galvin, J.C., & Scherer, M.J. (1996). *Evaluating, selecting, and using appropriate assistive technology*. Gaithersburg, MD: Aspen Publishers.

Glennen, S.L., & DeCoste, D.C. (1997). *Handbook of augmentative and alternative communication*. San Diego, CA: Singular Publishing Group. Inc.

Hall, J.W. (1992). *Handbook of auditory evoked responses*. Boston, MA: Allyn & Bacon.

Harkins, J.E. (1994). Telecommunications for deaf and hard of hearing children: Educating the schools. *Technology and Disability, 3*, 195–198.

Hearing health industry world directory (2002). *The Hearing Journal, 54 (December)*.

Jensema, C., & Rovins, M. (1998). Correction: Frequently-used words in TV captions. *Perspectives in Education and Deafness, 16*, 5.

Kampfe, C.M. (1993). Parental expectations as a factor in evaluating children for the multichannel cochlear implant. *American Annals of the Deaf, 138*, 297–303.

Kwiatkowski, J. (2000). Sweet sounds. *Buffalo News*, (February 22, Section C), 1–2.

Lang, H.G. (2002). A phone of our own: The Deaf Insurrection against Ma Bell. Washington, DC: Gallaudet University Press.

Monikowski, C. (1997). Electronic media: Broadening deaf students' access to knowledge. *American Annals of the Deaf, 142*, 101–104.

Moseley, K.A., & Moseley, P.L. (1994). The TTY: A tool for inclusion. *Perspectives in Education and Deafness, 13*, 12–15.

National Directory of TTY numbers. (2002–2003). Washington, DC: Telecommunications, Inc.

Noe, C.M., & Mishler, P.J. (1997). The use of large group assistive listening devices with and without hearing aids in an adult classroom setting. *American Journal of Audiology, 6*, 48–63.

Pollard, R.Q. (1996). Conceptualizing and conducting preoperative psychological assessments of cochlear implant candidates. *Journal of Deaf Studies and Deaf Education, 1*, 16–28.

Schragle, P.S., & Bateman, G. (1994). Impact of captioning. In M.D. Garretson (Ed.), Deafness: Life and culture (pp. 01–104). *A Deaf American Monograph*. Silver Springs, MD: National Association of the Deaf.

Schragle, P., Verlinde, R. (1986). *How to write and caption for Deaf people.* Silver Springs, MD: T.J. Publications, Inc.

Seelman, K.D. (1993). An assessment of public policy and technology: The case of older people with hearing impairment. *Technology and Disability, 2*, 34–42.

Singer, B.R. (1991). Captioning your own videotapes. *Perspectives in Education and Deafness, 9*, 12–13.

Sternberg, M.L. (1994). *American Sign Language Dictionary on CD-ROM.* NY: Harper Collins Publishers.

Tobey, E., & Hastenstaub, S. (1991). Language development in children receiving Nucleus multichannel cochlear implants. *Ear and Hearing, 12 (Supplement), S55–S65.*

Tucker, B.P. (1998). *Cochlear implants: A handbook.* Jefferson, NC: MacFarland and Co.

Warick, R., Clark, C., Dancer, J., & Sinclair, S. (1997). *Assistive listening devices.* A report of the National Task Force on Quality of Services in the Postsecondary Education of Deaf and Hard of Hearing Students. Rochester, NY: Northeast Technical Assistance Center, Rochester Institute of Technology.

Wayner, D.S. (2002). The hearing aid handbook: User's guides for clinicians, adults and children. Washington, DC: Gallaudet University Press.

ORGANIZATIONS

American Academy of Audiology
8201 Greensboro Drive, Suite 300
McLean, VA 22102
(703) 610-9022 TTY/Voice

Academy of Rehabilitative Audiology
Department of Psychology
University of Maryland, Baltimore City
5401 Wilkens Avenue
Baltimore, MD 21228
(301) 455-2364 Voice

Acoustic Society of America
500 Sunnyside Blvd.
Woodbury, NY 11797
(516) 576-2360

American Academy of Audiology
8201 Greensboro Drive, Suite 300
McLean, VA 22102
(703) 610-9022
(800) AAA-2336

American Loop Systems
29 Silver Hill Road, Suite 100
Milford, MA 01757
(800) 955-7204 TTY
(800) 438-5667 Voice

Assistive Device Center
Buffalo Board of Education
School #84
462 Grider Street
Buffalo, NY 14215
(716) 897-8080
(716) 897-8081 FAX

The Caption Center
125 Western Avenue
Boston, MA 02134
(617) 492-9225 TTY/Voice
(617) 562-0590 FAX

Captioned Films for the Deaf
Modern Talking Pictures Services, Inc.
5000 Park Street North
St. Petersburg, FL 33709
(800) 237-6213 TTY/Voice

Captioned Media Program
(formerly Captioned Films/Videos Program)
National Association of the Deaf (NAD)
1447 E. Main Street
Spartanburg, SC 29307
(800) 237-6819 TTY
(800) 237-6213 Voice
(800) 538-5636 FAX
info@cfv.org (email)

Global Assistive Devices
4950 North Dixie Highway #121
Fort Lauderdale, FL 33334
(954) 784-0035

IBM Special Needs Systems
P.O. Box 1328
Boca Raton, FL 33429-1328
(800) 426-3383

International Deaf/Tek
P.O. Box 2431
Framingham, MA 01701
(508) 620-1777

International Hearing Society
20361 Middlebelt Road
Livonia, MI 48152
(313) 478-2610 Voice
(800) 521-5247 Hearing Aid Helpline
(313) 478-4520 FAX

Motorola Pagers
1500 Gateway Blvd.
Boynton Beach, FL 33426
(800) 548-9954 TTY/Voice

National Captioning Institute
5203 Leesburg Pike, suite 1500
Falls Church, VA 22041
(703) 998-2400 TTY/Voice

National Center for Accessible Media
125 Western Avenue
Boston, MA
(617) 492-9258

National Hearing Aid Society
20361 Middlebelt Road
Livonia, MI 48152
(313) 478-2610 TTY/Voice
(800) 521-5248 Hearing Aid Helpline

Nationwide Flashing Signal Systems
8120 Fenton Street
Silver Spring, MD 20910
(301) 589-6670 TTY
(301) 589-6671 Voice

Organization for the Use of the Telephone, Inc. (OUT)
PO Box 175
Owing Mills, MD 21117
(301) 655-1827 Voice

Phone TTY, Inc.
202 Lexington Avenue
Hackensack, NJ 07601
(201) 489-7889 Voice

Phonic Ear Inc.
250 Camino Alto
Mill Valley, CA 94941
(415) 3834000

Special Office for Materials Distribution
Indiana University
AudioVisual Center
Bloomington, IN 47401
(This center distributes educational captioned films and other teaching aids
    for deaf and hard of hearing people.)

Telecommunications for the Deaf, Inc.
814 Thayer Avenue
Silver Spring, MD 20910
(301) 589-3006 TTY/Voice

Tele-Consumer Hotline
1910 K Street, NW, Suite 610
Washington, DC 20006
(202) 223-4371 TTY/Voice

Telex Communications, Inc.
9600 Aldrich Avenue South
Minneapolis, MN 55420
(612) 884-7430

INTERNET

www.cfv.org

Web page for the Captioned Media Program, which is a free-loan open-captioned media system.

www.geccities.com/cicentral

Cochlear Implant Central: A collection of information and resources on cochlear implants.

www.cici.org

Cochlear Implant Association

www.cochlear.com

Information on cochlear implants.

www.deafbroadcastingcouncil.org.uk

A consumer organization representing deaf, deafened, and hard of hearing television viewers in the UK.

www.deafmall.net

This website offers technology, products, and other resources.

www.deaftech.force9.co.uk/

An international organization promoting Deaf awareness technology.

www.deaftek.org

Facilitates employment opportunities for deaf people and persons that serve this population.

www.fda.gov/cdrh/safety/cochlear.html

Food and Drug Administration investigation on the safety of cochlear implants.

www.iol.ie/~nad/deaftech.html

Deaftech equipment available from the National Association of the Deaf.

www.ip-relay.com

IP-Relay Text lets you call anyone you want. IP-relay also has IP-Relay VRS—a video relay service.

www.thehearingjournal.com

Website for *The Hearing Journal,* which focuses on hearing care and technology.

www.phonak.com

Phonak Hearing Systems offers the newest technology in digital hearing aids.

www.sonus.com

A hearing health company with online access to hearing aids, batteries, a nationwide network of audiologists, dispensers, and physicians resources.

www.tedpa.org/statprogram/map/htm

Some states offer telecommunications equipment and have equipment distribution programs. This website will inform you of a distribution program in your state.

www.t-mobile.com

National and international site for pager and phone technology.

www.ultratec.com

Only USA TTY manufacturer to win prestigious BABT award for excellence in quality.

www.unitedtty.com

Website on assistive technology.

www.wynd.com

Website for Wynd communications is the nation's leading provider of two-way wireless communications services for consumers that are deaf or hard of hearing.

GENERAL TOPICS

BOOKS AND JOURNAL ARTICLES

American Academy of Pediatrics. (1999). Newborn and infant hearing loss: Detection and intervention. Task Force on Newborn and Infant Hearing. *Pediatrics, 103,* 527–530.

Andrews, J.F., & Jordan, D.L. (1993). Minority and minority-deaf professionals: How many and where are they? *American Annals of the Deaf, 138,* 388–396.

Backenroth, G.A.M. (1995). Deaf people's perception of social interaction in working life. *International Journal of Rehabilitation Research, 18,* 76–81.

Backenroth, G.A.M. (1997). Deaf employees' empowerment in two different communication environments. *International Journal of Rehabilitation Research, 20,* 417–419.

Benderly, B.L. (1980). *Dancing without music: Deafness in America.* New York: Anchor Press/Doubleday.

Berkay, P.J. (1990). Making adult education accessible to the deaf: A model of direct instructor communication in ASL. *American Annals of the Deaf, 135,* 396–401.

Berkay, P.J. (1991). The establishment of a deaf employment task force in a major corporation. *Journal of the American Deafness and Rehabilitation Association, 24,* 81–85.

Bess, F.H. (1998). *Children with hearing impairment: Contemporary trends.* Nashville, TN: Vanderbilt Bill Wilkerson Center Press.

Bowe, F.G. (1994). Technologies that hear and talk. *Technology and Disability, 3,* 1–10.

Bragg, B. (1989). *Lessons in laughter: the memoirs of a Deaf actor.* Washington, DC: Gallaudet University Press.

Branch, T. (2003). *Tips for Communities with Deaf and hard of hearing in the work place.* Retrieved November, 2003 from www.worksupport.com/archives/deafhardhearing.asp.

Brown, S.C. (1986). Etiological trends, characteristics, and distributions. In A.N. Schildroth and M.A. Karcher (Eds.), *Deaf children in America* (pp. 3354). San Diego, CA: College Hill Press.

Bullis, M. (1995). The school to community transition experiences of hearing young adults and young adults who are deaf. *Journal of Special Education, 28,* 405–423.

Christensen, K.M., & Delgado, G.L. (1993). *Multicultural issues in deafness.* White Plains, NY: Longman.

Clark, J.G., & Martin, F.N. (1994). *Effective Counseling in audiology: Perspectives and practice.* Upper Saddle River, NJ: Prentice Hall.

Cohen, O., Fischgrund, J., & Redding, R. (1990). Deaf Children from ethnic linguistic and racial minority backgrounds. *American Annals of the Deaf, 135,* 67–73.

The Community Ear Magazine. 300 NE Multnomah Street, Suite 2, Portland, Oregon, 97232.

Danek, M.M. (1992). Working with people who are deaf or hard of hearing. *American-Rehabilitation, 18,* 12–15, 35–36.

Deaf USA (Promoting information and marketing Opportunities). EF Training Center, Inc., 7712 Lankershim Blvd., North Hollywood, CA 91605–2815.

Dowler, D.L., & Hirsch, A. (1994). Accommodations in the workplace for people who are deaf or hard of hearing. *Technology and Disability, 3,* 15–25.

Dugan, M.B. (2003). Living with hearing loss. Washington, DC: Gallaudet University Press.

Foster, S.B. (1992). *Working with deaf people: Accessibility in the workplace.* Springfield, IL: Thomas Publishers.

Gallaudet Research Institute. (January, 2001). *Regional and National Summary Report of Data from the 1999–2000 Annual Survey of Deaf and Hard of Hearing Children & Youth.* Washington, DC: GRI, Gallaudet University.

The Gallaudet Survival Guide to Signing. (1987). Washington, DC: Gallaudet University Press.

Gallaudet University for Assessment and Demographic Study. (1998). Thirty years of the annual survey of deaf and hard of hearing children and youth: A glance over the decades. *American Annals of the Deaf, 142,* 72–76.

Garretson, M. (1992). *Viewpoints on deafness.* Washington, DC: Gallaudet University Press.

Glass, L.E., & Elliott, H. (1993). Work place success for persons with adult-onset hearing impairment. *Volta Review, 95,* 403–415.

Goldberg, B. (1995). Families facing choices. *ASHA,* May, 39–47.

Hadadian, A. (1998). Deaf or hard of hearing children: Issues in personnel training. *CAEDHH Journal, 24,* 73–81.

Hall, J.W. (1992). *Handbook of auditory evoked responses.* Boston, MA: Allyn & Bacon.

Hearing Health. (2002). *Resource consumer guide for communication assistance, 16.* Washington, DC: Deafness Research Foundation, 1050 17th Street, NW, Suite 701, Washington, DC 20036.

Heppner, C.M. (1992). *Seeds of disquiet: One woman's experience.* Washington, DC: Gallaudet University Press.

Hodges, C. (1995). *When I grow up.* Hollidaysburg, PA: Turtle Books, Jason & Nordic Publishers.

Holt, J., Hotto, S., & Cole, K. (1994). *Demographic aspects of hearing impairment: Questions and answers.* 1–13. Washington, DC: Center for Assessment and Demographic Studies, Gallaudet University.

Johnson, C.D., Benson, P.V., & Seaton, J.B. (1997). *Educational audiology handbook.* San Diego, CA: Singular Publishing Group, Inc.

Kayser, H. (1995). *Bilingual Speech-Language Pathology: An Hispanic Focus.* San Diego, CA: Singular Publishing Group.

Kisor, H. (1990). *What's that pig outdoors: A memoir of deafness.* New York: Hill & Wang.

Kramlinger, J. (1996). Making noise in a silent world: A profile of the deaf college experience. *Volta-Voices, 3,* 20–21.

Langdon, H.W. & Cheng, L.L. (1992). *Hispanic Children and Adults with Communication Disorders: Assessment and Intervention.* Gaithersburg, MD: Aspen Publishers.

Low, S., & Livadas, G. (1999). Deaf professionals break the sound barrier. *Democrat and Chronicle,* Monday, April 12.

Luterman, D.M., Kurtzer-White, E., Seewald, R.C. (1999). *The young deaf child.* Timonium, MD: York Press, Inc.

Mace, A., Wallace, K., Whan, M., & Stelmachoica, P. (1991). Relevant factors in the identification of hearing loss. *Ear and Hearing, 12,* 287–293.

MacLeod-Gallinger, J.E. (1992). The career status of deaf women. *American Annals of the Deaf, 137,* 315–325.

Mason, J., & Hermann, K.R. (1998). Universal infant screening by automated auditory brainstem response measurement. *Pediatrics, 101,* 221–228.

Mendow-Orlas, N.P., Merters, D.M. & Suss-Lehrer, M.A. (2003). Parents and their deaf children. Washington, DC: Gallaudet University Press.

Meyers, D.G. (2000). *A quiet world: Living with hearing loss.* Yale University Press.

Million, H. (1991). Emergency: Your community needs sign language. *Perspectives in Education and Deafness, 9,* 6–8.

Moore, B. (1997). *An Introduction to the Psychology of Hearing.* New York, New York: Academic Press.

Moore, M., Beazley, S., & Maelzer, J. (1998). *Researching disability issues.* UK: Open University Press.

Mowry, R.L., & Anderson, G.B. (1993). Deaf adults tell their stories: Perspectives on barriers to job advancement and on-the-job accommodations. *Volta Review, 95,* 367–377.

NIDCD's 2003 information resources directory. (2003). National Institute on Deafness and Other Communication Disorders, National Institutes of Health, 31 Center Drive, MSC 2320, Bethesda, MD: 20892–2320.

Parlato, S.J. (1995). *All about deafness: Where to turn for answers to questions about hearing loss.* Rochester, NY: S.J. Parlato.

Parratt, D. (1995). Working with deaf people. *Disability and Society, 10,* 501–519.

Pollard, R.Q. (2002). Ethical conduct in research involving deaf people. In V.A. Gutman (Ed.), *Ethics in mental health and deafness,* pp. 162–178. Washington, DC: Gallaudet University Press.

Pollard, R.Q. Miner, I.D., & Cioffi, J. (2000). Hearing and vision loss. In T.R. Elliott & R. J. Frank (Eds.), *Handbook of rehabilitation psychology*, (pp. 205–234). Washington, DC: American Psychological Association.

Pollard, B. (2001). Special interest section on deafness, *APA Newsletter*, *10*, 1–4.

Poon, B. (1996). Attitudes toward deaf or hard of hearing individuals: Factors and strategies. *CAEDHH-Journal*, *22*, 130–139.

Preston, P.M. (1996). *Mother Father Deaf: Living between sound and silence*. Cambridge, MA: Harvard University Press.

Prieve, B.A. (1997). Establishing infant hearing programs in hospitals. *American Journal of Audiology*, *6*, 84–87.

Recruitability (2003). *Tips for employing people who are deaf or hard of hearing*. Retrieved November 3, 2003, from www.disabledperson.com/Recruitabity/empdeaf.htm

Research at Gallaudet. A publication of the Gallaudet Research Institute, Gallaudet University.

Rezen, S.V., & Hausman, C. (2000). Copy with hearing loss: Plain talk for adults about losing your hearing. Melbourne: Aus. Barriecade Books.

Rose, H.M., & Smith, A.R. (2000). Sighting sound/sounding sight: The "violence" of deaf-hearing communication. In D.O. Braithwaite, D.O., & T.L. Thompson (Eds.), *Handbook of communication and people with disabilities: Research and application*. LEA's communication series. (pp. 369–388). Mahwah, NJ: Lawrence Erlbaum Associates.

Ryan, E. (1992). A deaf child in the family: New reasons to hope? *Perspectives*, *11*, 14–17.

Sandlin, R.E., & Olsson, M.A. (2000). Tinnitus through the ages. *Hearing Health*, *16*, 90–96.

Schrader, S.L. (1995). Silent alarm: on the edge with a Deaf EMT. Washington, DC: Gallaudet Press.

Sevigny-Skyer, S. (1990). Personally speaking. *Journal of Counseling and Development*, *68*, 336–337.

Schreider, M. (2003). "Do you hear me?" Language for OHH people by little people. Eau Claire WI: Thinking publication.

Solit, G., Taylor, M., & Bednarczyk, A. (2002). *Access for all: Integrating deaf, hard of hearing, and hearing preschoolers*. Washington, DC: Laurent Clerc National Deaf Education Center, Gallaudet University, 800 Florida Avenue, NE, 20002.

Sonnen Strahl, P.M. (2003). Deaf crisis in America: Colonized to contemporary. San Diego, CA: Dawnsign Press.

Spradley, T.S., & Spradley, J.P. (1978). *Deaf like me*. New York: Random House.

Stenross B. (1999). Missed connections. Hard of hearing in a hearing world. Philadelphia, PA: Temple University.

The Volta Review. (Available from the Alexander Graham Bell Association for the Deaf, 3417 Volta Place, NW, Washington, DC 20007).

Weisel, A. (Ed.). (1998). *Issues unresolved.* Washington, DC: Gallaudet University Press.

Wilding-Daez, M.M. (1994). Deaf characters in children's books: How are they perceived? In B. D. Snider (Ed.), *Post Milan: ASL and English Literacy: Issues, Trends, Research.* Washington, DC: Gallaudet University College for Continuing Education.

Woodcock, K. (1996). The Association of Late-Deafened Adults; rationale, highlights, history. In M.D. Garretson (Ed.), *Deafness: Historical Perspectives: A Deaf American Monograph, 46*, pp. 155–166, Silver Spring, MD: NAD.

Yoshinaga-Itano, C., & Apuzzo, M.L. (1998). Identification of hearing loss after age 18 months is not early enough. *American Annals of the Deaf, 143*, 380–387.

Yost, W.A. (1994). *Fundamentals of hearing: An introduction.* (3rd ed.), New York: Academic Press.

Zahn, S.B., Kelly, L.J. (1995). Changing attitudes about the employability of the deaf and hard of hearing. *American Annals of the Deaf, 140*, 381–385.

ORGANIZATIONS

ADARA: Professionals Networking for Excellence in Service Delivery with Individuals who are Deaf or Hard of Hearing
(formerly AMERICAN DEAFNESS AND REHABILITATION ASSOCIATION)
ADARA National Office
Attn: Sherri Gallagher, National Office Coordinator
P.O. Box 727
Lusby,MD 20657
650) 372-0620 TTY/Voice
(650) 372-0661 FAX

ADCO
5661 South Curtice Street
Littletown, CO 80120
(303) 794-3928 TTY/Voice
(303) 794-3704 FAX
Sales@adcohearing.com Email

Sign language gifts

Advocates for Hearing-Impaired Youth
PO Box 75949
Washington, DC 20013
(301) 868-7593 TYY/Voice; evenings and weekends

Alexander Graham Bell Association for the Deaf
3417 Volta Place, NW
Washington, DC 20007
(202) 337-5220 TTY/Voice

ALTA Book Center
14 Adrian Court
Burlingame, CA 94010
800) 258-2375

American Academy of Audiology
Acting Exec. Director: Cheryl Kreider Carey
8300 Greensboro Drive, Suite 750
McLean, VA 22102
(703) 790-8466 TTY/Voice
(800) AAA-2336 TTY/Voice
(703) 790-8631 FAX

American Academy of Otolaryngology-
Head and Neck Surgery
Exec. Vice President: G. Richard Holt, MD
1 Prince Street
Alexandria, VA 22314-3357
(703) 519-1585 TTY
(703) 836-4444 Voice
(703) 683-1553 FAX

American Association of the Deaf-Blind, Inc. (AADB)
814 Thayer Avenue
Silver Spring, MD 20910
(301) 589-7279, after 6:00 p.m. TTY/Voice

American Athletic Association of the Deaf
2015 Wooded Way
Adelphi, MD 20783

American Hearing Research Foundation
55 E. Washington Street, Suite 2022
Chicago, IL 60602
(312) 726-9670 Voice

American Society for Deaf Children
Operations Manager: Linda Zumbrun
PO Box 3355
Gettysburg, PA 17325
(800) 942-ASDC (Parent Hotline) TTY/Voice
(717) 334-7922 (Business) TTY/Voice
(717) 334-8808 FAX

American Tinnitus Association
P.O. Box 5
Portland, OR 97207
(503) 248-9985 Voice
(503) 248-9076 FAX

Association of Late-Deafened Adults
P.O. Box 641763
Chicago, IL 60664-1763
(815) 459-5741 TTY
(815) 459-5753 Voice

Better Hearing Institute
PO Box 1840
Washington, DC 20013
(703) 6420580
(800) EARWELL

The Blue Book
Telecommunications for the Deaf, Inc.
814 Thayer Avenue
Silver Spring, MD 20910
(301) 589-3006 TTY/Voice

The Blue Book is the 2003 TDI National Directory and
Resource Guide. This guide provides equal access in
telecommunications and media for people who are deaf, late-
deafened, hard of hearing, or deaf-blind.

Children of Deaf Adults International, Inc.
P.O. Box 30715
Santa Barbara, CA 93130
(800) 382-6328

Clearinghouse on the Handicapped
Switzer Building, Room 3132
Washington, DC 20202
(202) 7321245

DawnSign Press
2124 Kittredge Street, #107
Berkeley, CA 94704
(415) 430-9451 TTY
(415) 430-9419 Voice

Deaf Family Research Press
DFR Press
P.O. Box 8417
Alexandria, VA 22306-8417

Deafness and Communication Disorders Branch
Rehabilitation Services Administration
Department of Education
330 C Street, SW Room 3316
Washington, DC 20201
(202) 7321298 TTY
(202) 7321401 Voice

Deaf and Hard of Hearing Entrepreneurs
814 Thayer Avenue
Silver Springs, MD 20910
(301) 587-8596

Deaf Networks, Inc.
P.O. Box 365
Safety Harbor, FL 34695
(800) 752-7345 TTY/Voice
(727) 796-7609 FAX
deafnetinc@aol.com Email

Deaf USA
7712 Lankershim Blvd.
North Hollywood, CA 91605-2815
818-764-4311 TTY
818-764-4066 FAX
Deafusa@aol.com EMail

The EAR Foundation
2000 Church Street, Box 111
Nashville, TN 37236
(615) 329-7807 TTY/Voice

The Endeavor
Published by the American Society
of Deaf Children
814 Thayer Avenue
Silver Spring, MD 20910

Episcopal Conference of the Deaf
429 Somerset Avenue
St. Louis, MO 63119
(314) 461-1805 TTY/Voice

Forest Bookshop
8 Crucible Court
Coleford, Glos
GL16 8RF
email: deafbooks@forestbooks.com

Friends of Libraries for Deaf Action
(FOLDA)
2930 Craiglawn Road
Silver Spring, MD 20904-1816

A public service of Library for Deaf Action providing deaf-related organizations with the tools to form partnerships with local libraries.

Gallaudet University,
Audiology Department
800 Florida Avenue, NE
Washington, DC 20002
(202) 6515358 TTY/Voice

Gallaudet University Bookstore
800 Florida Avenue, NE
Washington, DC 20002
(202) 651-7107 TTY/Voice

Gallaudet University Press Bookstore
800 Florida Avenue, NE
Washington, DC 20002
(202) 651-5380 TTY/Voice
(800) 451-1073 TTY/Voice

Greater Los Angeles Council on Deafness, Inc.
(GLAD) Bookstore
616 South Westmoreland Avenue
Los Angeles, CA 90005
(213) 3832220 TTY/Voice

Hard of Hearing Advocates
245 Prospect Street
Framingham, MA 01701
(508) 875-8662

Hearing Health Magazine
P.O. Box 2663
Corpus Christi, TX 78403-2663

A magazine designed for people who experience degrees of hearing loss, tinnitus, or other ear disorders.

HEAR NOW
Hearing Assistance
4248 Park Glen Road
Minneapolis, MN 55416
(800) 648-HEAR TTY/Voice
(952) 828-6946 FAX

Hellen Keller National Center for Deaf-Blind
Youths and Adults
111 Middle Neck Road
Sands Point, NY 11050
(516) 944-8900 TTY/Voice

House Ear Institute
256 South Lake
Los Angeles, CA 90057
(213) 484-2642 TTY
(213) 483-4431 Voice

International Hearing Society
20361 Middlebelt Road
Livonia, MI 48152
(800) 521-5247

International Lutheran Deaf Association
1333 S. Kirkwood Road
St. Louis, MO 63122
(314) 965-9971, X684 TTY/Voice

League for the Hard of Hearing
71 West 23rd Street
New York, NY 10010
(212) 741-7650

Modern Signs Press
PO Box 1181
Los Alamitos, CA 90720

National Association of the Deaf Bookstore
814 Thayer Avenue
Silver Spring, MD 20910
(301) 587-1788
(301) 587-6282 TTY/Voice

National Catholic Office for the Deaf
814 Thayer Avenue
Silver Spring, MD 20910
(301) 587-7992 TTY/Voice

National Center on Employment of the Deaf
National Institute for the Deaf
Rochester Institute of Technology
One Lomb Memorial Drive
Rochester, NY 14623
(716) 475-6205 TTY
(716) 475-6219 Voice

National Center for Law and the Deaf
Gallaudet University
800 Florida Avenue, NE
Washington, DC 20002
(202) 6515373 TTY/Voice

National Congress of Jewish Deaf (NCJD)
9102 Edmonston Court
Greenbelt, MD 20770
(301) 345-8612 TTY

National Healthcare Foundation for the Deaf
12034 1/2 Otis Street, NE
Washington, DC 20017
(202) 832-6681 TTY/Voice

National Information Center on Deafness
Gallaudet University
800 Florida Avenue, NE
Washington, DC 20002
(202) 651-5052 TTY
(202) 651-5051 Voice
(800) 6726720 X5052 TTY, X5051 Voice

National Organization on Disability
910 Sixteenth Street, NW
Washington, DC 20006
(202) 293-5968 TTY
(202) 293-5960 Voice
(202) 293-7999 FAX

President's Committee on Employment
of People with Disabilities
1331 F Street, NW
Washington, DC 20004
(202) 376-6200

Tinnitus Reprints
Hearing Health
PO Drawer V
Ingleside, TX 78362-0500
(361) 776-3278 FAX

TJ Publishers Bookstore
817 Silver Spring Avenue, #206
Silver Spring, MD 20910
(301) 585-4440 TTY/Voice
(301) 585-5930 FAX

World Around You (Children and Youth)
Pre-College Programs
Gallaudet University
800 Florida Avenue, NE
Washington, DC 20002

World Recreation Association of the Deaf, Inc.
PO Box 3211
Quartz Hill, CA 93586
(805) 943-8879 TTY
(805) 947-2109 Voice

INTERNET

www.ADCOhearing.com

Sign language novelties and gifts

www.agbell.org/

One of the oldest and most comprehensive organizations focused on pediatric hearing loss.

www.alda.org

Website for the Association of Late-Deafened Adults

www.altaesl.com

Provides ESL materials, some specifically for use with deaf or hard of hearing people.

www.ata.org

Website for the American Tinnitus Association

www.audiology.org/consumer/

Consumer information, news announcements, and professional resources.

http://clerccenter.gallaudet.edu

Laurent Clerc National Deaf Education Center is a comprehensive website offering a variety of informative links and vast amounts of information related to deaf and hard of hearing individuals.

www.coda-international.org

Website for Children of Deaf Adults (CODAs)

www.deafchild.org/

Website for Deaf Child International, which offers information on events,
schools, deaf role models around the world, and games and chat rooms
for children.

www.deafhh.org

Deaf and hard of hearing service center.

www.deaflibrary.org

A virtual library on-line that offers a collection of reference materials and
links intended to educate the public about Deaf Culture as well as hard
of hearing topics.

www.deaflinx.com

Links to everything you ever wanted to know about deafness, Deaf Culture,
organizations, issues, and education topics.

www.deafness.about.com

General information about deaf issues.

www.deafology.com

Offers courses such as Deafology 101 which presents Deaf Culture as seen
through the eyes of a Deaf comedian.

www.deafredbook.com

Deaf Red Book Directory on-line.

www.deafzone.com

A comprehensive guide to deaf resource links.

www.dogsforthedeaf.org

Founded in 1977, its mission is to rescue and professionally train dogs to
assist deaf and hard of hearing people and enhance their lives.

www.dpa.org.sg/DF/

Information related to Project HIIT, which lists various world wide
websites for those interested in the Deaf and hard of hearing
populations.

www.drf.org/

The website for the Deafness Research Foundation, which is a national organization whose goal is the cure and prevention of hearing loss.

www.forestbooks.com

Website for Forest Bookshop which has books, videos, and CD-ROMs about deafness and Deaf issues.

www.gallaudet.edu/site_index.htm

Comprehensive information index and directory of Gallaudet University sites.

www.geocities.com/gregoryjrummo/deaf.htm

The *Live Wire* on the web, which provides news articles about deaf issues prepared by Gregory J. Rummo.

http://gri.gallaudet.edu

Gallaudet's research institute and center on deafness.

www.gupress.gallaudet.edu/annals/past.htm

Gallaudet University Press website that offers past issues of the *American Annals of the Deaf* on-line.

www.hearingfocus.com

A website for people with hearing loss and their families and friends.

www.hearinglossweb.com

Information about hearing loss, events, medical topics, resources, and technology.

www.hearnet.com

A non-profit hearing information source for musicians and music lovers.

www.hohadvocates.org

Advocate support agency for hard of hearing people.

www.hearingexchange.com

Resources and publications concerning deaf and hard of hearing people such as the law, advocacy, and other community services.

www.icdri.org

The website for the International Center for Disability Resources on the Internet.

www.lhh.org

The website for the League of the Hard of Hearing, the world's leading not-for-profit rehabilitation and human services agency for infants, children, and adults who are deaf, hard of hearing, and deaf-blind.

www.ndcs.org

The National Deaf Children's Society is a UK charity solely dedicated to the support of all deaf children and young deaf people, their families, and the professionals working with them.

www.publisher@dhhig.org

A comprehensive site with a variety of resources, sponsored by federal government employees who are Deaf or hard of hearing.

http://wally.rit.edu/internet/subject/deafness.html

A comprehensive, subject-based, Deaf-links page that provides general to specific resources and information on hearing loss.

www.zak.co.il/deaf-info/old/index-abbrev.html

A comprehensive international website concerning Deaf and hard of hearing people.

REFERENCES

CHAPTER 1

Adams, J.W. (1997). *You and your deaf child*. Washington, DC: Gallaudet University Press.

Adams, J.W. (July, 2001). *Mental health issues and the Deaf consumer*. Paper presented at the biannual meeting of the Empire State Association for the Deaf, Buffalo, NY.

Adams, J.W., & Tidwell, R. (1989). An instructional guide for reducing the stress of hearing parents of hearing-impaired children. *American Annals of the Deaf, 134*, 323–328.

Baker, C., & Cokeley, D. (1980). *American Sign Language: A teacher's resource text on grammar and culture*. Silver Spring, MD: T J Publisher.

Brick, K.N. (2000). Standing up for Access. *Silent News, 32*, 10.

Brueggemann, B.J. (1999). *Lend me your ear*. Washington, DC: Gallaudet University Press.

Candlish, P. (1996). *Not deaf enough: Raising a child who is hard of hearing with hugs, humor, and imagination*. Washington, DC: Alexander Graham Bell Association.

DeafDigest. (November 25, 2001). *Famous deaf people*. Retrieved December 10, 2001, from *www.deafdigest.org*.

Deafness Research Foundation. (October 8, 2001). *Rush Limbaugh announces severe hearing loss*. Retrieved from *www.drf.org*.

Dralegal. (n.d.). Disability Rights Advocates: Bates vs. UPS. Retrieved September, 2001 from http://www.dralegal.org/cases/bates.

Drudge Report. (October 8, 2001). *World's most listened to voice announces: I am deaf; Rush Limbaugh vows to continue*. Retrieved from *www.drudgereport.com*, January, 26, 2003.

Gallaudet Research Institute. (January, 2001). *Regional and National Summary Report of Data from the 1999–2000 Annual Survey of Deaf and Hard of Hearing Children & Youth*. Washington, DC: GRI, Gallaudet University.

Garbarino, J. (1992). *Children and their families in the social environment*. 2nd Ed. New York: Aldine De Gruyter.

Hall, J.W. (2000). *Handbook of otoacoustic emissions*. San Diego, CA: Singular Publishing Group.

Hallahan, D.P., & Kauffman, J.M. (1997). *Exceptional learners: Introduction to special education*. Boston, MA: Allyn & Bacon.

Hard of Hearing Advocates. (n.d.). Hearing loss statistics. Retrieved July 10, 2003 from http:///www.hohadvocates.org.

Hardman, M.L., Drew, C.J., & Winston-Egan, M. (1996). *Human Exceptionality: Society, school, and family*. Boston, MA: Allyn & Bacon.

Henderson, D., & Hendershott, A. (1992). ASL and the family system. *American Annals of the Deaf, 136*, 325–329.

Hindley, P., & Kroll, L. (1998). Theoretical and epidemiological aspects of attention deficit and overactivity in deaf children. *Journal of Deaf Studies and Deaf Education, 3*, 64–72.

Johnson, C.D., Benson, P.V., & Seaton, J. (1997). *Educational Audiology Handbook*, San Diego, CA: Singular Publishing Group, Inc.

Kinsella-Meier, M.A. (1994). Is the audiogram important to consider when determining inclusion? In B.D. Snider (Ed.), *Inclusion? Defining quality education for deaf and hard of hearing students (pp. 63–77)*. Washington, DC: Gallaudet University Press.

Kirk, S.A., Gallagher, J.J., & Anastasiow, N.J. (1997). *Educating exceptional children*. Boston, MA: Houghton Mifflin Co.

Kluwin, T.N., & Gaustad, M.G. (1992). Predicting family communication choices. *American Annals of the Deaf, 136*, 28–34.

Kwiatkowski, J. (2000, February 22). Sweet sounds. *Buffalo News*, Section C, pp. 1–2.

Low, S., & Livadas, G. (1999, April 12). Deaf professionals break sound barrier. *Democrat and Chronicle*.

Luterman, D.M. (1996). (3rd ed.) *Counseling persons with communication disorders and their families*. Austin, TX: ProEd.

Marschark, M. (1997). *Raising and educating a deaf child*. New York: Oxford University Press.

Meadow, K.P. (1980). *Deafness and child development*. Berkeley, CA: University of California Press.

Moore, B. (1997). *An introduction to the psychology of Hearing*. New York, New York: Academic Press.

National Association of the Deaf. (1997–1998). *Deaf fact sheets*. Silver Spring, MD: NAD.

National Association of the Deaf. (2000). *Legal Rights: The guide for Deaf and hard of hearing people*. Washington, DC: Gallaudet University Press.

National Association of the Deaf Law Center. (n.d.) *Obligations of hospitals and nursing homes to provide interpreters and auxiliary aids for Deaf and hard of hearing patients*. Retrieved December 1, 2001, from *http://www.nad.org/infocenter/infotogo/legal/hospital.html*.

Nowell, R.C., & Marshak, L.E. (1994). *Understanding deafness and the rehabilitation process*. Boston, MA: Allyn & Bacon.

Ogden, P. (1996). *The silent garden: Raising your deaf child*. Washington, DC: Gallaudet University Press.

Padden, C., & Humphries, T. (1988). *Deaf in America: Voices from a culture*. Cambridge, MA: Harvard University Press.

Paul, P.V., & Jackson, D.W. (1993). *Toward a psychology of deafness: Theoretical and empirical perspectives*. Boston, MA: Allyn & Bacon.

Paul, P.V., & Quigley, S. (1990). *Education and deafness*. White Plains, NY: Longman.

Quigley, S.P., & Kretschmer, R.E. (1982). *The education of deaf children: Issues, theories, and practice*. Baltimore, MD: University Park Press.

Quinn, W.R. (1996). *Understanding clinical deafness: A word your ear*. San Fransisco, CA: Harper-Collins.

Rawlinson, S.L. (1998). The American Disabilities Act. Applications in postsecondary education of students who are deaf/hard of hearing. *Journal of Deaf Studies and Deaf Education, 3 and 4 Fall*, 339–340.

Sanderson, G., Siple, L., & Lyons, B. (2000). Interpreting for post-secondary deaf students. *Interpreting for Deaf students task report.*, 1–3.

Schneider, J. (1999/2000). A model employer. *Careers and the disabled. Winter*, 2–5.

Schwartz, S. (Ed.) (1996). *Choices in deafness: A parent's guide to communication options*. Bethesda, MD: Woodbine House.

Sevigny-Skyer, S. (1990). Personally speaking. *Journal of Counseling and Development, 68*, 336–337.

Slowman, L., Perry, A., & Frankenburg, F. (1987). Family Therapy with deaf family members. *The American Journal of Family Therapy, 15*, 242–252.

Spivak, L.G. (1998). *Universal newborn hearing screening.* New York, New York: Thieme Medical Publishers, Inc.

Stach, B.A. (1997). *Comprehensive dictionary of Audiology illustrated.* Baltimore, MD: Williams & Wilkins.

Starr, A., Pictin, T., Sininger, Y., Hood, L., & Buhn, C. (1996). Auditory neuropathy. *Brain, 119,* 741–753.

Stinson, M.S. (1991). Affective and social development. In R. Nowell & L. Marshak (Eds.), *Understanding deafness and the rehabilitation process,* Needham Heights, MA: Allyn & Bacon.

Stuckless, R., Ashmore, D., Schroedel, J., & Simon, J. (1997). *Introduction: A report of the National Task Force on the quality of services in postsecondary education of Deaf and hard of hearing students.* Rochester, NY: Northeast Technical Assistance Center, Rochester Institute of Technology.

Tucker, B.P. (1998). *Cochlear implants: A handbook.* Jefferson, NC: MacFarland & Co., Inc. Publishers.

Vernon, M., & Andrews, J.F. (1990). *The psychology of deafness.* New York, NY: Longman.

Vital and Health Statistics. (2004). *Data from the Health statistics for U.S. adults: National Health Interview Survey* (Series 10, No. 209). National Center for Health Statistics: Author.

Wheeler, J. (March, 1999). *Demographics,* Deafness Research Foundation, Retrieved December 15, 2002, from www.drf.org.

Wohar Torres, M.T. (1995). A postmodern perspective on the issue of deafness as culture versus pathology. *JADARA, 29,* 1–7.

Woodcock, K. (1996). The Association of Late-Deafened Adults: Rationale, highlights, and history. In M.D. Garretson (Ed.), *Deafness: Historical perspectives. A Deaf American Monograph, 46,* 155–161. Silver Spring, MD: National Association of the Deaf.

CHAPTER 2

Adams, J.W. (1997). *You and your deaf child.* Washington, DC: Gallaudet University Press.

Anderson, C., Bergan, J., Landish, B., & Lewis, N. (1985). *Communication in human relationships.* Washington, DC: Gallaudet University Press.

Baldridge, D.C., & Veiga, J.F. (2001). Toward a greater understanding of the willingness to request an accommodation: Can requesters' beliefs disable the Americans with Disabilities Act? *Academy of Management Review, 26,* 85–99.

Becker, G. (1980). *Growing old in silence.* Berkeley: University of California Press.

Bodner-Johnson, B. (1988). Conversation begins at home—around the table. *Perspectives for Teachers of the Hearing Impaired, November/December,* 13–15.

Colella, A. (2001). Coworker distributive fairness judgments of the workplace accommodation of employees with disabilities. *Academy of Management Review, 26,* 100–116.

Gersick, C.J.G., Bartunek, J.M., & Dutton, J.E. (2000). Learning from academia: The importance of relationships in professional life. *Academy of Management Journal, 43,* 1026–1044.

Hallahan, D.P., & Kauffman, J.M. (1997). *Exceptional learners: Introduction to special education.* Boston, MA: Allyn & Bacon.

Heifer, K.S., & Wilber, L.A. (1990). Hearing loss, aging, and speech perception in reverberation and noise. *Journal of Speech and Hearing Research, 33,* 149–155.

Humes, L.E., & Christopherson, L. (1991). Speech identification difficulties of hearing-impaired elderly persons: The contributions of auditory processing deficits. *Journal of Speech and Hearing Research, 34,* 686–693.

Kapetyn, T.S. (1977a). Satisfaction with fitted hearing aids. *Scandinavian Audiology, 6,* 147–156.

Kapetyn, T.S. (1977b). Satisfaction with fitted hearing aids: II. An investigation into the influence of psycho-social factors. *Scandinavian Audiology, 7,* 171–177.

Lane, H., Hoffmeister, R., & Bahan, B. (1996). *A journey into the deaf world.* San Diego, CA: DawnSignPress.

Marschark, M. (1997). *Raising and educating a deaf child.* New York: Oxford University Press.

Nowak, M., & Tesch-Romer, C. (May, 1994). Spouse support in hearing impaired subjects. Paper presented at the *Second International Conference on Communication, Aging, and Health.* Hamilton, Ontario, Canada.

Padden, C., & Humphies, T. (1988). *Deaf in America: Voices from a culture.* Cambridge, MA: Harvard University Press.

Pollard, R.Q. (1998). *Mental health interpreting: A mentored curriculum.* (139 page text with accompanying 32 minute videotape of interpreting vignettes) Rochester, NY: University of Rochester.

Sanders, D.S. (1982). *Aural rehabilitation: A management model* (2nd ed.). Englewood Cliffs, NJ: Prentice Hall.

Schein, S.L. (1998). Suffering in Silence: Psychologists who have a hearing problem. *California Psychologist, 31,* 8–9.

Simmons, M.K., Rosenbaum, M.S., & Sheridan, K.M. (1996). Counseling your client with hearing loss. Journal of *Mental Health Counseling, 18,* 80–88.

Trychin, S. (1991). *Manual for mental health professions, part II: Psycho-social challenges faced by hard of hearing people.* Washington, DC: Gallaudet University Press.

Weinberger, M., & Radelet, M.L. (1983). Differential adaptive capacity to hearing impairment. *Journal of Rehabilitation, Oct/Nov/Dec,* 63–69.

CHAPTER 3

Anders, G. (1995). Beauty and the battle. *USA Weekend, March, 1995,* 4–6.

Anderson, C., Bergan, J., Landish, B., & Lewis, N. (1985). *Communication in human relationships.* Washington, DC: Gallaudet University Press.

Armstrong, D.F. (1999). *Original signs: Gesture, sign, and and the success of language.* Washington, DC: Gallaudet University Press.

Bailes, C.N. (2001). Integrative ASL-English language Arts: Bridging paths to literacy. *Sign Language Studies, 1,* 147–174.

Becker, S. (1981). Counseling the families of deaf children: A mental health worker speaks out. *Journal Of Rehabilitation of the Deaf, 15,* 10–15.

Begley, S. (1999). Talking from hand to mouth. *Newsweek, March 15,* 56–58.

Body language. (1995). *Dateline NBC.* New York: National Broadcasting Company.

Bowe, F. (1998). Language development and deaf children. *Journal of Deaf Studies and Deaf Education, 3,* 73–77.

Cavanagh, M.E. (1990). *The counseling experience: A theoretical and practical approach.* Prospect Heights, IL: Waveland Press.

Christensen, K. (1990). American Sign language and English: Parallel bilingualism. In M.D. Garretson (Ed.), *Communication issues among Deaf people: A Deaf American Monograph,* (pp. 27–30). Silver Spring, MD: NAD.

Cohen, J. (1990). Total communication: A parent's perspective. In M.D. Garretson (Ed.), *Communication issues among Deaf people: A Deaf American monograph,* 31–34. Silver Spring, MD: NAD.

Conference of Executives of American Schools for the Deaf. (1976). Total communication definition adopted. *American Annals of the Deaf, 121,* 358.

Davis, F. (1973). *Inside intuition: What we know about nonverbal communication,* New York: McGrawHill.

Donovan, P. (2000). ECRC begins sign-language program. *University of Buffalo Reporter, 32,* (Thursday, September 14).

Drasgow, E. (1998). American sign language as a pathway to linguistic competence. *Exceptional children, 64*, 329–342.

Eastabrooks, W. (1996). *Cochlear implants for kids.* Washington, DC: Alexander Graham Bell Association For the Deaf.

Erting, C.J. (1987). Cultural conflict in a school for Deaf children. In P.L. Higgins & J.E. Nash (Ed.), *Understanding deafness socially*, 129–50. Springfield, IL: Charles C. Thomas.

Erting, L., & Pfau, J. (1997). *Becoming bilingual: Facilitating English literacy development using ASL in preschool.* Pre-College National Mission Programs, Gallaudet University.

Firth, A.L. (1994). The Americans with Disabilities Act: Where are we now? In M.D. Garretson (Ed.), *Deafness: Life and culture: A Deaf American monograph*, 31–34. Silver Spring, MD: NAD.

Garcia, J. (1999). *Sign with your baby.* Seattle, WA: Northlight Communications.

Greenberg, M.T. (1990). *Family communication and deaf children's self-esteem.* Keynote address presented at the Twelfth Biennial Convention of the American Society for Deaf Children, Vancouver, British Columbia.

Grossman, A.H. (1999). *A guide for parents of very young deaf children*, London, England: Deaf Children's Society.

Hall, J.W. (2000). *Handbook of otoacoustic emissions.* San Diego, CA: Singular Publishing Group.

Henderson, D., & Hendershott, A. (1992). ASL and the family system. *American Annals of the Deaf, 136*, 325–329.

Higgins, P.L., & Nash, J.E. (1987). *Understanding deafness socially.* Springfield, IL: Charles C. Thomas.

Jackendoff, R. (1994). *Patterns in the mind: Language and human nature.* New York: Basic Books.

Kannapell, B. (1993). *Language choice—identity choice.* Burtonsville, MD: Linstok Press, Inc.

Lane, H., Hoffmeister, R., & Bahan, B. (1996). *A journey into the deaf world.* San Diego, CA: DawnSignPress.

Lederberg, A.R. (1993). The impact of deafness on mother-child and peer relationships. In M. Marschark & M. Clark (Eds.), *Psychological perspectives in deafness*, 93–119. Hillsdale, N.J.: Lawrence Erlbaum Associates.

Livadas, G. Love echoes in boy's silence. *The Democrat and Chronicle*, pp. 1A, 6A.

Mahshie, S.N. (1995). *Educating deaf children bilingually.* Washington, DC: Gallaudet University, Pre-College Programs.

Marschark, M., & Clark, M.D. (Eds.). (1993). *Psychological perspectives on deafness.* Hillsdale, NJ: Lawrence Erlbaum Assoc.

Meador, H.E. (1994). The "how" of a language. In M.D. Garretson. (Ed.), *Deafness, life, and culture, A Deaf American Monograph, 44*, Silver Spring, MD: NAD, pp. 81–84.

Meadow, K.P. (1980). *Deafness and child development.* Berkeley, CA: University of California Press.

Melville, N.A. (May 28's 2001). *Sign language improves reading skills. HealthScoutNews.* Retrieved from May 29, 2001 from *www.dailynews.yahoo.com.*

Menchel, R.S. (2000). Hearing world must stop giving deaf people the cold shoulder. *Democrat and Chronicle.*

Mindel, E.D., & Vernon, M. (1987). *They grow in silence: Understanding deaf children and adults.* 2nd ed. San Diego, CA: College Hill Press.

Moores, D.F. (1987). *Educating the deaf: Psychology, principles, and practices.* 3rd ed. Boston, MA: Houghton Mifflin.

National Association of the Deaf. (2000). *Legal rights: The guide for deaf and hard of hearing people.* Washington, DC: Gallaudet University Press.

Ogden, P. (1996). The silent garden: Raising your deaf child. Washington, DC: Gallaudet University Press.

Ogden, P., & Lipsett, S. (1982). *The silent garden.* New York: St. Martin's Press.

Padden, C. (1980). The Deaf community and the culture of Deaf people. In C. Baker & R. Battison (Eds.), *Sign Language and the Deaf Community*, pp. 89–104. Silver Spring, MD: National Association of the Deaf.

Padden, C., & Humphries, T. (1988). *Deaf in America: Voices from a culture*. Cambridge, MA: Harvard University Press.

Paul, P.V., & Jackson, D.W. (1993). *Toward a psychology of Deafness: Theoretical and empirical perspectives*. Boston, MA: Allyn & Bacon.

Paul, P.V., & Quigley, S. (1990). *Education and deafness*. White Plains, NY: Longman.

Ruben, B.D. & Stewart, L.P. (1998). Communication and human behavior. Boston: Allyn & Bacon.

Scheetz, N.A. (1993). *Orientation to deafness*. Boston, MA: Allyn & Bacon.

Schirmer, B.R. (1999). *Language and literacy development in children who are deaf*. Boston, MA: Allyn & Bacon.

Schlesinger, H.S. (1985). Deafness, mental health, and language. In F. Powell, T. Finitzo-Hieber, S. Friel-Patti, & D. Henderson (Eds.), *Educating the hearing-impaired child*. (pp. 103–113). San Diego, CA: College Hill Press.

Schlesinger, H.S., & Meadow, K.P. (1972). *Sound and sign: Childhood deafness and mental health*. Berkeley, CA: University of California Press.

Stewart, D.A., Schien, J., & Cartwright, B. (1998). *Sign language interpreting: Explaining its art and science*. Boston, MA: Allyn & Bacon.

Trychin, S. (1990). You and me, and hearing loss makes three. *SHHH Journal, 11*, 7–11.

Vernon, M., & Daigle, B. (1994). Bilingual and bicultural Education. In M.D. Garretson (Ed.), *Deafness: Life and culture: A Deaf American monograph*, 121–126. Silver Spring, MD: NAD.

Walters, R.P. (1989). Nonverbal communication in group counseling. In G.M. Gazda (Ed.), *Group counseling: A developmental Approach*, 3rd 203–233. Boston, MA: Allyn & Bacon.

Wixtrom, C. (1999). Moving pictures of Deaf identity: They must be seen to be believed. *Deaf Nation, 4*.

CHAPTER 4

American Academy of Audiology. (n.d.) *Consumer resources: Hearing aids*. Retrieved from www.audiology.org/consumer/, August 14, 2002.

AT&T Consumer (2003). *AT&T relay services: How to make a video relay call*. Retrieved November 15, 2003 from www.consumer.att.com/relay/video/index.html.

Begley, S. (1999). Talking from hand to mouth. *Newsweek, March 15*, 56–58.

Benderly, B.L. (1980). *Dancing without music: Deafness in America*. New York: Anchor Press/Doubleday.

Bowe, F. (1998). Language development and deaf children. *Journal of Deaf Studies and Deaf Education, 3*, 73–77.

Brasel, K., & Quigley, S. (1977). The influence of certain language and communication environments in early childhood on the development of language in deaf individuals.

Brown, P. (1995). Showing sensitivity to Deaf Culture. *ASHA, May*, 46–47.

Brueggemann, B.J. (1999). *Lend me your ear*. Washington, DC: Gallaudet University Press.

Christensen, K. (1990). American sign language and English: Parallel bilingualism. In M.D. Garretson (Ed.), *Communication issues among Deaf people: A Deaf American monograph* (pp. 27–30). Silver Spring, MD: NAD.

CSD Catalogue. (2004). (Available from CSD, 15155 Technology Drive, Eden Prairie, MN 55344-2277.

D-Link. (2003). I-2-eye broadband videophone manual. Available from: D-Link Systems, Inc., 53 Discovery Drive, Irvine, CA 92618.

Daniels, M. (1993). ASL as a factor in acquiring English. In W. Stoke (Ed.), *Sign Language Studies, 78*, 23–29.

DeafDigest (2000, July). *Hamilton Telecommunications announces enhanced feature which saves time and money for relay service users.* Retrieved from August 16, 2000, from www.deafdigest.org.

DeafDigest (2001). Deaf vending machine. *DeafDigest Gold, November 25, 2001.*

Deaf Life (1997). For hearing people only: Are hard of hearing people part of the Deaf Community? *October*, 8–9.

Deyo, D., & Gelzer, L. (1991). *When hearing loss is diagnosed.* Washington, DC: Gallaudet University, National Information Center on Deafness.

Di Perri, K. (1998). *"I'm trying to tell you something: ASL to written English".* Paper presentation at NYSAED Regional convention, Saratoga Springs, NY.

Dolnick, E. (1993). Deafness as culture. *The Atlantic Monthly, September*, 37–53.

Donovan, P. (2000). ECRC begins sign-language program. *UB Reporter, 32, n.4.*

Drasgow, E. (1998). American Sign Language as a pathway to linguistic competence. *Exceptional children, 64*, 329–342.

Epstein, S. (1987). A medical approach to hearing loss. In S. Schwartz (Ed.), *Choices in deafness: A parent's guide* (pp. 1–14). Kensington, MD: Woodbine House.

Erting, C.J. (1987). Cultural conflict in a school for Deaf children. In P.L. Higgins & J.E. Nash (Ed.), *Understanding deafness socially* (pp. 129–150). Springfield, IL: Charles C. Thomas.

Ewolt, C., & Israelite, N. (1992). *Bilingual/bicultural education for deaf and hard of hearing students.* Toronto, Canada: MGS Publication Services.

Finn, G. (1995). Developing a concept of self. *Sign Language Studies, 86*, 1–15.

Firth, A.L. (1994). The Americans with Disabilities Act: Where are we now? In M.D. Garretson (Ed.), *Deafness: Life and culture: A Deaf American monograph* (pp. 31–34). Silver Spring, MD: NAD.

Glickman, N.S. (1996). The development of culturally Deaf Identities. In N.S. Glickman & M.A. Harvey (Eds.), *Culturally affirmative psychotherapy with Deaf persons* (pp. 115–153). Mahwah, NJ: Lawrence Erlbaum Associates.

Goldberg,B. (1995). Families facing choices. *ASHA, May*, 39–47.

Goodstein, H. (1990). American Sign Language. In M.D. Garretson (Ed.), *Communications issues among Deaf people: A Deaf American monograph* (pp. 47–49). Silver Spring, MD: National Association of the Deaf.

Grushkin, D.A. (1998). Why Shouldn't Sam Read? Toward a New Paradigm for Literacy and the Deaf. *Journal of Deaf Studies and Deaf Education, 3*, 179–204.

Hafer, J.C., & Ditman-Richard, E. (1990). Perspectives on deafness: Hearing parents of deaf children. In M.D. Garretson (Ed.), *Communication issues among Deaf people: A Deaf American monograph* (pp. 63–65). Silver Spring, MD: National Association of the Deaf.

Halpern, C.A. (1996). Listening in on Deaf Culture. *Standards*, Retrieved on December 15, 2002, from www.Colorado.edu/journals/standards/.

Hard of Hearing Advocates. (n.d.). *General information.* Retrieved from www.hardof-hearingadvocates.org, May 10, 2001.

Harris Communications Catalogue. (2002). *Volume 11.* (Available from Harris Communications, 15155 Technology Drive, Eden Prairie, MN 55344–2277.

Harris Communications Catalogue (2003). *Volume 12.* (Available from Harris Communications, 15155 Technology Drive, Eden Prairie, MN 55344–2277.

Hartman, C. (n.d.). Talking glove interprets sign language. Retrieved September 4, 2003 from www.datacenter.ap.org/wdc/glove.

Higgins, P.L., & Nash, J.E. (1987). *Understanding deafness socially.* Springfield, IL: Charles C. Thomas.

Holmes, K.M., & Holmes, D.W. (1981). Normal language acquisition: A model for language programming for the deaf. *American Annals for the Deaf, 126*, 23–31.

House, J.D. (2001). Pagers: Let your thumbs do the talking. *TDI*, 6–10.

Isenberg, G. (1996). Storytelling and the use of culturally appropriate metaphors in psychotherapy with deaf people. In N.S. Glickman & M.A. Harvey (Eds.), *Culturally affirmative psychotherapy with Deaf persons* (pp. 169–183). Mahwah, NJ: Lawrence Erlbaum.

Jackendoff, R. (1994). *Patterns in the mind: Language and human nature.* New York: Basic Books.

Jankowski, K.A. (1997). *Deaf empowerment: Emergence, struggle, and rhetoric.* Washington, DC: Gallaudet University Press.

Kemp, M. (1998). Why is learning American Sign Language a challenge? *American Annals of the Deaf, 143,* 255–259.

Lane, H. (1989). *When the mind hears.* New York, NY: Random House.

Lane, H. (1992). *The mask of benevolence: Disabling the Deaf community.* New York, NY: Knopf.

Lartz, M.N., & Lestina, L.J. (1995). Strategies deaf mothers use when reading to their young deaf or hard of hearing children. *American Annals of the Deaf, 140,* 358–362.

Lightman, W. (1998). A place at the table. *A Deaf American Monograph, (1998/1999),* 43–48.

Mahshie, S.N. (1995). *Educating deaf children bilingually.* Washington, DC: Gallaudet University, Pre-College Programs.

McKee, R.L., & McKee, D. (1992). What's so hard about learning ASL? Students' and teachers' perceptions. *Sign Language Studies, 75,* 129–157.

Meadow, K.P. (1980). *Deafness and child development.* Berkeley, CA: University of California Press.

Nover, S.M., Christensen, K.M., & Cheng, L.L. (1998). Development of ASL and English competence for learners who are deaf. *Topics in Language Disorders, 18,* 61–72.

Okwara, M.G. (1994). Discovering my identity and culture. In M.D. Garretson (Ed.), *Deafness: Life and culture: A Deaf American Monograph* (pp. 85–87). Silver Spring, MD: National Association of the Deaf.

Padden, C. (1980). The Deaf community and the culture of of Deaf people. In C. Baker & R. Battison (Eds.), *Sign Language and the Deaf Community* (pp. 89–104). Silver Spring, MD: National Association of the Deaf.

Padden, C. (1988). *Interaction of morphology and syntax in ASL.* New York: Garland Publication.

Padden, C., & Humphries, T. (1988). *Deaf in America: Voices from a culture.* Cambridge, MA: Harvard University Press.

Padden, C., & Ramsey, C. (1991). Deaf Culture and literacy. *American Annals of the Deaf, 138,* 96–99.

Paul, P.V. (1998). *Literacy and deafness: The development of reading, writing, and literature thought.* Boston, MA: Allyn & Bacon.

Paul, P.V., & Jackson, D.W. (1993). *Toward a psychology of deafness: Theoretical and empirical perspectives.* Boston, MA:: Allyn & Bacon.

People. (2004, April 12). How we will live: The next wave. pp. 252–253.

Prinz, P.M., Strong, M., Kuntze, M., Vincent, J., Friedman, J., Moyers, P.P., & Helman, E. (1996). A path to literacy through ASL and English for deaf children. In C.E. Johnson & J.H.V. Gilbert (Eds.), *Children's Language* (Vol. 9, pp. 235–251). Mahwah, NJ: Lawrence Erlbaum.

Rodda, M., & Grove, C. (1987). *Language, cognition and deafness.* Hillsdale, NJ: Lawrence Erlbaum Associates.

Rosen, R. (1986). Deafness: A social perspective. In D.M. Luterman (Ed.), *Deafness in perspective* (pp. 241–262). San Diego, CA: College Hill Press.

Rutherford, S. (1993). *A study of American Deaf folklore.* Burtonsville, MD: Linstok Press, Inc. Berkeley, California.

Scheetz, N.A. (1993). *Orientation to deafness.* Boston, MA: Allyn & Bacon.

Schragle, P.S., & Bateman, G. (1994). Impact of captioning. In M.D. Garretson (Ed.), Deafness: Life and culture (pp. 1–104). *A Deaf American Monograph.* Silver Springs, MD: National Association of the Deaf.

Stach, B.A. (1997). *Comprehensive dictionary of Audiology illustrated*. Baltimore, MD: Williams & Wilkins.

Stokoe, W.C. (1995). Deaf Culture working. *Sign Language Studies, 86*, 81–94.

Stokoe, W.C. (1998). A very long perspective. In M. Marschark & M.D. Clark, (Eds.), *Psychological perspectives on deafness* (Vol. 2, pp. 1–18). Hillsdale, NJ: Erlbaum.

Strong, M., & Prinz, P. (1997). A study of the relationship between American Sign Language and English literacy. *Journal of Deaf Studies and Deaf Education, 2*, 37–46.

Thomas, K. (2002). Glove lends the deaf a hand. *USA Today, January 16, 2002*, p. D.06.

T-Mobile Sidekick Reference Guide. (2002). (Available from Danger (c/o Voicestream), 1000 Park Road, Chanhassen, MN 55317).

Van Cleve, J.V., & Crouch, B. (1989). *A place of their own*. Washington, DC: Gallaudet University Press.

Vernon, M., & Andrews, J.F. (1990). *The psychology of deafness*. New York, NY: Longman.

Vernon, M., & Daigle-King, B. (1999). Historical overview of inpatient care of mental patients who are deaf. *American Annals of the Deaf, 144*, 51–61.

Wentzel, M., & Livadas, G. (1995). Deaf & Proud. *Democrat and Chronicle, Sunday, February 12, 1995, 1*, 7–9.

CHAPTER 5

Adams, J.W. (1997). *You and your deaf child*. Washington, DC: Gallaudet University Press

Associated Press, (2002). Class action suit by Deaf United Parcel Service workers. Retrieved December 15, 2002 from www.deafhh.org.

BBC News. (2001, October 18). Breakthrough for deaf children. [Online news]. London, England: BBC.

Brueggemann, B.J. (1999). *Lend me your ear*. Washington, DC: Gallaudet University Press.

Burek, D.M. (1993). *Encyclopedia Associations*. Detroit, MI: Gayle Research.

Clay, R. (1997). Do hearing devices impair deaf children? *APA Monitor, 28*, 1, 29–30.

Enerstvedt, R.T. (1999). New medical technology: To what does it lead? *American Annals of the Deaf, 144*, 242–49.

Fryauf-Bertschy, H.T., Kelsey, D.M., & Gantz, B.J. (1992). Performance over time of congenitally deaf and postlinguistically deafened children using a multichannel cochlear implant, *Journal Speech and Hearing Research, 35*, 913–920.

Gallaudet Research Institute. (January, 2001). *Regional and National Summary Report of Data from the 1999–2000 Annual Survey of Deaf and Hard of Hearing Children & Youth*. Washington, DC: GRI, Gallaudet University.

Glickman, N.S., & Harvey, M.A. (1996). *Culturally affirmative psychotherapy with Deaf persons*. Mahwah, NJ: Lawrence Erlbaum.

Guttman, N. (1998). High-tech ear implants offer new hope to profoundly deaf. *HSC Weekly, March 20, 4*, p. 1.

Hallahan, D.P., & Kauffman, J.M. (1997). *Exceptional learners: Introduction to special education*. Boston, MA: Allyn & Bacon.

Humphries, T. (1993). Multicultural issues in deafness. In K.M. Christensen & G.L. Delgado (Eds.), *Multicultural issues in deafness* (pp. 3–15). White Plains, NY: Longman.

Isenberg, G. (1996). Storytelling and the use of culturally appropriate metaphors in psychotherapy with deaf people. In N.S. Glickman & M.A. Harvey (Eds.), *Culturally affirmative psychotherapy with Deaf persons* (pp. 169–183). Mahwah, NJ: Lawrence Erlbaum.

Kirk, K.I. (2000). Challenges in the clinical investigation of cochlear implant outcomes. In J. Niparko (Ed.). *Cochlear implants: Principles and practices*. Philadelphia, PA: Lippincott, Williams & Wilkins.

Kwiatkowski, J. (2000, December 31). Soaking up the sounds of life. *Buffalo News*.

Lane, H. (1995). Constructions of deafness. *Disability & Society, 10*, 171–189.

Lane, H. (1994). The cochlear implant controversy. *World Federation of the Deaf News, 2–3*, 22–28.

Lane, H., Hoffmeister, R., & Bahan, B. (1996). *A journey into the deaf world*. San Diego, CA: DawnSign Press.

Lentz, E. (1995). *The treasure: Poems by Ida May Lentz*. (videotape). Berkeley, CA: In Motion Press.

Marschark, M. (1997). *Raising and educating a deaf child*. New York: Oxford University Press

Nevins, M.E., & Chute, P.M. (1996). *Children with cochlear implants in educational settings*. San Diego: Singular Publications.

Niparko, J. (2000). *Cochlear implants: Principles and practices*. Phildelphia, PA: Lippincott, Wilkins and Wilkins.

O'Brien, B. (2003, May 31). Implant restores deaf firefighter's hearing. *Buffalo News*.

Osberger, M.J., Robbins, A.M., Miyamoto, R.T., Berry, S.W., Myres, W.A., Kessler, K.S., & Pope, M.L. (1991). Speech perception abilities of children with cochlear implants, tactile aids or hearing aids. *American Journal of Otology, 12*(Suppl.), 105–115.

Pollard, R.Q. (1996). Professional psychology and Deaf people: Emergence of a discipline. *American Psychologist, 51*, 389–396.

Prinz, P.M., Strong, M., Kuntze, M., Vincent, J., Friedman, J., Moyers, P.P., & Helman, E. (1996). A path to literacy through ASL and English for deaf children. In C.E. Johnson & J.H.V. Gilbert (Eds.), *Children's Language* (Vol. 9, pp. 235–251). Mahwah, NJ: Lawrence Erlbaum.

Robbins, A.M., Osberger, M.J., Miyamoto, R.T., & Kessler, K.S. (1994). Language development in young children with cochlear implants. *Advances in Oto-Rhino-Laryngology, 50*, 160–166.

Sandlin, R.E., & Olsson, R.J. (2000). Tinnitus through the ages. *Hearing Health, January/February*, 89–97.

Shipp, D., Nedzelski, J., Chen, J., & Hanusaik, L.(1997). Prognostic indicators of speech recognition performance in post lingually deafened adult cochlear implant users. In I. Honjo & H. Takahashi (Eds.), *Cochlear implant and related sciences update. Advances in otorhinolaryngology, 52*, Basel: Karger, 74–77.

Staller, S.J., Beiter, A.L., Brimacombe, J.A., Mecklenberg, D., & Arndt, P. (1991). Pediatric performance with the Nucleus 22 channel cochlear implant system. *American Journal of Otology, 12*, 126–136.

Strong, M., & Prinz, P. (1997). A study of the relationship between American Sign Language and English literacy. *Journal of Deaf Studies and Deaf Education, 2*, 37–46.

Van Cleve, J.V. (1987). (Ed.). *Gallaudet encyclopedia of Deaf people and deafness*. New York: McGraw-Hill Books.

Voell, P. (1998, May 8). Loud and clear for those with a hearing loss: A whole new world of sound. *Buffalo News*.

Waltzman, S., & Cohen, N.L. (1998). Cochlear implantation in children younger than 2 years old. *American Journal of Otology, 19*, 158–162.

Wentzel, M., & Livadas, G. (1995). Deaf & Proud. *Democrat and Chronicle, Sunday, February 12, 1995*, 1, 7–9.

Wilson, B. (2003, June 28). Tips for hard of hearing people in the workplace. Retrieved November 3, 2003 from http://www.nurc.org.

Zucker, J. (Executive Producer) (2001, October 8). *The Today Show* [Television Broadcast]. New York: National Broadcasting Corporation.

CHAPTER 6

Cagle, K., & Cagle, S. (1990). *GA to SK etiquette*. Bowling Green, OH: Bowling Green Press.

Cornell University (2000). Hearing loss: Workplace tools & tips. In IRL *Access for all*. Retrieved November 3, 2003, from http://www.ilr.cornell.edu/ped/accessforall/hearing.htm.

Daiss, M.D. (1987). *Working together: Deaf and hearing people.* Rochester, NY: Rochester Institute of Technology.

Gallaudet Today (Spring, 2000). Deaf-friendly employer, p. 8.

Geballe, S.L. (1999, August 13). Deaf-friendly workplace. Retrieved November 3, 2003, from http://www.seattle.bcentral.com/seattle/stories.

Iacelli, L. (1992). *Working together, deaf and hearing people: A training program for managers and co-workers.* Rochester Institute of Technology.

iCan (2001, October 9). Creating a deaf-friendly workplace. Retrieved November 3, 2003, from http://www.ican.com/news.

Myers, P.C. (1992). *The ADA & you: A guide for Deaf and hard of hearing people.* Washington, DC: Gallaudet University Press.

National Association of the Deaf. (1997–1998). *Deaf fact sheets.* Silver Spring, MD: NAD.

National Association of the Deaf. (2000). *Legal rights: The guide for Deaf and hard of hearing people.* Washington, DC: Gallaudet University Press.

Rochester Institute of Technology, National Technical Institute for Deaf. (n.d.). Employers: How to work with a deaf person. Retrieved November 3, 2003, from http://www.ntid.rit.edu/nce/emp-work-group.asp.

RecruitAbility (n.d.). Tips for employing people who are Deaf or hard of hearing. Retrieved November 3, 2003 from http://www.disabledperson.com/RecruitAbility/empdeaf.htm.

Shellabarger, T. (2000). Hiring Deaf people benefits employers. *Deaf USA, 14,* 1, 4, 8.

Appendix A

State Definitions of Special Education Categories

CALIFORNIA STATE DEPARTMENT OF EDUCATION, CCR 3030, ELIGIBILITY CRITERIA

A pupil shall qualify as an individual with exceptional needs, pursuant to section 56026 of the Educational Code, if the results of the assessment as required by section 56320 demonstrate that the degree of the pupil's impairment as described in section 3030 (a through j) requires special education in one or more of the program options authorized by section 56361 of the Educational Code. The decision as to whether or not the assessment results demonstrate that the degree of the pupils impairment requires special education shall be made by the individualized education program team. . . .

a) A pupil has a hearing impairment, whether permanent or fluctuating, which impairs the processing of linguistic information through hearing, even with amplification, and which adversely affects educational performance. Processing linguistic information includes speech and language reception and speech and language discrimination (Statutes of 1981, CFR 300.5).

New York State Department of Education, Part 200,

(2) Deaf. A student with a hearing impairment which is so severe that the student is impaired which in processing linguistic information through hearing, with or without amplification, which adversely affects educational performance.

---

(5) Hard of hearing. A student with a hearing impairment, whether permanent or fluctuating, which adversely affects the child's educational performance but which is not included under the definition of deaf in this section. (April, 2001)

APPENDIX B

A COMPARISON OF TWO VIEWS OF DEAFNESS

1st View: Deafness as Pathology

With this perspective, a person might:

Define deafness as a *pathological condition* (a defect, or a handicap) which distinguishes *abnormal* deaf persons from normal hearing persons.

Deny, downplay or hide evidence of deafness.

Seek a "cure" for deafness; focus on ameliorating the effects of the "auditory disability" or "impairment.".

Give much attention to the use of hearing aids and other devices that enhance auditory perception and/or focus on speech. Examples: Amplifiers, tactile and computer-aided speech devices, cue systems. . . .

2nd View: Deafness as a Difference

With this perspective, a person might:

Define deafness as merely a *difference*, characteristic which distinguishes *normal* deaf persons from normal hearing persons. Recognize that deaf people are a linguistic and cultural minority.

Openly acknowledge deafness.

Emphasize the abilities of deaf persons.

Give much attention to issues of communication access for deaf persons through visual devices and services. Examples: telecommunication devices, captioning devices. light signal devices, interpreters. . . .

Place much emphasis on speech and speechreading ("oral" skills); avoid sign and other communication methods which are deemed "inferior."	Encourage the development of all communication modes, including—but not limited to—speech.
Promote the use of auditory-based communication modes; frown upon the use of modes which are primarily visual.	Strongly emphasize the use of vision as a positive, efficient alternative to the auditory channel.
Describe sign language as inferior to spoken language.	View sign language as equal to spoken language.
View spoken language as the most natural language for all persons, including the deaf.	View sign language as the most natural language for people who are born deaf.
Make mastery of spoken language a central educational aim.	In education, focus on subject matter, rather than on method of communication. Work to expand all communication skills.
Support socialization of deaf persons with hearing persons. Frown upon deaf/deaf interaction and deaf/deaf marriages.	Support socialization within the deaf community as well as within the larger community.
Regard "the normal hearing person" as the best role model.	Regard successful deaf adults as positive role models for deaf children.
Regard professional involvement with the deaf as "helping the deaf" to "overcome their handicap" and to "live in the hearing world."	Regard professional involvement with the deaf as "working with the deaf" to "provide access to the same rights and privileges that hearing people enjoy."
Neither accept nor support a separate "deaf culture."	Respect, value and support the language and culture of deaf people.

Source: Wixtrom, C. (1988). Two views of deafness. *The Deaf American, 38 (Winter)*, 3–10.

Appendix C

Cochlear Implant Manufacturers

Advanced Bionics Corporation
12740 San Fernando Road
Sylmar, CA 91342
(800) 678–2575

www.advancedbionics.com

Cochlear Corporation
61 Inverness Dr East
Englewood, CO 80112
(800) 523–5787

www.cochlear.com

Med El Corporation
2222 East Highway 54
Beta Building Suite 180
Durham, NC 27713
(888) MEDELCI (633–3524)

www.medel.com

APPENDIX D

COMPREHENSION COMMUNICATION ACCESSIBILITY CHECKLIST

A. Assistive listening systems
Amplification
Audio loops (for use with individual's hearing aid)
Wireless headphone systems (i.e., FM & Infrared)
Hard-wired devices

B. Electronic-based
Computer assisted note taking (CAN)
Computer-assisted real-time captioning (CART)
Computer bulletin board system
Internet & World Wide Web
Computer-aided transcription services
FAX & E-mail Telephone for All (TFA)

C. Films/Videotapes
Open and closed captioned
On-screen signing
Deafness related
Deaf culture & history related

D. Hearing-ear dogs

E. Interpreters
Voice to Sign & Sign to Voice
Cued speech and oral

F. Sign Language
American Sign Language (ASL)
In English order
Fingerspelling (manual alphabet)

G. Sign writing

H. Signage

I. Speech reading
Cued speech
With aid of hearing aid
Without aid of hearing aid

J. Telephone
Amplifier and amplified ringers
Visual paging, flashing lamps as ringers
TTY (Text Telephone)
Telecommunications relay services
Telebraille (converting teletype signals into Braille)
Video phone technology

K. Television

Closed caption decoder & Built-in decoder
Personal listening system
On-screen signing

L. Theater

Vacuum Fluorescent Display (VFD)
Rear-View Captioning
Assistive listening devices Interpreters

M. Others

Light and vibration signalers (e.g., alarm clock, baby cry, door beacon, phone strobe flasher, shake alarm, smoke detector)
Auxiliary aids and services specialized for people with hearing disabilities, including those who may have visual or other disabilities.

Source: *The Redbook* copyright by Alice L. Hagemeyer, 1996/1997. Silver Spring, MD: National Association of the Deaf.

APPENDIX E

SHOPPING GUIDE FOR EMPLOYERS OF
DEAF AND HARD OF HEARING PEOPLE

Shopping Guide for Employers of Deaf People

Text Telephones (TTYs)

A TTY or text telephone enables a deaf person to communicate by typing on a type writer-like keyboard over the phone lines. When making a call, the conversation can be read on the TTY screen. Calls are transmitted through a special coding called Baudot or ASCII. A TTY can come in printing and non-printing models. Basic TTYs or TTYs with many convenient features are available.

Signalers

A signaler plugs into a lamp to notify a deaf person that a phone is ringing or that someone is at the door. Both are simple to set up. Plug a lamp and phone into the telephone signaler and the lamp will flash when the phone rings. Plug a lamp into the doorbell signaler and it will flash when the doorbell is pushed.

Pagers

Use a vibrating pager to notify an employee who doesn't work by a phone. A pager can be a simple alerting device like the Private Page or a more sophisticated pager that can be used with TTY, fax and email messaging like the WyndTell Pager.

It doesn't have to be difficult to find the products that will assist your deaf employee. We suggest you first sit down with your deaf employee to find out the kind of products needed to help him/her on the job. Oftentimes the deaf person is familiar with the equipment available and can make valuable suggestions. Once you have a basic idea of your needs, our customer service representatives can guide you through selecting the product that makes the most sense for your deaf employee's work environment. Shown are general categories of products that will assist a deaf employee.

Smoke Detectors

Many companies are safety conscious but forget that a deaf person cannot hear a smoke alarm. Smoke alarms are available with strobe lights or with transmitters that will transmit to personal receivers.

Shopping Guide for Employers of Hard of Hearing People

There are many products available which will assist your hard of hearing employee. It is important to remember that hearing loss varies between individuals. What works for one employee, may not work for another. If possible, sit down with each hard of hearing employee to discuss his/her needs based on his/her work duties. Our customer service will assist you in finding the specific products that will work for that particular hard of hearing employee. The products available are usually easy to set up and will work with existing phone and sound systems. Shown are general categories of products.

Amplified Phones

A hard of hearing employee who uses an office digital telephone will often need amplification features beyond what is found in normal phones. Connecting an in-line amplifier is usually the best solution.

Voice Carry Over (VCO) Phone

Hard of hearing individuals who can't use an amplified phone may find using a Voice Carry Over (VCO) Phone a convenient alternative. Instead of listening to the conversation, the hard of hearing person will read the message on the VCO display and respond through the handset like a regular telephone.

Loud Phone Ringer/Signalers

For a hard of hearing employee to hear the phone, it may be necessary to use either a loud phone ringer or a signaling device. A loud phone ringer has volume and tone controls making it easier for a hard of hearing person to hear. If a loud phone ringer is too disruptive in the work environment, a lamp signaling device can be used as a notifying device.

Assistive Listening Devices

Hard of hearing employees who attend group meetings may need some accommodations. What products you need will depend on the group and room size. Most systems have personal receivers that will allow a hard of hearing employee to adjust the tone and volume as needed.

Source: CSD Product Catalogue (2004). ADA Compliance Products. 13, p. 40. (Obtained from CSD, 15155 Technology Drive, Eden Prairie, MN 55344-2277.)

INDEX

Fourth Century, A.D.

Early Christians demonstrate the first known examples of discrimination against the deaf. Christian leaders like St. Augustine view deafness in a child as a sign of parental sin.

Early 1970s

The Oral Approach to communication flourished until the birth of the Total Communication Philosophy. Total Communication promotes the use of manual signs, speech, and residual hearing as part of educational programming for the deaf and hard of hearing. (Image source: NAD.)

1988

The "Deaf President, Now" protest at Gallaudet University becomes the hallmark of modern Deaf history. As an outcome of the protest "heard" around the world, I. King Jordan becomes the first deaf president at Gallaudet University, the only liberal arts institute of higher learning specifically established for the deaf and hard of hearing. (Image source: Gallaudet University Archives.)

Early Twentieth Century

Hearing aids used to be cumbersome devices. (Images sources: *Oticon, Early Microphone Hearing Aid,* Eriksholm Museum, Denmark.)